Memory and Amnesia

An Introduction

Second Edition

ALAN J. PARKIN
University of Sussex

First published 1987
Second edition 1997
Reprinted 1998

Blackwell Publishers Ltd
108 Cowley Road
Oxford OX4 1JF, UK

Blackwell Publishers Inc
350 Main Street
Malden, Massachusetts 02148, USA

British Library Cataloguing in Publication Data
A CIP catalogue record for this book is available from the British Library

Library of Congress Cataloging in Publication Data
Parkin, Alan J.
Memory and amnesia: an introduction / Alan J. Parkin — 2nd ed.
p. cm.
Rev. ed. of Memory. 1993.
Includes bibliographical references and index.
ISBN 0–631–19702–8 (pbk: alk. paper)
1. Memory. 2. Memory—Age factors. I. Parkin, Alan J. Memory.
II. Title.
BF371.P277 1997   96–36178
153.1'2—dc20   CIP

Typeset in 10 on 12pt Bembo
by Photoprint, Torquay, S. Devon
Printed and bound in Great Britain
by MPG Books Ltd, Bodmin, Cornwall

This book is printed on acid-free paper

Contents

Preface to the First Edition

Interest in amnesia has increased greatly in the last twenty years. The various phenomena exhibited by amnesic patients have become of great interest not just to clinicians, but also to experimental psychologists concerned with explaining normal memory function. One aim of this book, therefore, is to provide an introductory text which can be read by psychology undergraduates pursuing a course in the psychology of memory or neuropsychology. The nature and consequences of memory loss are, however, of interest to other professional groups, most notably neurologists, neurosurgeons, psychiatrists, speech therapists, occupational therapists, nurses and lawyers. Accordingly, the book also offers an account of memory and amnesia which can be followed by professionals with no previous experience of psychological approaches to explanation.

These aims have necessitated a book divided into two parts. The first part provides a basic account of psychological theories about the nature of human memory. The study is somewhat selective in that it concentrates on those aspects of research and theory which are central to the subsequent discussion of memory disorders. Furthermore, some of my colleagues will note that the account is rather traditional, with no discussion of more recent theoretical developments such as distributed processing models. The reason for this lies in the current relationship between most research on memory disorders and theories of normal function. Attempts to explain amnesia have drawn, almost exclusively, on theories of normal function as their starting-point. As a result, theorizing in amnesia research tends to lag behind that in the normal field and accounts of amnesia have yet to embrace more recent developments.

The second part opens with an overview of assessment procedures followed by an account of the various kinds of memory disorders. Most space is given over to the amnesic syndrome, despite its comparative rarity in the clinical population. This reflects the considerable theoretical importance that the syndrome has acquired within experimental memory research. The rest of the book covers ageing and dementia, transient disorders, psychogenic memory loss, and remediation. In providing a bibliography I have tried to strike a balance between thorough coverage while avoiding mass citation. I hope that most of the references cited will lead the interested reader to more detailed information on a particular topic, and I have also made suggestions for further reading.

Finally, many people have helped in the preparation of this book by commenting on various sections. In particular I would like to thank Nick Leng, Andrew Mayes, and Barbara Wilson. In addition, Pete Clifton, Sue Leekam, Bronwyn Moorehouse and Nicola Stanhope provided useful comments. Much of the material for the book had to be obtained from sources outside my own university and I am indebted to Shirley Kirby-Turner and Jenny Marshman of Sussex University Library and Judy Lehmann of the Brighton Postgraduate Medical Library for their help in obtaining references. Last, I must thank Sylvia Turner for all her work preparing the manuscript, Philip Carpenter for his encouragement, and Jean Van Altena for her very thorough copy-editing.

Alan Parkin
Sussex University, July 1986

Preface to the Second Edition

Writing a second edition of a book provides a good opportunity to assess developments in one's field of research. In rewriting this book I have been struck by just how much new research has been carried out since 1987. There has been the emergence of implicit memory as a major theoretical research area, and the frontal lobes, which were not even indexed in my 1987 book, now have a chapter of their own. Work on age-related memory loss has also expanded markedly, and this is also reflected in the revised edition. Researching this book, I found very few areas where little new had occurred, and thus the reader will find a great deal of new material here. As with most new editions, this is a larger book, but I hope that the introductory feel of the first edition is still preserved.

I have a number of people to thank for help in the preparation of this book. First, I am again indebted to Jean van Altena for her very thorough copy-editing. Ella Squires provided me with invaluable editorial assistance, and Narinder Kapur provided very useful comments on the entire manuscript. I also owe a debt to my former student Sam Hutton whose review of the ageing and memory literature helped me considerably with chapter 8, and to Frances Aldrich for her support and for providing me with many useful insights into memory remediation.

Alan Parkin
Brighton, July 1996

Acknowledgements

I am grateful to Academic Press for permission to use the illustrations in figures 1.3, 1.4, 1.5, 2.4, 4.3, 6.3, 6.8, 7.1 and 10.1; Oxford University Press for figures 1.6, 5.2, 5.4 and 6.2a; University of Toronto Press for figure 2.6; American Psychological Association for figures 3.2, 3.3, 8.2 and 8.3; Guildford Press for figure 6.10; Elsevier Science for figures 5.5, 6.5 and 6.11; W. H. Freeman for figure 10.2; Davis for figure 6.4; Cambridge University Press for figure 6.6; Masson Italia for figure 6.7; John Wiley & Sons for figure 6.2c; Princeton University Press for figure 3.5.

Every effort has been made to obtain the necessary permissions. The author and publishers would be grateful to be notified of any corrections that should be incorporated in the next edition or reprint of this book.

Part 1
The Nature of Memory

1 A Model of Memory

One response to the question 'How does memory work?' might be to look at the anatomy and physiology of the brain. After all, memory is located there, so our knowledge of brain function might be expected to provide the answer. The brain is composed of millions of **neurones**, whose basic structure is illustrated in figure 1.1. Communication between neurones occurs by the transmission of nerve impulses along the **axon** of one neurone to the **dendrites** of another. The point of communication between an axon and a dendrite is called a **synapse**. Essentially it consists of two membranes separated by a minute gap. The impulse is transmitted by means of a chemical substance known as a **neurotransmitter**, which is released from the **pre-synaptic membrane** and travels to the **post-synaptic membrane**, where it sets up a new impulse. The level of interconnection between neurones is enormous, with a fully developed neurone averaging over a thousand dendritic and a thousand axonal synapses. The neuronal network therefore provides an ideal basis for the complex processes of memory.

In recent years neuroscientists have made major advances towards an understanding of the nervous system, but they have not reached the point where they can provide answers to many questions psychologists ask about memory. Thus we may be able to identify certain brain structures and neurotransmitters as being implicated in memory; but this does not tell us how memory is organized, why one learning strategy is better than another or, most mysteriously of all, how the interactions between these neurones give rise to our conscious recollections. We know that the neural networks of the brain underlie these activities, but unless we have a theory about how they are organized, we are no better off than someone who knows nothing about electronics trying to understand the circuits of a television.

Because the workings of memory are not apparent from the physical structure of the brain, explanations of memory must be based on **analogies** with things we do understand. The earliest and perhaps most famous example of a description of memory by analogy comes from Plato, who asks us to:

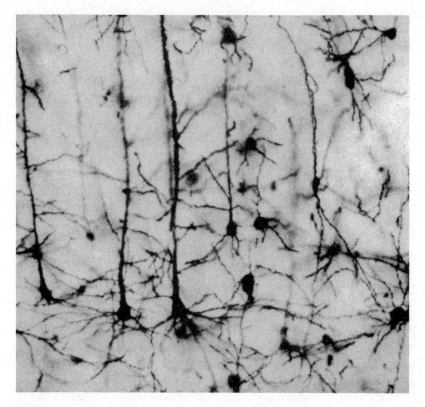

Figure 1.1 Cross-section of brain tissue showing neuronal network.

> Imagine . . . for the sake of argument that our minds contain a block
> of wax, which in this or that individual may be larger or smaller, and
> composed of wax that is comparatively pure or muddy, and harder in
> some, softer in others, and sometimes of just the right consistency . . .
> and say that whenever we wish to remember something we hear or
> conceive in our own minds, we hold this wax under the perceptions or
> ideas and imprint them on it as we might stamp the impression of a
> seal ring. Whatever is so imprinted we remember and know so long as
> the image remains; whatever is rubbed out or has not succeeded in
> leaving an impression we have forgotten and do not know. (*Theaetetus*,
> translated by Hamilton, 1961, p. 897)

By means of a simple analogy, Plato provides a basis for discussing the
formation of memories, memory capacity, and individual differences in
learning ability, and distinguishes between different explanations of forgetting. Another analogy appears later, when Plato describes memory as an

'aviary', in which pieces of knowledge are represented by 'birds' which have to be 'hunted down' if that knowledge is to be used. This argument extends the wax tablet analogy in two important ways. First, it conceives of memory as a space in which individual memories are stored at specific locations, and second, it makes a distinction between storing information and the active search processes required to retrieve it.

The origins of recent memory models can be traced back to William James (1842–1910). Although he relied entirely on **introspection**, James had many important ideas about memory and other psychological processes, and we will refer to him at a number of points. Like Plato, James used a spatial analogy to describe memory; he compared the act of remembering to the way we 'rummage our house for a lost object'. However, James introduced another important distinction, noting that new experiences do not disappear immediately from consciousness, but linger in awareness for a short period of time. He termed this phenomenon **primary memory**, and suggested that its contents did not need to be retrieved; hence 'an object of primary memory is not . . . brought back; it was never lost; its date was never cut off in consciousness from that of the immediately present moment . . . it comes to us as belonging to the rearward portion of the present space of time, and not to the genuine past' (James, 1890, pp. 646–7).

In James's system the contents of primary memory pass into **secondary memory**, a large repository within which all our acquired knowledge is permanently stored. Information in secondary memory, unlike that in primary memory, has to be retrieved before it can be used. Unfortunately, James's important insights into memory were ignored for more than half the twentieth century. This was largely attributable to the pervasive influence of **behaviourism** on the course of experimental psychology at this time. The behaviourists viewed any explanation which embodied consciousness as a concept unworthy of scientific interest; thus James's dichotomy, with its emphasis on the relationship between consciousness and remembering, failed to attract any experimental investigation.

The 'Multistore' Model of Memory

Analogies used to explain memory are now referred to as **models**. These models still conceive of memory in spatial terms, but they tend to compare the organization of memory with that of a computer. Figure 1.2 shows a typical example of this approach. Memory is seen as a series of 'stores', each representing a different stage in the processing of information. New information first enters a **sensory store**, a form of memory whose existence has been confirmed only by means of modern experimental techniques. New information enters the nervous system via one or more of

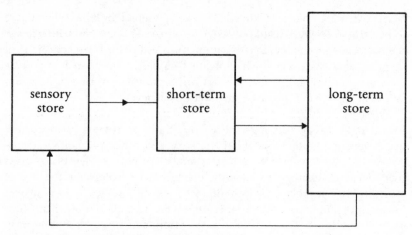

Figure 1.2 The 'multistore' model of memory.
(*After Atkinson and Shiffrin, 1968.*)

our senses. Experiments have shown that the pattern of stimulation set up remains for a short period after the stimulus itself has been terminated. For visual information this form of sensory storage is known as **iconic memory**, and its existence was elegantly demonstrated by 'Sperling in 1960. In his experiment, subjects were shown three rows of letters, such as TDR, SRN and FZR, for only 50 milliseconds. When the subjects were asked to name all the letters, they could report no more than four or five. Alternatively, subjects were shown the array, and immediately afterwards were given a signal indicating which of the three rows should be reported; they then named all three letters correctly on most trials. Since the subjects had no advance warning as to which row they would be asked to report, they must have had the whole array available when the signal was given, even though the stimulus itself was no longer present. Sperling examined the time course of this **partial report advantage**, and found that it could be obtained only with intervals of less than a second between terminating the stimulus and giving the report signal, thus confirming that iconic memory is extremely transient. Sensory storage in other modalities has also been investigated, but discussion of this topic goes beyond our present concern.

During the period of sensory storage, information undergoes basic processes of identification before it passes into **short–term store** (STS). This store is conceptually equivalent to James's primary memory, and provides the basis for our conscious mental activity. STS is the locus of control within the memory system; it determines what information is attended to and how information is processed, and governs retrieval of existing memory. STS can hold only a certain amount of information, and we refer to this capacity as our 'span of awareness' or, more typically, our

memory span. Measurement of memory span is most commonly undertaken using the **digit span** technique. This measures the number of randomly arranged digits that an individual can repeat back in the correct order immediately after hearing or seeing them. In normal adults, digit span is around seven (plus or minus two).

The need for an STS is evident from consideration of a number of different tasks. When reading, for example, the earlier parts of a sentence must be kept in mind for the sentence as a whole to be understood. In performing a mental calculation, the outcome of one stage may need to be held while the solution to another stage is derived. Anecdotal evidence suggests that information in STS is vulnerable, and can easily be lost if some distraction or aversive event occurs. The everyday experience of being distracted and then being unable to remember what you were just saying is one example, as is the inability of concussion victims to remember events immediately preceding their accident.

Once in STS, information can have one of two fates: it can be transferred to **long-term store** (LTS), a structure of large capacity analogous to James's secondary memory, or it can be forgotten. How transfer occurs will be considered a little later. For now it is sufficient to note that effective transfer of information to LTS involves the formation of a permanent memory trace, which subsequently provides the basis for restoring that information to consciousness. In figure 1.2 you will notice that there is an arrow going directly from LTS to sensory store. This acknowledges that LTS is needed for the identification processes carried out. These early processes are extremely complex in themselves, and include word identification and object recognition. Thus, by the time information reaches STS, a considerable degree of processing has been achieved. We are not aware of these initial processes, however; what passes into consciousness and hence into STS is just their end result. This relationship implies that only information that has been consciously perceived passes from STS to LTS. In general we will assume this to be the case, but allow for the possibility of remembering some things we are not aware of (e.g. see Eich, 1984).

Evidence for the STS/LTS Distinction

The distinction between STS and LTS is one that has strong intuitive appeal, but it is important to show that these hypothetical stores are separable components within the memory system. We will see later that evidence from amnesic patients bears on this issue; but for now, only experiments on normal memory will be considered. A number of techniques have been used; but we will concentrate on the free recall paradigm. This involves the sequential presentation of a series of items, usually words,

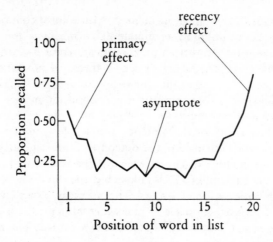

Figure 1.3 Typical finding from a free recall experiment, showing the three components of the serial position curve.
(*After Glanzer and Cunitz, 1966.*)

followed by the instruction to recall as many of the items as possible in any order.

The results are displayed by plotting the probability of an item being recalled as a function of its position in the list; figure 1.3 shows the resulting serial position curve. The first few items are remembered quite well relative to the items in the middle of the list; this is called the **primacy effect**. The best recall is obtained for the last few items in the list; this is termed the **recency effect**. The middle portion of the curve, where recall is poorest, is known as the **asymptote**.

Psychologists were quick to explain this result in terms of the STS/LTS distinction; the recency effect was interpreted as the output of STS, while recall from earlier in the list was thought to come from LTS. However, before this interpretation could be accepted, additional experimental evidence was required. If the serial position curve represented the joint operation of STS and LTS, it was necessary to show that the two parts of the curve responded differently when certain factors were manipulated. If one could isolate a factor which influenced recall from earlier parts of the list but had no influence on the recency effect and, by contrast, a factor which affected only the size of the recency effect, this would be consistent with the operation of two memory stores with different characteristics.

Subsequent experiments explored the serial position curve under a number of different conditions. Figure 1.4a shows that longer presentation time improves recall from early list positions but has no influence on recall of the last few items. A number of other factors were shown to have similar effects. Thus, recall from the primacy and asymptote portions of the curve was greater with word lists comprising of related items or more common words than with lists of uncommon or unrelated words. The only factor found to have the opposite effect was distraction prior to recall. This was shown by comparing the recall of subjects allowed to start remembering immediately after the last item had appeared with that when they were required to count backwards in threes for 30 seconds before recalling the items. Under these conditions, the recency effect was completely eliminated, without any change in recall from the other parts of the list (see figure 1.4b).

These results are most readily interpreted by assuming that recall from different parts of the list reflects the output of different memory stores. The ease with which the last few items are recalled and the susceptibility of this effect to distraction support the existence of an STS from which new information is immediately available, but which is vulnerable to disruption. Conversely, the fact that distraction does not affect recall from earlier in the list indicates that this information has achieved permanent storage in LTS. The identification of factors which influence recall from this part of the list but fail to influence the recency effect also supports the multistore interpretation of the serial position curve. Furthermore, the variables influencing recall indicate factors that are pertinent to the operation of LTS itself. For example, the finding of enhanced recall when items are meaningfully related confirms what we might expect: that memory is more effective for organized material.

If we conceive of memory formation as the transfer of information from STS to LTS, we must consider what factors might influence this process. The most obvious of these is that the brain itself should be working normally, and the consequences of brain malfunction on memory constitute a major part of this book. However, normal individuals often fail to remember things, and, under certain circumstances, this could be attributed to an ineffective transfer from STS to LTS. Proponents of the multistore model have suggested that successful transfer may depend on the amount of **rehearsal** the information receives. This concept stems from our natural tendency to repeat new information, either aloud or silently, in an effort to remember it. The relationship between rehearsal and memory was demonstrated by Rundus in 1971, using a modified version of the free recall technique. Subjects were presented with a list of words, and were encouraged to repeat them out loud during presentation. Figure 1.5 shows both the recall data and the number of times words at each list position were rehearsed. For the early serial positions, recall was highly correlated with rehearsal rate, but this was not observed for the last few items. The transfer of information from STS to LTS therefore seems to be related to the amount of rehearsal each item receives; it thus offers an explanation of the primacy effect in terms of higher rehearsal rates for the first few items. Furthermore, the increased recall with slower presentation rates probably stems from the extra rehearsal time made available in that condition.

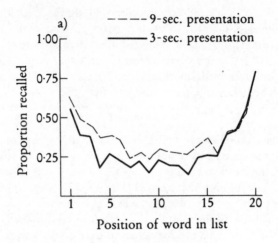

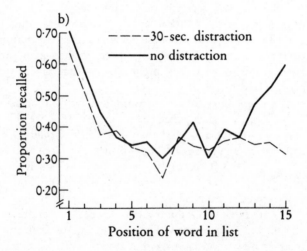

Figure 1.4 a) The effect of presentation time on the serial position curve. Presentation for 9 seconds improves recall relative to presentation for 3 seconds for early list positions, but does not influence the size of the recency effect. b) The effect of distraction prior to recall on the serial position curve. With distraction for 30 seconds, the recency effect disappears, but there is no effect on recall from other parts of the list.
(*After Glanzer and Cunitz, 1966.*)

Although rehearsal affects how well we perform in the free recall task, it is of little broader significance. In everyday life we are seldom aware of rehearsing new information, yet we remember large numbers of new facts everyday. Coupled with this, certain types of information, such as faces and

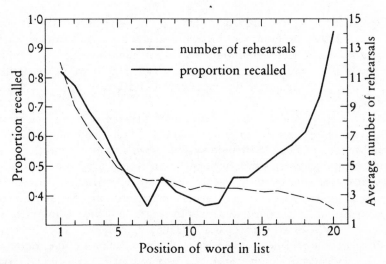

Figure 1.5 The relationship between the serial position curve and the number of times each word was rehearsed.
(*After Rundus, 1970.*)

smells, do not seem amenable to rehearsal. Finally, the rehearsal concept places too great an emphasis on the role of intentionality in learning. It is a perverse fact about human memory that we often remember things we would rather forget and forget things we want to remember. The writer Annie Dillard (1982) gives her own observation on this problem:

> I . . . looked at the painting on the hotel room wall. It was . . . a detailed and lifelike painting of a smiling clown's head, made out of vegetables. It was a painting . . . which you do not intend to look at but alas you never forget. Some tasteless fate presses it upon you. . . . Two years have passed and I have forgotten a great many things I wanted to remember – but I have not forgotten that clown painting or its lunatic setting in the old hotel. (p. 85)

Forming new memories depends on more than the conscious intention to do so. In later chapters we will consider what these other factors might be.

Problems with the Serial Position Curve

A central assumption about STS is that it has a limited capacity; so we should be able to measure what that capacity is. The recency effect in immediate free recall has been considered to reflect output from STS. Thus, if we can make a reliable quantitative estimate of the recency effect, we will have estimated the capacity of STS. Glanzer and Razel (1974), on the basis of 21 free recall experiments, concluded that the average size of the recency effect was 2.2 words. However, this neat conclusion was undermined when they tested free recall using proverbs (e.g. 'a watched pot never boils') rather than unrelated words, and found that the recency effect was 2.2 proverbs. Next they used unfamiliar sentences and found a recency effect of 1.5 sentences.

Glanzer and Razel's findings demonstrate that the size of the recency effect cannot be measured in simple 'words and units', and thus highlights a fundamental problem in attempting to measure human memory capacity. Artificial storage systems such as floppy discs, compact discs and magnetic tapes have measurable fixed capacities because information is stored by means of information units (e.g. 'bytes' of information). To measure the capacity of human memory, we would first need to reduce all information to basic units – something which at present is impossible.

Other recent evidence has also led to a reconsideration of the nature of the recency effect. A number of authors have examined the nature of serial position effects found with immediate free recall, delayed free recall and a new manipulation known as **continuous distraction** (see figure 1.6). In the latter task each item was separated by a period of distraction lasting 12 seconds and, following the last item, a further 20-second period of distraction was applied. Figure 1.6 shows that immediate free recall generated a typical serial position curve, and that no recency effect was found in delayed free recall. However, there was also a significant recency effect in the continuous distraction condition – even though the terminal item was followed by a period of distraction sufficient to remove the recency effect in delayed free recall.

It has been proposed (e.g. by Glenberg et al., 1980) that the pattern of recency effects obtained in the three different conditions shown in Figure 1.6 can be accounted for by a single function in which recall probability is calculated by the following ratio:

$$\text{probability of item recall} = \frac{\text{presentation interval between items}}{\text{time elapsed between item presentation and start of recall}}$$

According to this **constant ratio rule** the critical factor determining recall success is not the absolute amount of time that elapses between presentation of an item and the test, as would be the case with a simple displacement account of STS. Instead, the rule predicts that enhanced recall of terminal items will be greater when the presentation interval between items and the time elapsing before recall are constant. Test conditions which utilize this constant will therefore generate recency effects regardless of the time interval between items.

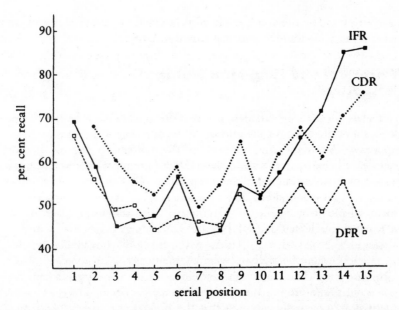

Figure 1.6 Recency effects for immediate free recall (IFR), delayed free recall (DFR), and recall under conditions of continuous distraction (CDR). (*From Baddeley, 1986.*)

A formula that predicts the shape of recency effects obtained under different conditions is not, in itself, an explanation. It does, however, suggest that a single theory might explain standard recency effects and those found with continuous distraction. At present we have little idea about what the common mechanism underlying recency effects might be. One possibility is that recency effects could be attributable to a retrieval process known as **scanning** (Craik and Jacoby, 1976). This can be thought of as a 'looking back' process, in which the contents of the immediate past are made available in some automatic effortless fashion, and the task of the retrieval mechanism is to discriminate the target information from any other information also present. Recency effects arise because, as information goes further back in time, it becomes less discriminable from other information, rather in the same way that a line of telegraph poles gradually merges as they become further away. The constant ratio rule may reflect the fact that this scanning process is more efficient if target information is located at regular intervals – as is the case when the retention interval and the inter-item intervals are the same length. Scanning can be contrasted with the **reconstructive** processes needed to retrieve information that is further back in time. Reconstructive processes form the means whereby we retrieve most information, and we will consider these processes more thoroughly in chapter 3. For the moment we will simply note that retrieval via reconstruction involves the effortful interaction between information currently in consciousness and that stored in LTS.

Short-term and Long-term Storage from a Biological Perspective

At a physical level we can define a **memory trace** as some permanent alteration of the brain for the purpose of representing some aspect of a past experience. Many differing views about the biological nature of memory traces have been put forward. In the Middle Ages memories were thought to be contained within the cerebrospinal fluid of the ventricles. Later, Descartes rightly considered that it was the solid substance of the brain that contained memory, but he wrongly located it in the pineal gland. Much later, when the nucleic acids (RNA and DNA) were discovered, a number of scientists proposed that RNA, with its modifiable ability to store information, might be the basis whereby memories were stored. However, it became clear that, although nucleic acids are involved in memory formation, they were not the actual substance of memory.

It is now universally accepted that the biological substrate of memory must lie in some permanent alteration in the synaptic interconnections between neurones. There are at least two good reasons why synaptic interconnectivity is the favoured view of memory formation. First, modification of synapses appears to be the only mechanism capable of storing the huge amounts of information that memory contains. It has been estimated that the brain contains 10^{13} synapses, a number that is adequate to handle the levels of information storage in memory. Second, synapses make very low demands on energy, requiring only that the basal metabolic rate of the brain be maintained – thus accounting for the preservation of memory during periods of coma, when the brain's electrical activity is substantially reduced. The exact means by which synapses are modified is not yet known. One possibility is that changes occur in the amounts of neurotransmitter released at particular synapses; another is that memory formation involves the growth of completely new synapses.

The process by which neurones become modified to produce new memories is known as **consolidation**. Hebb (1949) formulated an influential theory concerning this relationship between brain physiology and memory. He suggested that the initial presentation of a stimulus led to the activation of groups of neurons, which he called 'cell assemblies'. The activity of these cell assemblies maintained a representation of that stimulus long enough to allow the formation of a permanent long-term trace. If consolidation is time-based, it is logical to ask how long the process takes. Hebb suggested around 30 minutes, but evidence from studies of disrupted memory suggests that the transition from active to passive storage normally occurs much more rapidly than this.

An important feature of Hebb's explanation of consolidation is that the active and passive modes of storage make use of different underlying mechanisms. This being so, performance based on the active storage of information should continue even when the mechanisms of consolidation have been made inoperative (note that the reverse is not possible, because passive storage relies on the input provided by the active storage mechanism). Thus we might expect to observe situations in which information can be recalled immediately, because it is in active storage, but has been forgotten a few minutes later. In this book you will find many examples of this dissociation in various pathological disorders of memory, but for now we will restrict ourselves to experimental evidence from normal individuals.

Neuropharmacology offers a new and important means of investigating human memory (e.g. Warburton and Rusted, 1991; Polster, 1993). As we have seen, the neural pathways underlying all brain function depend on neurotransmitters as the means whereby nervous impulses are transmitted across synapses. The exact involvement of different pathways in memory can be explored by employing neuropharmacological agents which either inhibit or facilitate the activity of particular neurotransmitters. Drugs that inhibit activity are called **antagonists,** and those that facilitate it are **agonists**.

The **cholinergic blockade** technique involves administration of a drug known as **scopolamine (hyoscine),** an antagonist of **acetyl-choline**, a neurotransmitter known to be essential for consolidation. Figure 1.7 shows the effect of scopolamine on subjects' ability to perform three types of memory task. Digit span requires subjects to reproduce a sequence of numbers in the same order as they were presented, and, typically, normal subjects manage seven plus or minus two. It is generally agreed that digit span is a good measure of short-term storage, and the absence of any decline in digit span under the influence of scopolamine indicates that short-term store is not dependent on cholinergic activity. Digit supra-span involves subjects repeating back slightly longer sequences, and again there appears to be minimal disruption from scopolamine. By contrast, the recall task, which involves learning a list of words and recalling them after a 60-second period of distraction, is markedly affected by scopolamine, thus indicating that long-term storage is dependent on cholinergic mechanisms and that active storage processes are not involved after a 60-second delay.

Active storage therefore appears to be short-lived, but it would be wrong to conclude that the act of consolidation is fully executed within a minute or so. Many theorists hold the view that consolidation is a multistorage process in which an initial fixation is established quite rapidly, followed by subsequent 'elaborative' consolidation in which the new memory trace becomes more fully integrated with pre-existing memories – aspects of memory which a simple list recall task may not be sensitive to. The time period over

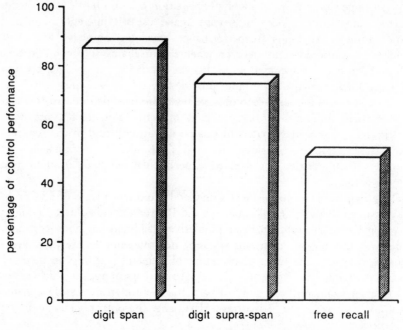

Figure 1.7 The performance of subjects under the influence of scopolamine in comparison with control subjects on three tests of memory. (*Data from Drachman and Sahakian, 1979, p. 354.*)

which this additional consolidation occurs might be measured in minutes, hours or even years! (Squire, 1987; Remple-Clower et al., 1996).

Explanation of memory in purely biological terms is not yet possible. We know that complex patterns of neuronal interconnectivity underlie memory function, but the manner in which memory is created is not evident from this alone. Psychologists have therefore constructed models of memory by drawing analogies between memory function and entities we do understand. Current psychological theories conceive of memory as a series of stores each with its own functional characteristics. In this chapter we have emphasized the distinction between STS and LTS. Phenomena such as the recency effect indicate that recently experienced events are dealt with in a different way from events experienced further back in time. However, it has not proved possible to provide accurate measures of how long information resides in STS or to estimate the latter's capacity. The idea of STS and LTS receives support from biological studies of memory. In particular, it has been shown that pharmacological agents which block the activity of the neurotransmitters essential for long-term storage have no effect on STS tasks such as digit span.

2 Beyond the Multistore Model

In chapter 1 we examined the evidence for a fundamental distinction between STS and LTS. We saw that there was both psychological and biological evidence to suggest that important differences exist between our memory for the immediate past and our longer-term memories. In this chapter we will consider the nature of long-term store in more detail, and then examine alternative ways of developing our ideas about human memory.

The Organization of LTS

In any individual, LTS contains a vast amount of information, and to be effective, it must be organized. The question of organization can be approached in many ways. Psycholinguists, for example, may be concerned with how we represent our knowledge of words and their meanings. Our initial approach will be more general, and will be based on the proposal that information in LTS takes one of three basic forms. As a starting-point for discussion, let us return to the serial position curve in figure 1.3. This shows that subjects remembered only about 20 per cent of the words from the middle part of the list. Clearly, memory has failed here; but what exactly has gone wrong? Free recall experiments involve common words, so the failure to remember cannot be because the subjects no longer know the words. Memory fails because the subjects are unable to remember that a given word was presented at a particular time.

In 1972 Tulving put forward a conceptual view of memory which provides a framework for discussing forgetting in the free recall task. He proposed that memories in LTS could be classified as either episodic or semantic. **Episodic memory** is described as an 'autobiographical' memory responsible for storing a record of the events in our lives. It enables us to answer questions such as 'What were you doing yesterday?' or 'When did you last go to the cinema?' The essential point about an episodic memory is that recollection involves some feeling of re-experiencing the event itself. Most commonly this would involve some image of the event in our 'mind's eye'.

Semantic memory is our store of general knowledge about the world: concepts, rules and language. The essential feature of semantic memory is that it can be used without reference to the events that account for its formation in the first place. Thus, when using language or doing arithmetic, we are not aware of the original circumstances under which we learnt to do these things; they are simply something we 'know'. Returning to the free recall task, the forgetting of words can be considered as a failure of episodic memory, since the locus of difficulty is in remembering a specific past event – namely, that a particular word was presented in a list we saw or heard at a specific time.

Semantic memory can also store information about ourselves and events that have happened to us. When we are asked what we have done, what our opinions are and so on, we do not, as would be the case with episodic recall, remember specific past experiences in order to answer. Instead, we have access to a general account of ourselves, which is often sufficient to answer a wide range of personal questions. In normal individuals, this information can be used in conjunction with the recollection of specific past experiences to provide a more detailed answer to a question. Thus, when asked your opinion about a particular piece of music, your positive reaction might be reinforced by recounting some occasion when you found it particularly enjoyable.

More recently Tulving (1985), among others (e.g. Anderson, 1995), has argued for an additional form of memory, a form that has been termed **procedural memory**. This can be defined as information in LTS that cannot be inspected consciously. Riding a bicycle, for example, is a complex skill that most of us acquire; but if we try to explain how we do it, we can give only the most superficial explanation. Similarly, native speakers of a language can usually give no account of the complicated grammatical rules that enable them to produce correct utterances. This type of memory is contrasted with episodic and semantic memory, both of which can be inspected consciously, and their contents described fully to another individual.

Although it is necessary to distinguish them conceptually, episodic, semantic and procedural memory represent a highly interactive system, and, at any one time, the behaviour of a normal individual may be directed by information from one or more of these sources. In addition, the contribution of these different memories to determining behaviour may change across time. The formation of new semantic memories may depend initially, for example, on information from episodic memory. Consider the problem of learning computer terminology. To newcomers, the jargon is wholly unfamiliar and difficult to assimilate. Thus the instruction to 'boot' the system is quite mysterious unless you remember that on a previous occasion it meant to start up the computer. However, with repeated use, the term becomes part of your general knowledge, and can be defined without recourse to episodic memory. These kinds of interactions also occur while learning skills. Take learning to type, for example. At first, this involves remembering the layout of the keyboard in order to place your fingers correctly. However, as practice continues, the skill becomes increasingly automatic and independent of the ability to remember the keyboard's layout. At this stage, typing has ceased to rely on episodic and semantic memory, and has become incorporated in procedural memory. Indeed, when skilled typists are asked to recall the layout of the keyboard, they often find it difficult, remembering the location of some letters only by trying to type them and noticing where their finger is placed (Posner, 1973).

Tulving's account of memory is essentially introspective, with each form of memory being associated with a different kind of conscious experience. We are not consciously aware of procedural memories; their existence is inferred from the fact that an organism responds in a consistent manner to a particular stimulus. Because of this, it is a form of memory that we can assume to be present in any organism capable of learning. For this reason, it is thought to be the most primitive kind of memory. Semantic memory is open to conscious examination, because we can inwardly contemplate the features of the external world. Its contents are confirmed or altered in the light of new experience. For example, someone might believe initially that all cars run on petrol, but then he or she encounters a car that runs on diesel. This new observation then modifies that person's knowledge about cars. Episodic memory is associated with an additional and qualitatively distinct conscious awareness. It has a self-referential quality, enabling us to be aware of ourselves in the past and to imagine ourselves in the future. The truth of episodic memories is determined entirely by their subjective familiarity, rather than by observation. When we recall personal experiences, we do not have external proof that our memories are correct; the manner in which they enter our consciousness seems to assure their authenticity.

Semantic and episodic memory are assumed to be higher and more recently evolved forms of memory, and are inextricably linked with consciousness. As yet, we cannot establish whether other animals experience consciousness, which makes it difficult to consider these memory systems in relation to species other than man. Many psychologists have proposed conceptual distinctions similar to Tulving's, and there is agreement that a classification of this kind makes intuitive sense; but experimental evidence to support the distinctions is only beginning to emerge. At present, major support for this view comes from studies of the human amnesic syndrome, which will be considered in chapter 6.

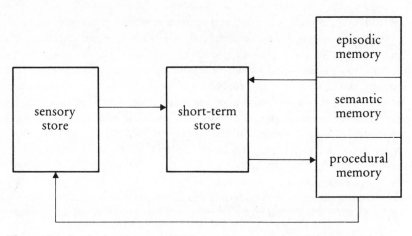

Figure 2.1 Revised multistore model showing tripartite division of LTS.

Figure 2.1 represents our revised view of human memory; the multistore model is retained, but with the addition of a tripartite division of LTS into episodic, semantic and procedural memory. The division of LTS into three stores has been a popular theory, but there have been arguments against the distinction between episodic and semantic memory. It has been argued that a simpler distinction between procedural and **declarative memory** gives a better account of memory. Here a distinction is made solely in terms of whether information is consciously accessible or not. We have already seen that procedural memory is not consciously accessible; declarative memory is the converse: any permanent memory we can consciously describe irrespective of whether it is an autobiographical recollection or a piece of general knowledge. We will return to this issue in chapter 6.

Levels of Processing

In chapter 1 we saw that there were difficulties in developing the STS/LTS distinction to solve more specific problems such as measuring the capacity or time course of STS. Problems of this kind led Craik and Lockhart (1972) to propose an alternative framework for understanding memory, which they called **levels of processing**. It is important to note that they did not reject the STS/LTS distinction. They simply argued that the model was unable to provide any further insights into the operation of memory, and that attempts to develop it further would be counterproductive.

The levels of processing concept is based on the reasonable assertion that the memory trace represents a record of the analyses carried out during the conscious processing of new information. It follows, therefore, that memory function can be explored by investigating how variations in the way

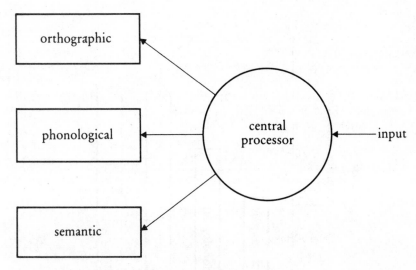

Figure 2.2 The 'levels of processing' approach to memory. Processing of new information is controlled by the central processor and can occur at one or more levels. Diagram shows how the theory relates to verbal memory.

new information is processed affect our subsequent ability to remember it. This idea was formalized by suggesting that analysis of a new stimulus proceeds through a series of levels, each representing a different dimension of the stimulus. The analogy was then extended by suggesting that more complex processing occurs at 'deeper' levels than simpler processes. For words, three levels were conceived: **orthographic**, **phonological** and **semantic**, the latter representing the deepest level. Processing of new information was said to be under the control of a **central processor** (see figure 2.2). This entity, like STS, represents the locus of conscious mental activity. However, the concern of Craik and Lockhart was not with the processor's structural aspects, but with how variations in its deployment might affect the retention of new information.

To explore this issue, Craik and Lockhart made use of the **incidental learning** technique. This involves presenting subjects with a series of items and requiring them to make a decision about each one. By manipulating the type of decision required, it is possible to create various orienting tasks, each of which addresses a different level of processing. The following are examples of **orienting tasks** involving orthographic, phonological and semantic levels of processing: 'Is the word in capital letters?' (orthographic); 'Does it rhyme with "grog"?' (phonological); 'Does it hop about?' (semantic). All these would evoke a 'yes' response for the word FROG. For convenience, orthographic and phonological tasks are classified together as 'non-semantic'. An important feature of incidental learning is that the subjects do not expect their memory to be tested; hence, the pattern

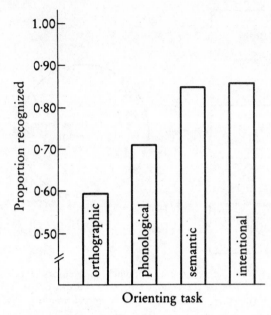

Figure 2.3 Typical effect of different levels of processing on memory performance.
(*Data from Craik, 1977.*)

of retention observed can be attributed to the processing evoked by
the orienting task, as opposed to subjects' own attempts at deliberate
memorization.

Figure 2.3 shows the results of an incidental learning experiment
involving memory for words. It employed not only semantic and non-
semantic orienting tasks, but also a control task in which subjects were
instructed to learn the words. The most important result is that the
semantic orienting task produced much better memory performance than
the non-semantic tasks. But note that the semantic task was as effective as
the control condition; this emphasizes the point made earlier that the
intention to remember is not an important determinant of whether or not
we remember something. On the basis of these findings, it was asserted that
'deeper' semantic processing gave rise to a better, more durable memory
trace. The superiority of semantic over non-semantic processing was
demonstrated in numerous studies, and led to the generation of a principle:
that the probability of remembering something is a positive function of the
depth to which it is processed.

Craik and Lockhart's approach grew in popularity with the demonstration of levels of processing effects for different types of information. This
contrasted with experiments on the multistore model, which had been
concerned almost exclusively with verbal memory. Winograd (1976), for

example, showed subjects a long sequence of unfamiliar faces, and required them to make a decision about each one. This involved either a judgement about physical characteristics ('Does he have straight hair?'), personality ('Does he look friendly?') or role ('Does he look like an actor?'). Subsequently the subjects' ability to recognize the faces was tested, and it was found that judgements about physical characteristics produced poorer recognition than the other types. This finding resembles findings in studies with words, since it shows that memory is best when subjects attend to meaning during learning. However, subsequent research has shown that the relationship between different orienting tasks and facial memory is more complex than was originally thought (see Parkin, 1993).

More subtle distinctions than that between semantic and non-semantic processing levels can be made. Craik and Tulving (1975) maintained that within the level of semantic processing, one could distinguish between different degrees of **elaboration**. This concept arose from experiments showing that the more extensively subjects processed the meaning of information, the more successfully they remembered it. The importance of elaboration in memory was recognized by James (1890), and his account captures the essential point:

> The more other facts a fact is associated with in the mind, the better possession of it our memory retains. Each of its associates becomes a hook to which it hangs, a means to fish it up by when sunk below the surface. . . . The 'secret of a good memory' is thus the secret of forming diverse and multiple associations with every fact we care to retain. (p. 662)

In modern terminology, elaboration can be described as the formation of a more richly encoded memory trace, which is more easily accessible because there are many different ways of contacting it in the process of retrieval.

Depth and elaboration were just two of a number of concepts that arose from the levels of processing approach. But interest in the approach subsided when certain methodological problems surfaced. The most important of these concerned the explanatory power of the levels concept. In the experiment illustrated in figure 2.3, subjects in the semantic orienting condition remembered more words than those in the non-semantic groups. This effect was explained by arguing that the semantic task produced a 'deeper' level of encoding. But how could we assume that? The answer was: 'Because it produced better retention.' Unfortunately, this argument is *circular*, since differences in depth are assumed on the basis of differences in retention, while this, in turn, is explained as a consequence of different depths of processing. The problem of circularity has proved a major stumbling-block in developing the levels of processing concept. I have demonstrated some ways of overcoming it, but progress has not been great (Parkin, 1979).

Despite these difficulties, the levels of processing idea has made a significant contribution to our understanding of memory. Prior to its development, memory theories tended to oversimplify the psychological factors involved in the formation of new memories. Work with the multistore approach had identified only rehearsal as a significant factor in remembering. However, as we noted in chapter 1, this is a rather limited concept, which can account for only a tiny fraction of what we learn. The recognition that acquisition is not a rigidly defined process, and that variations in the way information is handled can affect how well it is remembered, has had an important impact on the way psychologists investigate memory. In attempting to explain a wide range of memory phenomena, it is now accepted that changes in the processing strategy adopted by the subject may provide the basis for an explanation.

Working Memory

The **working memory** model of Baddeley and Hitch (1974) represents a third framework for studying the operation of memory. Its aim is to establish how memory is organized so as to support the kinds of mental activity that characterize our everyday life. Essentially, it is a development of the STS concept described in chapter 1. The major difference is that STS is no longer a unitary system. Instead, it is conceived of as 'an alliance of temporary storage systems co-ordinated by an attentional component [termed] the central executive' (Baddeley, 1984, p. 15).

The starting-point for the development of this model was the assumption that if digit span reflects the capacity of STS and, in turn, if STS is a single structure, then any task requiring the subject to retain a sequence of digits comparable to their memory span should make it extremely difficult for the subject to carry out any other task requiring STS capacity at the same time.

To test this idea, it was necessary to devise a **dual task paradigm** in which the subject performs a primary task while carrying out, simultaneously, a **secondary task**. In one experiment subjects had to learn lists of visually presented words while simultaneously either retaining a sequence of three or six spoken digits or copying down pairs of digits as they were spoken.

If digit span reflects maximum STS capacity, we should expect subjects doing the list learning and retaining six digits at the same time to be quite impaired on the task – this follows because the maximum digit span of normal adults is seven plus or minus two. The additional load of six digits did generally reduce performance, but to nowhere near the extent one would expect if STS capacity were largely used up maintaining the digits. Furthermore, the recency effect, which we have also attributed to short-term storage processes, was affected very little by the six-digit load.

Baddeley and his colleagues went on to explore the influence of secondary task performance on primary tasks involving other kinds of conscious processing. In one study subjects were asked to verify sentences of the kind 'Canaries have wings', 'Dogs have feathers'. Before each of these sentences was presented, subjects were given a sequence of digits to remember which ranged from nought to eight numbers. The subjects had to repeat the sequence continually until they had verified the sentence in front of them. Even when subjects were keeping in mind seven or eight random digits, they could still perform a reasoning task in two seconds with 95 per cent accuracy. It is extremely difficult to reconcile this and other similar results (e.g. Baddeley and Hitch, 1974) with a unitary concept of STS in which digit span is assumed to be a fundamental measure of capacity, because, if so, one would expect verification performance to be severely disrupted when subjects were repeating seven or eight digits.

These experiments led to the view that the system responsible for memory span, as measured in the digit span task, was not the same as the memory system supporting all our conscious mental activity. Instead, it seemed possible that the task of retaining short sequences of digits might, to a large extent, be carried out by a different system from that involved in tasks such as learning word lists and reasoning. Using a variety of lines of evidence, Baddeley and Hitch (1974) suggested that the system under-lying the retention of digits was speech-based, and they named it the **articulatory loop**.

Evidence for the existence of an articulatory system underlying memory span came from experiments based on the observation that memory span for sequences of short words (e.g. SUM, WIT) is better than that for long words (e.g. ALUMINIUM, UNIVERSITY). Baddeley and colleagues (1975) examined whether this **word length effect** depended on the number of syllables in short and long words or on differences in the spoken duration of each word type. They compared memory span for items that have equal numbers of syllables but relatively shorter or longer spoken durations (e.g. WICKET versus HARPOON). Memory span was found to be lower for words with longer spoken durations; therefore they concluded that the system underlying memory span was speech-based.

More evidence for an articulatory loop came from a second study, in which the word length effect was examined under conditions of **articu-latory suppression**. In this, the secondary task entailed repeating a meaningless spoken sequence (e.g. 'the, the, the . . .) while carrying out the primary task. Figure 2.4 shows that articulatory suppression causes the word length effect to disappear. Note in particular that performance on short words is reduced to the same level as that on long words. This is strong

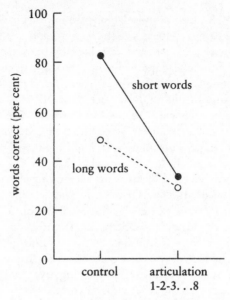

Figure 2.4 The influence of articulatory suppression on the word length effect. (*Data from Baddeley et al., 1975, p. 584.*)

evidence that the advantage in recalling short words in a memory span task depends on an articulatory coding system. When this is not the case, as with articulatory suppression, short and long words are dependent on the same memory processes, and are therefore recalled to the same degree.

These findings led to the first specific model of working memory, illustrated in figure 2.5. It identifies three components: the articulatory loop, a **visuo-spatial scratch pad** and a **central executive** (the latter two of which we will consider in due course). On the basis of experimental evidence, the articulatory loop was characterized as a structure capable of holding and recycling a small amount of speech-based information. The articulatory loop was assumed to underlie subjects' ability to perform mental tasks relatively easily while simultaneously holding digits, the argument being that part or all of the digit load could be placed in the articulatory loop, thus making little or no demand on other components of working memory. In terms of normal mental life, it is thought that the loop plays a particular role in silent reading by providing a temporary phonological storage system which aids comprehension by, for example, retaining the order of words or enabling intonation to be represented. Baddeley and Lewis (1981) examined how articulatory suppression interfered with subjects' abilities to detect anomalous words in texts. These sentences were quite complex (e.g. 'She doesn't mind going to the dentist to have fillings, but doesn't like the pain[rent] when he gives her the injection at the beginning'). Detection of anomalies was less accurate if subjects engaged in

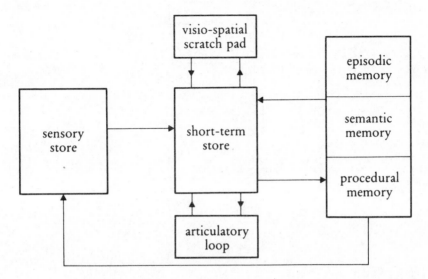

Figure 2.5 Multistore model revised to incorporate the concept of working memory.

articulatory suppression, but this did not affect their ability to classify meaningful sentences correctly. Finally we should note that the articulatory loop concept has undergone further development, and there is now good evidence that it comprises two subsystems: a phonological store and an articulatory control process (see Baddeley, 1990).

In a later chapter we will consider the phenomenon of **mental imagery**. Briefly, this is the experience we all have of being able to see things in our mind's eye. Thus, if I asked you to imagine an object such as an umbrella, you could form that **image** without difficulty. Furthermore, if I asked you to imagine the umbrella rotating, you could also do that. These introspections, which have been backed up by substantial experimental evidence (for reviews see Anderson, 1995; Parkin, 1993), suggest that, in some way, we have an internal medium within which images and other spatially arranged representations can be held and manipulated. Within the working memory model this function is undertaken by the visuo–spatial scratch pad (VSSP).

Evidence for a VSSP comes from dual task studies such as that used by Brooks (1968). Subjects were asked to keep in mind a letter F and then imagine an asterisk travelling around the F (see figure 2.6). At each change of direction, subjects had to indicate whether the asterisk was at an extreme or intermediate point of the F. Three modes of responding were used: vocal yes–no, tapping – one tap for yes, two taps for no – and a pointing response. In the latter, subjects had a visual array of spatially distributed Y and N symbols in front of them. As they imagined the asterisk moving,

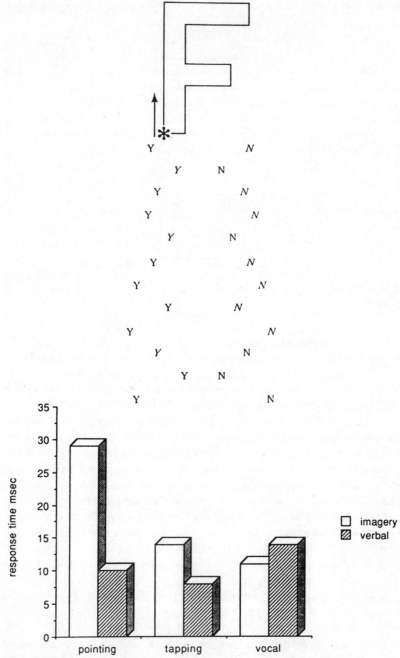

Figure 2.6 Simple diagram used by Brooks (1968) to study the scanning of mental images (*top*). Pointing response arrangement (*middle*). Response times in the different experimental conditions (*bottom*).
(*From Brooks, 1968, pp. 350–3.*)

subjects had to indicate their response by pointing to the next Y or N location available as they worked their way down the array.

These three modes of responding were also used in a verbal task in which subjects had to work through a proverb and indicate whether each successive word was a noun or not. For the verbal task the three response modes produced comparable reaction times. For the visual task, however, the pointing response produced far slower reaction times than the other two response modes. The fact that pointing caused a significant delay only when responding to the visual task suggests strongly that subjects were retaining a spatial image and that this interfered with responding which was also determined by spatial constraints.

The articulatory loop and visuo-spatial scratch pad contribute to only a small percentage of our conscious mental activity. In terms of the model, the bulk of what we do is carried out by the central executive. The central executive has much in common with both the original STS idea and Craik and Lockhart's notion of a central processor, in that it represents the locus of conscious control. Thus it is within the executive that decisions concerning how information should be encoded and how it should be retrieved are made. Being the most complex, it is not surprising that it is the aspect of the model that is least developed. However, we shall see later that evidence from certain types of brain-damaged patient have recently been instrumental in illustrating some aspects of executive function.

In this chapter we have extended the multistore model by dividing LTS into three separate forms of memory: episodic, semantic and procedural. We have noted that the multistore model is limited as a means of explaining how various parts of the system work. Two alternative approaches have been considered: levels of processing and working memory. Both these approaches still embody a distinction between some form of STS and LTS, but the emphasis is different. Levels of processing concentrates on how different processing strategies affect memory, whereas working memory considers how STS might have various components to deal with different types of information.

3 Remembering and Forgetting

The act of remembering involves the location of memories in LTS and their restoration to consciousness. Theoretical explanations of this **retrieval process** must explain how we are able rapidly to access specific memories from among the vast amount of information stored in LTS. For this to occur, retrieval must be guided in some way; thus William James writes: 'Suppose I am silent for a moment, and then say . . . "Remember!, Recollect!" Does your . . . memory obey the order, and reproduce any definite image from your past? Certainly not. It stands staring into vacancy, and asking, "What kind of a thing do you wish me to remember?" ' (1899, pp. 117–18). James's point is that retrieval is a reconstructive process, in which currently available information serves to initiate and direct the search for memories in LTS. Modern retrieval theories have attempted to offer a more detailed explanation of how this interaction occurs.

Modern Theories of Retrieval

Before we can discuss retrieval, it is necessary to distinguish three different kinds of remembering. Figure 3.1 illustrates a hypothetical experiment in which subjects have attempted to learn a list of words. Condition A represents **free recall**, where the subjects try to remember the words without any external information to help them. Condition B represents **cued recall**, in which the subjects are given some explicit information to help them remember (e.g. 'One of the words you are trying to remember begins with WA . . .'). Condition C involves **recognition**, the subject being presented with a word and then asked whether it is one that he or she is trying to remember (e.g. 'was WATCH on the list?'). The results are typical of the many experiments that have tested memory in these three different ways: performance is best with recognition testing, followed by cued recall and then free recall. These findings concur with our everyday experience of memory. We may fail to recall the answer to a question, for example, but

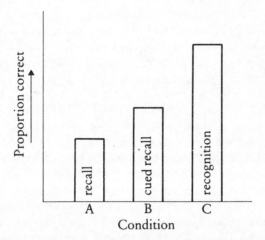

Figure 3.1 Typical relationship between different types of retrieval test.

recognize it immediately when it is shown to us. Similarly, we may be unable to name someone, but remember the name easily when we are prompted with their initials.

Any theory of retrieval must account for the superiority of recognition over recall. One explanation is to conceive of memories as varying in 'strength', and to say that greater trace strength is required for recall than for recognition (Kintsch, 1970). However, this explanation is not consistent with certain experimental findings. One of these is that lists of common words (e.g. TABLE) are recalled more easily than lists of rare words (e.g. SPOOL), whereas in recognition testing, rare words are identified more readily than common words. A 'strength' theory of memory cannot account for this, since it would predict that words recalled best should also be those most easily recognized.

The identification of factors which have different effects on recall and recognition has led to the idea that they are separate processes. This proposal forms the basis of the **generation–recognition** (GR) model of retrieval. The most well-known examples of GR models are those of Anderson and Bower (1972) and Kintsch (1970). These models specifically address how subjects retrieve words in a verbal learning experiment; but it must be borne in mind that the intention was to produce a general account of how retrieval happens. These models assume a structure rather like semantic memory in which each known word is represented by a **node**. When a subject studies a word, it is assumed that some form of 'occurrence marker' or 'tag' is set up to indicate that the word was part of the target list. When recall is attempted, various candidates are generated, and the corresponding nodes examined for markers, which, if detected, result in recognition and hence retrieval. Cued recall is more efficient than uncued recall, because the cue guides the generation of candidates. In recognition, access to the node was considered to be automatic and the recognition was dependent simply on detection of a marker.

The GR model provides us with a testable prediction. For a memory to be recalled, both the generation and recognition phases must have been successful. From this it follows that any information that can be recalled must be capable of being recognized. Thus, if we are able to recall WATCH from a word list, we should also be able to recognize it, since in recalling WATCH, the act of recognition was carried out.

In 1973 Tulving and Thomson carried out an experiment which examined this prediction. The experiment consisted of four phases. In phase 1 subjects were presented with target words to learn. Each of these was accompanied by a 'cue' word which the subjects were asked to attend to, but not deliberately try to remember. A typical example might be the target ENGINE paired with 'black'. In phase 2 subjects were presented with another list of words, for each of which they were required to generate associations. The stimulus words were carefully chosen so that there would be a high probability of their generating one of the targets learnt in phase 1. Thus for the 'black'–ENGINE pairing, the word 'steam' might be a stimulus in phase 2. As a result, a large number of phase-1 targets were produced. In phase 3 subjects had to look at the words they had generated and pick out any that were targets in phase 1. In phase 4 subjects were presented with the cue words from phase 1 and asked to recall the target word that accompanied each one. The most important result was that in phase 4 subjects often recalled words that they failed to recognize in phase 3.

The experiment failed to confirm the prediction that we must be able to recognize any word that we can recall. This led to a rejection of the GR model by Tulving and Thomson, who replaced it with the **encoding specificity principle**. The essence of this is that recall and recognition are not separate stages of the retrieval process. Instead, retrieval is viewed as a single process in which information currently available interacts directly with the contents of memory. The success of retrieval depends on overlap between the stored information and that currently available. The greater the overlap, the greater the likelihood of a memory being successfully retrieved. To explain the usual superiority of recognition over recall, it was argued that recognition tests typically present subjects with more information about what they are trying to remember. But then, why did Tulving and Thomson find cued recall better than recognition? Their explanation centred on the manner in which the target had been encoded. It was argued that the phase-1 cue words led subjects to encode the target words in a specific way. When these cue words were subsequently generated in phase 2, it was in response to different cues; thus the target words were presented in a different **context** to that in which they were originally learnt. Thus, in the recognition test there was less overlap with the target memory trace than with the original cue, and it was this difference that led to cued recall being better than recognition.

The encoding of contextual information is an essential prerequisite for an efficiently organized LTS. Contextual information can be defined broadly as the information associated with a memory that enables that memory to be distinguished from all others. Hewitt (1973) has proposed a distinction between **intrinsic** and **extrinsic context**. A change in intrinsic context arises when some aspect of the target itself is changed (e.g. the colour of someone's hair), whereas in a change of extrinsic context, the target itself remains the same, but the information accompanying the target is different. A good example of the latter is meeting someone you know very well in an unexpected place. There may be nothing different about their appearance, but the fact that you do not normally meet them under these circumstances can make it more difficult to recognize them.

An important feature of episodic memory is its capacity for answering questions requiring location of a particular point in the past. Episodic memory must therefore have some form of organization which distinguishes events in time. But how is this achieved? Logical constraints obviously play a role – e.g. school-days must have preceded college days. Similarly, 'key events', such as getting married, can be used as 'landmarks' for identifying events as having occurred before or after an event. But there are numerous occasions on which our ability to remember an event requires more sophisticated discrimination. Consider the question 'What did you watch on television last night?' Watching television is presumably something you have done many times before, so how do you distinguish the events of last night from those of previous similar occasions? To explain this ability, it has been proposed that contextual information has a specific time-based component which defines a given event in time. Psychologists label this **temporal context**, but there are no strong theories of how LTS represents this information.

The encoding specificity principle has come in for serious criticism. Consider a hypothetical experiment in which a subject learns some new information. Two cues, X and Y, are then presented successively, but only Y enables the subject to remember the target information. The encoding specificity principle asserts that a retrieval cue will be effective only if it has information in common with the memory trace. It would thus be concluded that Y has an overlap with the memory trace, whereas X does not. However, if X were the only effective cue, the opposite conclusion would be reached. This circular line of reasoning has led many psychologists to reject encoding specificity as a valid scientific theory. There are also 'ecological' objections to it. By arguing that cues are effective only if they have some informational overlap with a memory trace, considerable inflexibility is attributed to the retrieval system, since novel information cannot be used to access memories. By contrast, the generation-recognition model allows for completely new information to facilitate recall, provided it guides the generation process in an appropriate manner.

Although the encoding specificity principle is limited as a scientific theory, it was important in drawing attention to the role of context in the retrieval process. Earlier theories of retrieval had taken little account of contextual influences. Tulving and Thomson's demonstration that altering the conditions under which target information is presented can lead to failure of recognition ensured that all subsequent theories of retrieval would specifically address the effects of context. The generation-recognition model can be adapted to accommodate the effects of context (Reder et al., 1974) , but this still does not make it an adequate explanation of the retrieval system. One difficulty is that our memory does not normally seem to generate possibilities prior to recall. Most of what we remember appears to come to us effortlessly, and it is only on rare occasions that we apply a conscious generative strategy to help us remember. Related to this is the problem of specifying how the generation process starts. This may be straightforward when a specific cue is presented, but this situation is not characteristic of normal memory. The generation-recognition model provides an account of how retrieval operates when explicit information is available about the memories to be recalled. This does not deny the basic contention that retrieval is a reconstructive act, but the normal process of retrieval is more complex than that specified by the generation-recognition model.

Recognition versus Familiarity

So far we have considered recognition as a unitary process, but more detailed analysis shows that this is not the case. The literal meaning of the term recognition is 'previously known', and Mandler (1980) has proposed two ways in which our memory system indicates this. His analysis is based on an experience that we all have from time to time. He notes that we often encounter someone or something and experience it as 'familiar', even though we cannot identify who or what it is. Thus we may meet someone in the street and be aware that he or she is familiar, even though we do not know just who the person is. In order to identify the person, a second process must be initiated, in which LTS is searched until the person's identity can be established. This process might well involve generating possibilities about the person's role (is he the milkman? or the postman?). Mandler argued that this phenomenon suggested two stages to recognition: an initial **familiarity** response and identification following **context retrieval**. Within this theory, therefore, recognition can be either **context-free**, when only familiarity information is available, or **context-dependent**, when the prior occurrence of a stimulus has to be specified in place or time.

Recently Jacoby (1991) proposed the **process dissociation framework** as a means of measuring the extent to which a subject's recognition response is determined by familiarity or contextual retrieval. In a typical experiment subjects are presented with two successive lists of words, one spoken, the other visually presented. Two types of recognition test follow. In the **exclusion** condition, subjects are required to make a contextual recollection, in that they are required to identify only words from the second list. In the **inclusion** condition, no contextual demands are imposed; subjects are just told to recognize words they have seen before. The assumption of this methodology is that recognition of a list-1 word in the exclusion condition indicates that the subject has forgotten the context of that word's presentation, and that the recognition response is based on familiarity. The extent to which familiarity-based responding is occurring is determined by comparing incorrect recognition of list-1 words in the exclusion condition with the recognition rate for those words in the inclusion condition.

Using this task, Jacoby explored the effects of divided attention on the two components of recognition. In this case the subject is required to perform a main task, such as learning a list of words, and a secondary task, such as monitoring a sequence of digits for particular patterns. Divided attention is used as a means of discovering whether a psychological process is automatic or depends on conscious effortful processing. If divided attention has a negative effect on performance, it is assumed that the task depends on conscious effort. If no negative effect is observed, the task is considered to be performed automatically. Divided attention was found to reduce the number of heard words correctly identified and increase the number of seen words. Divided attention thus made subjects less able to meet the demand of the exclusion instructions, with a resulting decrease in context-based recognition and an increase in familiarity-based responding.

An alternative approach to trying to understand recollective and familiarity-based recognition is the recognition and conscious awareness (RCA) task. This task, originally devised by Tulving (1985), is based on the earlier observation that memory of an event can be based either on an episodic type of memory, in which some sense of actually experiencing the event is brought back to mind, or on a more general knowledge that the event happened, but without episodic recollection. The subjects were first shown a list of words to remember. They were then presented with a recognition test, and asked to indicate those words they recognized from the list. On recognizing a stimulus, they were required to classify their response as either 'remember' (R) or 'know' (K). An R response represented recognition in which the response was associated with some episodic recollection of the word's prior occurrence (e.g. an image or emotion it evoked), whereas a K response represented recognition without any specific recollection (i.e. familiarity).

A number of recent studies have collectively demonstrated that R and K responses appear to have different properties (see Gardiner and Java, 1993, for a review). Gardiner and Parkin (1990) asked subjects to learn a list of words under either focused attention conditions or while performing a secondary task. On testing, the level of R responding was directly related to the demands of the secondary task, whereas K responses were unaffected. This result suggests that R responses are dependent on consciously mediated processing operations, but K responses are not – a conclusion supported by additional findings that R responses are also affected by levels of processing, intentional learning instructions, and tranquillizers that affect our conscious processing resources (Gardiner, 1988; Gardiner and Java, 1993; Curran et al., 1993).

From the above we conclude that there is good evidence for supposing that recognition has two components: context-based retrieval and familiarity. Both the process dissociation data and findings using the RCA task indicate that context-based recognition requires effortful processing, whereas familiarity-based responding does not. The significance of this will be considered again in the next section.

Explicit and Implicit Memory

Up until now we have considered remembering as a deliberate act. Thus, in all the experiments we have considered, subjects are deliberately trying to remember specific pieces of information, such as words in a list. However, within the last ten years or so, psychologists have become increasingly interested in contrasting performance on tasks where memory is tested directly with that on tasks in which subjects' memory for an event is tested indirectly.

This area of research makes a fundamental distinction between tests of **explicit** and **implicit** memory. Tests of explicit memory are the ones we are already familiar with, such as recall and recognition. Tests of implicit memory are ones in which an individual's memory of an event is tested without requiring the event itself to be remembered. It is important to note that these terms are used to describe the demands of memory tasks, and are not referring to hypothetical underlying memory systems.

Tulving and colleagues (1982) devised an experimental procedure for investigating implicit memory. They began by asking subjects to learn a list of multisyllabic and relatively infrequent words such as TOBOGGAN. Following a retention interval of either 1 hour or 1 week, subjects returned and undertook two types of memory test. The first was a yes–no recognition test which examined subjects' explicit memory for the target stimuli. The second was not, ostensibly, related to the original learning event, and involved a task known as **fragment completion**. Subjects were presented with incomplete words – e.g. __O__BG__N? – and asked to fill in the blanks to make a word. In this task the solutions to half of the fragments were words from the target list, but subjects were not informed of this. Fragment completion therefore served as a test of implicit memory.

Tulving and his co-workers found that subjects were more likely to complete fragments correctly when the solution corresponded to a target word – a phenomenon known as **repetition priming**. You may not find this result surprising. One might, for example, argue that subjects notice that some of the solutions are target words and then use their explicit recollection to help them do the test. If correct, this argument would mean that repetition priming was just another form of explicit memory. However, an ingenious aspect of Tulving and colleagues' study ruled out this simple interpretation. In the experiment each target word was tested for recognition and fragment completion, and it was shown that the probability of correct fragment completion was no greater for target words that were recognized as such than for target words that subjects failed to identify. This **stochastic independence** suggested that the repetition priming effect was unrelated to explicit memory performance.

In chapter 1 we saw that one approach to establishing the existence of different forms of memory was to demonstrate that each form has different characteristics. To recap, this method assumes that if two different memory systems exist, they must have different properties, and that it must be possible to find experimental variables which affect each of these systems differently. Tulving and co-workers examined both recognition and repetition priming at retention intervals of 1 hour and 1 week. Figure 3.2 shows that recognition declined significantly after a week, but that the extent of priming did not change significantly. This demonstration that tests of implicit memory are far less affected by time than measures of explicit memory has now been shown a number of times. It is now known, for example, that repetition priming effects can be detected after intervals of up to 16 months (Sloman et al., 1988).

It is well established that divided attention reduces explicit memory. In the last section we saw, for example, that divided attention reduced the extent to which subjects were able to perform context-based recollection. Parkin and colleagues (1990b) examined how the imposition of the same secondary task would influence fragment completion priming. Divided attention significantly reduced recognition performance, but had no effect on repetition priming. This finding has been replicated using a different form of implicit memory test known as **picture completion priming** (Parkin and Russo, 1990), and collectively the data indicate that memory tested under implicit memory conditions is formed **automatically**, by

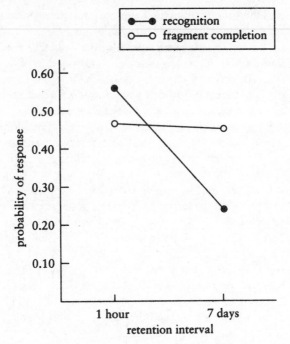

Figure 3.2 The influence of retention interval on fragment completion priming and recognition.
(*From Tulving et al., 1982, p. 339.*)

contrast with explicit memory, which is dependent on the degree of conscious effort made available This conclusion is consistent with Nissen and co-workers' (1988) finding that scopolamine (see chapter 1), a substance known to inhibit effortful memory functions such as free recall, has no effect on fragment completion priming.

Graf and co-workers (1984) examined repetition priming using a variant of the fragment completion paradigm known as **stem completion**. Subjects again studied a list of words such as WATCH and then, sometime later, were confronted with a series of word stems, e.g. WAT__? The stem can serve as an explicit memory test by acting as a cue for recall, or as an implicit test by requiring the subject to report the first word that 'pops' into their mind beginning with those three letters. Graf and colleagues found that cued recall instructions resulted in better recall for words learned under semantic than non-semantic orienting instructions – a finding consistent with the levels of processing research considered in chapter 2. However, when the word stems were used as an implicit memory test, subjects completed the stems more often with target than non-target words, a repetition priming effect; but this was uninfluenced by the level at which these target words were processed during learning.

However, to be sure of two memory systems, we need to find variables that influence implicit memory but not explicit memory. Jacoby and Dallas (1981) used an implicit memory test called **perceptual identification**, in which subjects are given a brief exposure to a stimulus and then required to identify it. Priming is shown in terms of increased efficiency in identifying repeated items compared with new items – a phenomenon we have already encountered, known as **perceptual fluency**. In one experiment the modality of presentation was varied across repetitions of the same item. Thus, on first presentation an item would be visually presented, and on second presentation it would be spoken. This **modality shift** greatly reduced the extent of priming compared with conditions where the modality was unchanged. However, the same modality shift had little or no effect on subjects' explicit memory for the target stimuli. Modality shifts also reduce performance on other types of implicit memory test such as stem and fragment completion (e.g. Bassili et al., 1989), and there are even demonstrations that shifts within a modality can influence performance. Repetition priming in fragment completion, for example, is substantially reduced if there is a change in the typescript used at learning and test (e.g. Roediger and Blaxton, 1987).

In sum, it appears that explicit memory is sensitive to a range of variables, including secondary tasks, levels of processing and retention interval. Implicit memory, by contrast, appears much more sensitive to the perceptual or **surface features** of stimuli. These differences thus give us some idea about how the forms of memory underlying implicit and explicit performance might be organized; we return to this in a later section.

What is Implicit Memory?

In the last section implicit memory was defined in terms of a set of task demands, conditions imposed on the subject at retrieval. However, there have been recent attempts to specify the type of memory underlying priming effects. Schacter (1990) has proposed that implicit memory effects are caused by a **perceptual representation system** (PRS) which comprises a series of subsystems each dealing with a particular **domain** of information. Each of these subsystems contains information about the form and structure of a particular stimulus category, but does not store information about meaning; it is therefore termed **pre-semantic**.

Evidence for a PRS being involved in implicit memory comes from studies by Schacter and his colleagues (e.g. Schacter et al., 1990; Schacter,

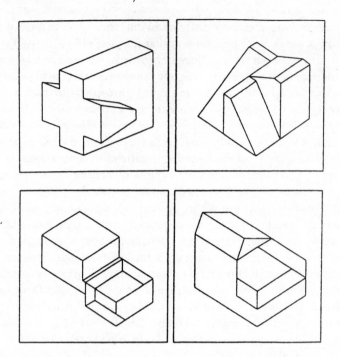

Figure 3.3 Possible and impossible stimuli used in Schacter et al.'s experiment. The upper stimuli are possible objects, the lower ones impossible objects. (*From Schacter et al., 1990, p. 7.*)

1992). In one experiment normal subjects were presented with a series of line-drawings half of which depicted possible objects, the other half impossible objects (see figure 3.3). As each object appeared, subjects had either to decide the main direction in which the object was pointing (left versus right) or to think of a real world object that the line-drawing reminded them of in the elaborative condition. Two tests were then given. In the implicit memory test subjects had to decide as quickly as possible whether a line-drawing was or was not a real object. A priming effect was demonstrated, in that subjects made quicker decisions about real objects that had been presented in the first phase of the experiment. However, there was no effect on the type of processing undertaken, and also no priming effect for impossible objects. By contrast, recognition was significantly better for line-drawings subjected to the elaborative task.

Schacter and his colleagues interpret these findings as showing priming at the level of the structural description PRS. Real objects show priming because possible relations between the element of the stimulus allow the system to derive a structural description. The setting up of this description subsequently provides a basis for recognizing this object on a subsequent occasion, and thus facilitates the object decision relative to a novel possible object. The view that this priming occurs at a pre-semantic level comes from the demonstration that a manipulation which enhances recognition (elaboration) does not have any effect on priming.

Schacter and co-workers' account of a PRS-type implicit memory system has been extended to the domains of auditory and visual word recognition. However, as with objects, memory is thought to be mediated at the pre-semantic level. A question therefore arises as to whether implicit memory occurs only at non-meaningful levels of processing. A number of investigators have demonstrated **cross-modal priming** of fragment completion. Hirshman and colleagues (1990), for example, showed that presentation of words could prime both fragment completion and picture identification. Priming in the latter case is reduced, and is assumed to arise at the level of semantics, because there is no physical overlap between words and pictures. For this reason this phenomenon is known as **conceptual priming** (see also Hamann, 1994).

Implicit Learning

In parallel with work on implicit memory there has been a growing body of evidence concerned with **implicit learning**. This can be defined as learning that takes place without the subject being able to explain how it occurs. Thus the subject may remember the learning episodes, but nothing of what they remember is relevant to what they have learned. Two types of experimental tasks have been used to investigate this: artificial grammar learning and the control of complex systems. In the former, subjects are asked to learn a set of strings of letters generated by a synthetic grammar which defines permissible and impermissible sequences of letters. Next they are told that the strings of letters are rule-governed, and are required to decide whether novel strings of letters are grammatical or not. There are now many demonstrations that subjects can learn these grammars, even though they cannot explain what the rules are (Reber, 1989; Berry and Dienes, 1992).

A typical complex control task is one in which subjects take on the role of managing a sugar production factory. They are required to maintain a specified level of sugar output by manipulating the number of workers. Several studies have shown that subjects can learn to perform optimally on this task even though they cannot explain the principle that is governing their performance (e.g. Berry and Broadbent, 1984). Indeed, there is evidence that subjects who attempt to form hypotheses about what the underlying principles are perform worse than those who do not attempt to do so.

Forgetting

If someone asks you what you have just been reading, it is likely that you will be able to tell them quite a lot. However, if you are asked sometime later, your recollection will not be as good. This indicates that forgetting is a time-dependent process. But at what rate does it actually occur? The first systematic investigation of this problem was carried out by Hermann Ebbinghaus (1885), who is regarded as the founder of experimental research on memory. Ebbinghaus's approach to experimentation was extremely thorough, with every effort made to exclude the influence of extraneous factors. His techniques have been considered artificial by some, but the rigours he practised are still present in much recent research. The experiments, which he conducted on himself, involved learning lists of nonsense syllables until he could recall them perfectly. To measure his forgetting rate, he would record the number of repetitions he needed to learn a list, and then test himself after a certain time. He then recorded the number of repetitions he needed to relearn the list. Forgetting was measured in terms of the difference between the number of repetitions originally required to learn the list and the number required when retested. Figure 3.4 shows the amount of 'savings' in relearning after different periods; this pattern is now known to be typical of forgetting in general. At first, forgetting is rather rapid, with a 60 per cent saving in learning time after 20 minutes reduced to 45 per cent after an hour. After this, forgetting occurs much more slowly, with only a 5 per cent difference between 2 and 31 days.

The next and more difficult question concerns how forgetting occurs. One theory is the 'law of disuse' (Thorndike, 1913), which states that memories naturally deteriorate over time. This view held considerable popularity until McGeoch (1932) raised two important objections. First, in many situations, disuse was shown to have no effect on retention. Second, and more important, even if disuse does lead to forgetting, this does not constitute an explanation. McGeoch drew an analogy with the fact that a nail becomes increasingly rusty over time. However, time is not the cause of the rust, but merely the logical prerequisite for the process of oxidation to occur. Similarly, if a memory fades through disuse, it is not time that has caused the forgetting, but something that has happened during that time.

McGeoch put forward an alternative explanation of forgetting, which led to the development of interference theory. The basis of this theory is that all learning involves the formation of associations (e.g. A→B). As more learning takes place, some of the new associations will have elements in

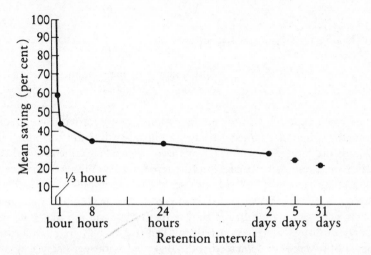

Figure 3.4 Forgetting rate, as measured by Ebbinghaus. (Note that forgetting is most rapid in the hour or so following learning.)
(*From Baddeley, 1976, p. 8.*)

common with those already formed (e.g. A→C), and this 'interference' will give rise to forgetting. One extensively used technique for exploring interference effects is that of **paired–associate learning**. The subject is first required to learn a series of arbitrary associations between, most commonly, pairs of words. Thus a subject would learn that the stimulus PIANO is associated with the response 'cigar' (A→B). A second series of pairs is then presented, in which the stimulus terms remain the same, but the responses are changed. Now the subject has to learn that PIANO is associated with 'giraffe' (A→C). Within this paradigm two forms of interference can be distinguished: **retroactive interference** (RI), in which subsequent learning (A→C) impairs recall of older memories (A→B), and **proactive interference** (PI), in which older memories impair subsequent learning.

The two forms of interference have been demonstrated in a number of different ways, but in most cases the experiments have involved either lists of single words or simple binary associations. This has led to the criticism that interference theory lacks external validity, because it is derived from experiments with learning tasks that are uncharacteristic of everyday life. This criticism is not altogether valid, for the common mistake of giving your previous address instead of the one to which you have just moved can be thought of in A→B, A→C terms. However, most of what we learn and then forget is difficult to conceive of as patterns of simple association. Further, interference theory has yet to explain how forgetting occurs in simple tasks such as paired-associate learning. These difficulties lead us to consider forgetting from a different, less theoretical, perspective.

The Penfield Phenomenon

During the 1940s Wilder Penfield carried out many brain operations on epileptic patients in order to relieve their intractable seizures. Patients were first fully anaesthetized; the appropriate area of the skull was then removed, and the brain exposed. Consciousness was then restored, with only a local anaesthetic being maintained (see figure 3.5). During the operation the surface of the brain was stimulated with an electrode. Penfield noted that stimulation in one particular region (the temporal lobe) resulted in patients recalling 'experiences'. One patient said: 'I just heard one of my children speaking . . . it was Frank, and I could hear the neighbourhood noises.' Another said: 'Something brings back a memory. I can see the Seven-Up bottling company . . . Harrison Bakers' (Penfield, 1958). In general, these recollections were vivid, detailed and concerned with seemingly insignificant past events. Penfield was deeply impressed by this phenomenon, and believed that he had located 'the stream of consciousness'. The apparent triviality of the patients' recollections led him to propose that 'nothing is lost [from memory], the record of man's experience is complete'. For Penfield, difficulties in remembering stemmed entirely from failure to gain access to memories.

Penfield's view of memory as a video-recorder faithfully recording every detail of our lives has come under serious criticism. Loftus and Loftus (1980) took a close look at the evidence on which Penfield based his claims. Penfield reported that recollections occurred only when the temporal lobe region was stimulated, a finding that is consistent with the known involvement of this area in memory function (see chapter 6). However, of the 520 patients stimulated in this way, only 40 showed the phenomenon, and of these, only 12 appeared to experience genuine recall. When the responses of these 12 were examined in more detail, they were found to have more in common with the content of dreams than actual memories.

Interest in brain stimulation and memory has continued until the present day, and the data largely support the conclusion of Loftus and Loftus. Gloor (1990), for example, concluded that stimulation similar to that used by Penfield can produce fragmentary recollections which assume authenticity because the stimulation induces an illusory degree of vividness similar to that experienced with real recollection. Bancaud et al. (1994) also report 'memories' being recollected due to stimulation, but are unwilling to assert that many of these are actually authentic. Instead, they view these memories as a type of 'dreamy state'.

It seems both implausible and impractical that our memory system should be burdened with the storage of millions of trivial experiences that are no longer of any use to us. A more attractive hypothesis is that memory

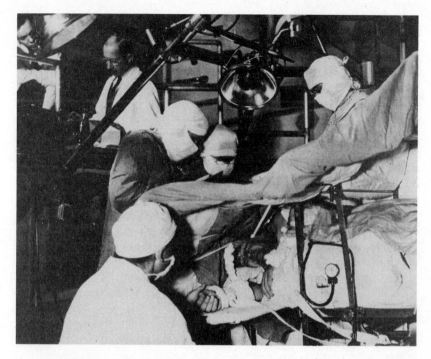

Figure 3.5 Photograph of 'open-head' surgery taking place. Note that the patient is awake. During procedures such as this, patients' brains were stimulated, and, apparently, this gave rise to spontaneous recollections.
(*From Penfield and Roberts, 1959.*)

is a selective process in which only certain aspects of our experiences are committed to LTS. In this connection we should note that possession of an STS in which information can be held temporarily provides an ideal locus for sorting out what does and does not need to be remembered. Thus, far from being a disadvantage, the labile nature of short-term memory traces has permitted the development of a more effective memory system. What needs to be stored can undergo consolidation, while the rest will simply be lost when the period of active storage is over. Forgetting can thus arise either as a result of **storage failure** or because of **retrieval failure**.

Storage failure is most readily demonstrated in experiments involving the administration of drugs such as scopolamine which block the cholinergic system (see chapter 1). Another drug of this type is **imipramine**, and Calev and colleagues (1989) explored how this drug affected the memory of people being treated for depression. They found that imipramine subjects had as much difficulty learning new information as patients who had memory loss following electroconvulsive therapy (ECT; see chapter 9).

However, in contrast to ECT patients, the imipramine subjects had no problems remembering events before the treatment.

Drug studies are rather difficult to carry out, and standard laboratory investigations of forgetting have tended to concentrate on retrieval deficits, because these can be investigated without tampering with subjects' brains.

Context Effects

There are many formal demonstrations that context exerts powerful effects on our ability to identify things. In a classic experiment Light and Carter-Sobell (1970) demonstrated how changes in the intrinsic context associated with a target could reduce recognition memory. Subjects studied simple sentences which biased them towards encoding one particular meaning of an ambiguous word (e.g. 'They were stuck in a traffic JAM'). Retention testing involved subjects identifying the target words, which were again embedded in biasing sentences, but in half of these, the sentence was biased towards a different meaning to that used at encoding (e.g. 'They enjoyed eating the JAM'). It was found that recognition of the targets was significantly reduced when the biasing context at learning was different to that at test.

Disruptive effects of changing the intrinsic context between learning and testing are perhaps unsurprising, because, in effect, what is being shown is that subjects are worse at remembering a different stimulus than the one they studied. More interesting, and potentially more relevant, is the possibility that the extrinsic context could exert effects on remembering.

Environmental Effects

Godden and Baddeley (1975) examined memory performance in two distinct environments: on land and under water. It was found that free recall was better when the learning and test environments were the same than when they were different. However, Godden and Baddeley (1980) found no evidence of an environmental influence when a recognition test was used. Smith (1986) reports another study, in which subjects undertook a number of memory span trials either in a room or while immersed in a flotation tank. Subjects were then given an unexpected final memory test for the items, and a significant *environment-dependent effect* was found for both recall and recognition. A subsequent study examined whether changing rooms could exert environment-dependent effects on recall and recognition. Memory span again served as the basic task, but half the subjects were also told that their memory of the words would be tested again later.

Here it was found that an environment-dependent effect occurred only when subjects did not know that recognition would be tested later.

Environmental context also appears to influence eyewitness accuracy. Smith and Vela (1992) staged an incident in which a confederate entered an introductory psychology class and announced that it was a fictitious person's birthday. He asked the class if 'she' was present, and when no one came forward, he left. After varying intervals the subjects were given a recognition test for the confederate, in either the same room or a different one. Of those in the different room, some were asked to try and reinstate mentally the original encounter with the confederate, while others were left to their own devices. Correct identification of the confederate was significantly better in the same context group, compared with the different context group. In addition, those subjects in the different context asked to reinstate the original context did particularly poorly – an interesting finding given that mental reinstatement under other conditions is held to improve eyewitness memory (e.g. Malpass and Devine, 1981).

State-dependent Learning

Various psychoactive states involving alcohol and drugs can result in **state-dependent learning**. This can be defined as enhanced memory when the psychoactive condition of the person is the same at retrieval as during learning. Goodwin (1974) measured recall and recognition tasks after subjects consumed either a soft drink or a substantial amount of high-strength vodka. The next day the subjects were required to perform the same tasks again, either in the same state or a different state. A change in state (e.g. learn sober, test intoxicated) produced reliably lower recall performance, but there was no state-dependent effect on recognition.

During the next decade there was considerable interest in the ability of various drugs to induce state-dependent effects, but the results were very inconsistent. Analysing these studies, Eich (1980) noticed that 88 per cent of studies showing evidence for state-dependent effects had measured free recall, whereas 90 per cent of the studies failing to show state-dependency had used either cued recall or recognition. Thus, like environmentally dependent memory, such effects are reliable only with recall.

State-dependent learning is not easy to explain, but one possibility is that psychoactive states lead people to adopt unusual strategies when trying to learn and retrieve information. Thus information learnt in an intoxicated state will be incompatible with the type of retrieval strategy adopted when sober. Evidence for this idea is slight, although there are a number of studies indicating that marijuana intoxication causes people to make unusual associations to stimuli (e.g. Block and Wittenborn, 1985). In the context of a memory experiment, this could lead to the formation of unusual representations or promote atypical retrieval strategies. This would be fine when learning and retrieval both occurred in the drugged state, but when they occurred in different states, retrieval would be more difficult.

Mood and Memory

The effect of mood on memory has received considerable attention (see Blaney, 1986). Bower (1981) asked subjects to keep a diary of the emotional aspects of their lives. After one week of this they were subjected to a **mood induction** procedure, in which hypnotic suggestion was used to make subjects either 'happy' or 'sad'. Subjects were then required to recall events, and it was found that there was a **mood–congruency** effect, with subjects in a pleasant mood recalling more pleasant memories and those in an unpleasant mood recalling more unpleasant memories. A second study by Bower and colleagues (1981) again used mood induction to create 'happy' or 'sad' subjects, who then listened to a story about Paul Smith. Half the events happening to Paul were positive and half negative, and a mood-congruence effect at recall was again found. Findings like these were incorporated in a network model in which mood state selectively biased which aspects of an experience were remembered (Bower et al., 1981). However, since then, there has been controversy over whether mood-congruence effects occur reliably. Also, as we shall see in the next section, the use of hypnosis as a means of inducing moods adds a further degree of uncertainty to the interpretation of positive mood effects.

Eich and Metcalfe (1989) reasoned that 'internal events', events that originate from mental operations such as reasoning and imagination, might be more influenced by current mood state than externally mediated events. If true, memory of these internal events should be more susceptible to mood-congruence effects than external events. To test this idea, subjects were first placed in either a good or a bad mood by listening to appropriate classical music (e.g. Mozart's *Eine Kleine Nachtmusik* or Albinoni's *Adagio in G minor*). During the learning phase subjects either read a target item paired with a category name and a related example (e.g. milk shake flavours: chocolate – VANILLA), or they generated the target item with a high probability when given the initial letter (e.g. milk shake flavours: chocolate – V___). The authors assumed that production of the response under generating conditions would correspond to an internal event, whereas reading conditions would be perceived as external. A subsequent retention test in which either the same or a different mood was induced prior to learning revealed two principal findings: mood-congruence effects were much more substantial for generated than read items, but only when free recall was measured. No effect of mood emerged with recognition testing.

While we may have some doubts as to whether mood can affect memory in normal people, there seems little doubt that abnormal mood states do have a profound effect on memory. Lloyd and Lishman (1975) found that the time taken by depressed patients to recall negative experiences decreased as they became more depressed. Clark and Teasdale (1981) exploited the natural mood swings of depressed patients. When the patients were relatively happy, they recalled more pleasant than unpleasant memories, but when they sank into deep depression, unpleasant memories dominated their recall (see also Williams et al., 1988, for a recent review of this area). Williams and Broadbent (1986) found that depressed suicidal patients found it more difficult to retrieve memories when prompted with positive cue words and, even when successful, these memories were less specific than with negative cue words (see chapter 6 for a further discussion of this latter result). In a similar kind of study Burke and Mathews (1992) presented clinically anxious and non-anxious subjects with neutral cues, and found that the anxious subjects produced more anxiety-related memories. Collectively these studies indicate that clinical mood states do exert important influences over the pattern of memories retrieved – findings that may have significance for understanding the nature and maintenance of these disorders.

Hypnosis

Anyone who has ever watched a hypnotist at work will be impressed by the fact that something very unusual is going on when people are being hypnotized. Why, for example, should hypnotized people believe and act as if the magic glasses they are wearing enable them to see through people's clothes or eat and enjoy an apple that is really a raw onion? Contemporary research into hypnosis is organized around two competing accounts: the **state**, or **special process**, view, and the **non-state, social-psychological** view (Spanos, 1986). According to the special-process theory, hypnosis produces involuntary behaviour that differs qualitatively from that in the non-hypnotic state. By contrast, the social-psychological view argues that hypnotic behaviour is purposeful, in that subjects deliberately comply with the aims of the hypnotic situation: the hypnotized subject may know that the raw onion they are eating is not an apple, but the power of **compliance** (Wagstaff, 1981) ensures that they continue to act as if it was.

In a **hypnotic amnesia** experiment subjects are given material to learn, and then some hypnotic instruction to forget part or all of that information. Subjects are then challenged to recall the material, and are then given a 'cancellation cue' and again asked to recall the material. Hypnotic amnesia is demonstrated when the subject fails to recall the information until the cancellation cue is given. Special-process theorists argue that this amnesia represents a genuine dissociation of memory involving the creation of 'amnesic barriers'. Social-psychological theorists argue that the hypnotized subjects are simply complying with the experimenter's wish for them not to recall the material while apparently hypnotized. Which of these theories is correct?

One widely used method for evaluating hypnotic amnesia is the 'owning up' control in which subjects failing to remember information following a hypnotic suggestion are given an opportunity to admit that they were pretending to be hypnotized. These studies typically show a lessening of hypnotic amnesia, but, importantly, the amnesia persists in subjects who are known to be highly susceptible to hypnosis (e.g. Kihlstrom, 1980). Special-process theorists interpret subjects behaving in this manner as showing a genuine interference with the usual processes of information retrieval. Social-psychological theorists, by contrast, argue that attempts to 'breach' the hypnotic amnesia merely provide highly suggestible subjects with a further opportunity to comply with what they perceive to be the aim of the experiment. This latter interpretation is the one favoured by most experimentalists (e.g. Spanos, 1992).

A different approach is to consider whether hypnosis can facilitate the recall of normal memories. Geiselman and Machlovitz (1987) examined 38 studies to determine whether hypnosis could act as a memory aid. Five studies showed positive results, and they concluded that these were ones in which the methods employed most closely resembled conditions under which hypnosis was used in real-life witness interviews. However, the question of whether hypnosis is acting as a special process or merely providing a more relaxed environment for recall is not clear. Dinges and colleagues (1992) examined whether hypnosis enhances retrieval or merely increases a person's willingness to report recollections regardless of their accuracy. In two experiments hypnosis failed to enhance memory, although it did increase the amount of incorrect information recalled. Some authors have claimed memory enhancement via hypnosis (e.g. Shields and Knox, 1986), but subsequent studies have failed to replicate this finding (e.g. Wagstaff and Mercer, 1993).

A major problem in attempting to use hypnosis as an aid to retrieval is that subjects become highly suggestible during the hypnotic interview. It has been shown repeatedly that subjects can, for example, be made to believe that various fictitious events have happened to them (e.g. Lynn and Nash, 1994). This fact has become increasingly relevant with the widespread use of hypnosis to 'recover' memories of child sexual abuse, because, very often, it has been found that these memories are false memories linked to suggestions made during the hypnotic interview (see chapter 10). This situation is further exacerbated by the erroneous belief of many psycho-therapists that memories obtained under hypnosis are more reliable than those retrieved in a normal waking state (Yapko, 1994). More worrying still is evidence that some psychotherapists mistakenly believe that hypnosis can allow people to regress to the moment of birth and access past lives (Loftus, 1994).

Retrieval takes three distinct forms: recall, cued recall and recognition. The process of retrieval is a reconstructive act in which currently available information guides a search of LTS. Generation-recognition theory and encoding specificity represent contrasting approaches to explaining retrieval. The former views recall and recognition as separate processes, whereas the latter sees them as different aspects of one retrieval mechanism. Recognition is no longer considered a single process, but one that comprises two components: recollection and familiarity. While most human remembering involves recollection (explicit memory), there is good evidence that memory can be expressed indirectly (implicit memory). The only general theory of forgetting so far developed is interference theory, but this has failed to provide a satisfactory explanation. An alternative approach is to consider factors that affect how well information is remembered. Experiments have shown that changes in intrinsic and extrinsic context can affect recall adversely. Furthermore, intoxication with psychoactive drugs, environmental context and mood can influence free recall. There is no convincing evidence that hypnosis enhances memory.

4 Improving Memory

I was once invited to participate in a television programme featuring two men both of whom had phenomenal memories. Unlike someone I shall consider shortly, neither of them had been born with a remarkable memory. Both had deliberately set out to improve their memories. One of them, Jonathan, proved his extraordinary memory by looking through a pack of playing cards for about a minute or so and then recalling the sequence of all 52 cards with complete accuracy. The other, Dominic, showed his powerful memory by introducing himself to around 50 guests. From encounters lasting no more than a few seconds each, he was subsequently able to recall the names of all those people along with other information he had learned about them.

It is obvious that we can improve our memories, and later in this chapter I will shed light on how the above feats of memory were achieved. But first I will consider various ways of improving memory, though you must remember that not every claim is true. In chapter 3, we saw that hypnosis is not a reliable means of improving memory, and one must be cautious of the claims made about other learning methods. A good example of these is **Suggestive Accelerated Learning and Teaching Techniques (SALTT)**, which employ a combination of various methods with the aim of enhancing learning. Thus the method might include a package of physical relaxation exercises, alternation of active and passive review (the latter usually accompanied by Baroque music), co-operative learning, suggestions that learning will be fun, overviews, songs and rhythms, and frequent self-testing all as a means of enhancing learning. When the method was first publicized, claims were made that it could enhance learning to a rate 'several hundred times' that of normal learning. However, when independent studies of SALTT were carried out, these claims, or even more modest ones, were not confirmed. One study compared a group of students who had learned Russian under SALTT conditions devised by a trained instructor and another group taught in a conventional way. SALTT training took five weeks less to cover the same material, but the students trained in this method had examination scores 40 per cent below those of the conventionally taught group (for further discussion of this and other 'New Age' techniques for enhancing mental ability, see Druckman and Swets, 1994).

Organization and Memory

One of the most effective ways of improving memory is to organize material so that it is easier both to learn and to retrieve. Many experiments have shown that subjects spontaneously organize material as they learn it. Jenkins and co-workers (1952), for example, gave subjects a list comprising 24 pairs of highly associated words (e.g. TABLE–HAIR) to remember. The list was scrambled so that the associated words were not adjacent to each other; nevertheless, at recall, subjects tended to recall the words in associated pairs. This and similar studies have shown that subjects will exploit experimenter-imposed organization when remembering lists of words. But what happens when information has no inherent organization? A number of studies (e.g. Tulving, 1962) have shown that people impose their own subjective organization on lists of words that have no obvious organization of their own. Thus, with repeated recall of the same word list, subjects will tend to recall the items in the same order.

It is clear that organization also plays a vital role in everyday memory. Learning of any set of facts will be enhanced if we can establish some link between them, so that recall of one will serve as a cue for remembering others. Furthermore, our ability to absorb new facts is related to what we know about the subject already. Noting unusual links between something you are trying to learn and something you know already can also improve memory. Thus, remembering my surname may be easier if you know that it means 'gingerbread'. The importance of organization increases as the material to be remembered becomes more complex. Learning a list of words may not pose any great organizational problem, but attempting to internalize the contents of a chapter of a book certainly does. One approach is to devise a 'tree diagram' which covers the basic conceptual framework. This is relatively easy to remember, and provides a basis for accessing memory in more detail and understanding the relationship between the various topics (Buzan, 1972).

It would be impossible to list the many different ways in which people organize information in order to remember it more efficiently. However, **mnemonics**, particularly those involving **imagery**, have been particularly well researched, and their role in memory improvement will be considered shortly.

Imagery and Memory, the Strange Case of 'S'

In 1968 the Russian neuropsychologist A. R. Luria published a book called *The Mind of a Mnemonist*. In it he described the case of a man called S who possessed an almost perfect memory. Figure 4.1a shows a meaningless mathematical formula which S was able to reproduce exactly, after studying it for only a few minutes. More remarkably, S was able to reproduce it again 15 years later, without prior warning. Luria studied S's memory skills in great detail, and discovered that his predominant means of remembering things was to create elaborate visual images of the information he was trying to learn. In the above example the start of the formula was remembered using the following image: 'Neiman (N) came out and jabbed at the ground with his cane (.). He looked up at a tall tree which resembled the square root sign ($\sqrt{}$), and thought to himself: "No wonder the tree has withered and begun to expose its roots. After all, it was here when I built these two houses" (d) . . .' (p. 42). Interestingly, this method is very similar to that used by the memory expert Jonathan. In order to remember the cards, he would create an identity for each one, and weave them into a complicated and often bizarre story which then became the framework for his recall.

Luria's account of S alerts us to the importance of visual imagery as an aid to memory. However, we must qualify this by noting two additional aspects of S's phenomenal memory. First, it is clear that S's experience of imagery was extremely unusual. Figure 4.1b shows a table of numbers which S could accurately reproduce in many different ways after studying them for three minutes. It is interesting to note how S explained his performance:

b)

6	6	8	0
5	4	3	2
1	6	8	4
7	9	3	5
4	2	3	7
3	8	9	1
1	0	0	2
3	4	5	1
2	7	6	8
1	9	2	6
2	9	6	7
5	5	2	0
x	0	1	x

a)

$$N. \sqrt{d^2 \times \frac{\cdot 85}{vx} \cdot \sqrt[3]{\frac{276^2 \cdot 86x}{n^2 v \cdot \pi 264}}} \; n^2 b = sv \; \frac{1624}{32^2} \cdot r^2 s$$

Figure 4.1 a) Meaningless equation; b) random table of numbers both learnt by S. (*From Luria, 1968, pp. 42 and 21, respectively.*)

He told us that he continued to see the table which had been written on a blackboard or a sheet of paper, that he merely had to 'read it off' successively enumerating the numbers. . . . Hence it generally made no difference whether he 'read' the table from the beginning or the end, whether he listed the elements that formed the vertical or the diagonal groups, or 'read off' the numbers of the horizontal rows. The task of converting the individual numbers into a single, multi-digit number appeared to be no more difficult for him than for others . . . asked to perform this task visually. (Luria, 1968, p. 23)

When most of us experience mental images, we do not perceive them as something we are looking at directly. Images appear to be 'inside our head', visible only to our 'mind's eye'. By contrast, S's report has more in common with **eidetic imagery**, a rare phenomenon in which the individual seems able to form vivid and detailed images which are experienced as if they were actual percepts.

Another unusual feature of S's memory was **synaesthesia**, in which stimulation in one sensory modality produces a sensation in another. Whenever anyone spoke, the person's voice would cause S to experience visual images. This ability was used extensively by S to remember sounds, nonsense syllables and words. However, his synaesthesia also had its drawbacks:

To this day I can't escape from seeing colours when I hear sounds. What first strikes me is the colour of someone's voice. Then it fades off . . . for it does interfere. If a person says something I see the word; but should another person's voice break in, blurs appear. These creep into the syllables of the words and I can't make out what's being said. (Ibid., p. 26)

Recently there has been considerable research into the underlying basis of synaesthesia, and many people with this ability have been found. Paulescu and colleagues (1995) have carried out a neuro-imaging study of people with synaesthesia. In the study subjects report when they are experiencing synaesthesia, and their brain activity is monitored using a procedure known as **positron emission tomography** (PET; this is explained in more detail in chapter 6). The PET scans show quite clearly that synaesthesia results in abnormal brain activation with, for example, hearing a word leading to the activation of the brain's hearing and visual centres.

S's memory capacity also affected his life adversely. His tendency to remember everything in terms of mental images often prevented him from grasping abstract concepts. When remembering tables of numbers, for example, it made no difference to him whether the numbers were meaningfully organized. He was also hindered by his inability to forget. At one stage in his life, S was a professional mnemonist, giving several performances each night. Problems arose when he began to confuse the information he had just committed to memory with that from previous performances. He eventually solved the problem by devising a forgetting strategy which, although effective, was never properly understood.

Imagery and Normal Memory

Images appear to play a central role in mental experience. Much of our memory takes this form, and we experience imagery when solving problems and planning actions. Thus it is surprising that mental imagery has been investigated seriously only during the last 20 years. The reason for this omission once again lies with the behaviourists. Prior to the rise of behaviourism, the predominant movement in psychology was introspectionism, in which the nature of psychological processes was inferred from the subjective impressions of observers. Not surprisingly, the characteristics of images featured strongly in these accounts. But Watson (1914), the founder of behaviourism, was vehemently opposed to this approach. 'Psychology, as the behaviorist views it', he wrote, 'is a purely objective, experimental branch of natural science, which needs introspection as little as do the sciences of chemistry and physics' (p. 9). And again: 'It is possible to define as "the science of behavior" and never to go back upon the definition: never to use the terms consciousness, mental states, mind, content, will, imagery, and the like' (p. 27). There is no doubt that Watson's view is extreme. Bolles (1975) has speculated that Watson's dismissal of mentalistic concepts stemmed from 'his own peculiar subjective world', the claim being that Watson did not have visual imagery. None the less, the behaviourist doctrine came to dominate experimental psychology, ensuring that mental imagery was hardly investigated before its rediscovery in the mid-1960s.

Renewed interest in the topic arose from the work of Paivio, who argued that mental imagery was susceptible to serious experimental analysis (see Paivio, 1986, for an extensive account). Initially, experiments on mental imagery made use of existing experimental techniques such as paired-associate learning (see chapter 3), which required subjects to learn arbitrary associations between single words (e.g. PIANO–cigar). Using this paradigm, it was an easy step to investigating how instructions to form images during learning might affect the learning of associations. Bower (1970) required subjects to learn lists of 30 word-pairs under one of three kinds of instruction. Group A had to repeat the word-pairs aloud as they appeared (rote learning); group B had to form an image of the two items interacting in some way (e.g. a piano smoking a cigar); and group C had to form separate images of the two words (e.g. imagine a piano, then a space, then a cigar). Subjects were first given a recognition test for the first member of each word-pair. If successful, they were then asked to recall the word that it had been paired with. The groups performed similarly on recognition, but group B showed a marked superiority on recall. This shows that forming mental images is superior to rote learning, but only when the instructions require the subject to imagine elements of the two items interacting in some way.

Interacting images may produce better recall because this type of instruction leads subjects to create bizarre images (such as a piano smoking a cigar), and it is this that underlies superior memory. This view is certainly held in the classical and anonymous work *Ad Herennium*, which suggests rules for the use of imagery. We remember what is 'exceptionally base, dishonorable, unusual, great, unbelievable, or ridiculous', whereas 'ordinary things easily slip from memory' (cited by Paivio, 1971, p. 160). Wollen and co-workers (1972) investigated whether experimental demonstrations of enhanced recall using interactive images did in fact stem from their tendency to encourage bizarre imagery. Like Bower, they found that interactive imagery was better than separate images, but that bizarreness had no additional effect. They concluded that it is primarily the interactional quality of images that determines their effectiveness.

It is now accepted that interactive imagery is a powerful aid to memory under certain circumstances. There are problems, however, in specifying the processes that underlie our subjective experience of mental imagery. Some argue that images are a distinct form of internal representation (Kosslyn, 1983); indeed, we saw in chapter 2 that the working memory model has a specific component, the visuo-spatial scratch pad, whose function is to provide a medium for spatial representations such as visual images. Others, however, view images as an 'epiphenomenon' stemming from the operation of 'propositional knowledge' (Pylyshyn, 1979). The debate is complex and unlikely to affect the conclusions about mental effectiveness of imagery as a memory aid reached here. Those interested in what is known as the 'imagery debate' are referred to recent reviews of the issue (e.g. Kosslyn, 1994; Parkin, 1993).

Mnemonics

Mnemonics are specific devices for improving memory, and have been used since classical times. It is unlikely that any of us have come through life without relying on a mnemonic at some time or another. At school or college, we may well have used **first-letter** mnemonics to remember facts in the correct order. The phrases 'Richard Of York Gained Battles In Vain' and 'Real Old Yokels Guzzle Beer In Volume' both enable us to remember the order of colours in the spectrum (red, orange, yellow, green, blue, indigo, violet). Rhymes are also useful, such as this one for diluting acid:

> *May his rest be long and placid,*
> *He added water to the acid!*
> *The other boy did what he oughter:*
> *He added acid to the water.*

Another useful kind of mnemonic is the **reduction mnemonic**, in which a string of letters is used to represent much more information. If the word they form is not a real word, they are known as **acronyms**; whereas if they form a real word, they are **acrostics**. These are particularly useful in medicine, where it is often necessary to learn clusters of symptoms corresponding to a particular diagnosis. Short and co-workers (1992) present a number of these, including STOMACH as a means of diagnosing generalized anxiety disorder:

> **S**canning and vigilance
> **T**wo or more worries
> **O**rganicity (rule out)
> **M**otor tension
> **A**nxiety unrelated
> **C**ourse of mood or psychotic (rule out)
> **H**yperactive autonomics

Armed with this mnemonic, the clinician is able to recall the key symptoms of the disorder and also to remember to rule out organic disease and the possibility that the anxiety reflects the course of a mood disorder or psychosis. There are large numbers of verbal mnemonics dealing with all kinds of technical information, and they can be found in various dictionaries of mnemonics (for a review see Malhotra, 1991). However, psychologists have been most interested in mnemonic systems that employ imagery as their principle ingredient.

One of the best-known imagery mnemonics is the **Method of Loci**. Its invention is attributed to the Greek poet Simonides, who lived around 500 BC. According to Cicero, Simonides was invited to recite at a dinner given by a local nobleman called Scopas. His poem was supposed to be entirely in praise of Scopas's recent achievements, but half of it concerned the twin gods Castor and Pollux. Scopas was angry, and paid Simonides only half his fee. Later, Simonides was called away from the table to speak to two young men (Castor and Pollux), at which point the roof of the building collapsed on the guests, crushing them into an unrecognizable pulp. When the relatives arrived, there was confusion because the various remains could not be identified. However, the problem was solved by Simonides, who could remember where everyone had been sitting during the dinner.

From this grisly experience, Simonides gained the following insight in how to improve memory. He reasoned that the clarity of his memory of the guests arose because each one had been seated in a separate location. He went on to suggest that memory in general could be made more effective if the things to be remembered were placed at different locations in the same imaginary space. The method is very simple. First, imagine a suitable setting, such as a room, with enough different locations for the items you want to remember. Next, use mental imagery to link each item with a location. If you are trying to memorize a shopping list and the first item is milk, you might imagine a milk bottle on a window-ledge. Finally, when all the items are in place, you can 'walk' through the room naming each in turn.

Another related method involves the peg-word device. Some quite complex **peg-word systems** have been devised (Higbee, 1977), but to illustrate the point, we will describe a simple example. The method involves learning a list of 'pegs'; these are easily learnt words which can be used as mental locations for remembering other items of information. The pegs are generated using the rhyming principle 'One is a bun, two is a shoe, three is a tree', and so on. Each item you wish to learn can then be associated with one of the pegs by forming a composite image. Using the shopping list example again, we could remember milk as the first item on the list by imagining a bun cut in half with a milk bottle sandwiched in between.

So far, the imagery techniques described have been quite simple. However, there are other, more sophisticated techniques, in which the generation of effective images requires considerable ingenuity. A good example is the face–name mnemonic devised by Lorayne and Lucas (1975), similar to the method used by Dominic. The idea is to link a person's face with a distinctive interacting image which can be decoded to give the person's name. There are three steps to this process:

1 Choose the most prominent feature of the person's face.
2 Select a word or phrase that sounds similar to the name (name trans- formation). This word or phrase must denote something that easily gives rise to an image.
3 Create an image in which the objects denoted by the phrase interact with the chosen facial feature.

McCarty (1980) gives the example of someone called Conrad, whose most prominent facial feature is his nose. The name transformation is con and rat, and the visual image involves a prisoner (con) riding on a rat that is sliding down a nose. When that person is encountered again, the prominent feature acts as a retrieval cue for the image, and the name transformation is derived from the image and decoded to give the name. This may sound rather complicated, but McCarty found that with college students this strategy produced better performance than simple face–name association learning.

There are many other mnemonics which use mental imagery as an essential ingredient (see Paivio, 1971; and Yates, 1966). However, a difficulty arises with regard to the practical application of these discoveries. For example, when the method of loci first evolved, it was of considerable value to orators as a means of remembering the points in their speeches. But modern speakers would be highly unlikely to use such a method, and would rely instead on either notes or an 'autocue' machine. Furthermore, Hunter (1977) has argued that the method is 'useless for all practical purposes', because the conditions needed for it to be effective are rarely encountered in real life. The face–name mnemonic has more potential, but, as McCarty himself notes, 'It is conceivable that in practice, the face–name mnemonic would be so complicated and time-consuming that most people would not use it' (p. 155).

One very effective imagery strategy, which I can recommend from personal experience, is the **keyword method** of learning new vocabulary in a foreign language (e.g. Atkinson, 1975; Grunberg, 1987). It works in the following way: 'herisson' is the French word for 'hedgehog'. To learn the word, first think of a key word or words in English that the French word sounds like. Here the example is 'hairy son'. Next imagine some interaction between that hairy son and a hedgehog. Now you have an image for the sound of the word, but what about the gender? For this Grunberg suggests that each masculine word should incorporate an inter-action with a boxer and each feminine word be characterized by an interaction with perfume. Thus for hedgehog you would imagine the boxer trying to take the hedgehog from the hairy son.

A rather different type of mnemonic was devised in Japan by Nakane. Known as **Yodai mnemonics**, their aim is to promote the learning of principles, procedures and rules rather than facts. They are particularly suited to problem solving such as multiplying binomials. Thus the problem $(a + b)(c + d)$ can be conceived of as a tag wrestling match. Each term in each bracket represents a wrestler of either the east or west team. Each wrestler on the east team wrestles each wrestler on the right team so that the solution becomes $ac + ad + bc + bd$ (Higbee and Kunihira, 1985).

Memory and Practice

Much of what we learn requires some form of practice before memory is firmly established. A fundamental question is whether practice is most effective when concentrated in short periods of time, or if learning is more

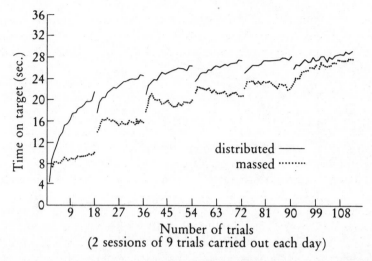

Figure 4.2 The effects of massed versus distributed practice on pursuit rotor learning.
(*After Digman, 1959; taken from Holding, 1965.*)

efficient when practice is spread over a longer period. The effects of 'massed' versus 'distributed' practice have been studied ever since experimental studies of memory began. On the basis of his classic studies of memory, Ebbinghaus was in no doubt that learning was more efficient when practice was distributed. Studies of motor skill learning also show a clear advantage for distributed practice. Figure 4.2 shows the results of an experiment in which subjects practised the pursuit rotor task under massed or distributed conditions. The task requires that the subject maintain contact with a revolving target by means of a hand-held stylus, and performance is measured as percentage of time on the target. In the massed condition, subjects were allowed only 2 seconds between each trial, whereas in the distributed condition, subjects were given 1.5 minutes' rest between trials. With distributed practice there is a rapid improvement on day 1, an initial drop on day 2, followed by further improvement in performance. With massed practice there is little improvement on day 1 after the first few trials. However, on day 2 performance is at a more accurate level than that achieved by the end of day 1. This phenomenon is known as **reminiscence**, and suggests that some of the deleterious effects of massed practice can be avoided if a lengthy rest period is given.

In attempting to master new facts, we often repeat them. In our earlier discussion of rehearsal (chapter 1), we saw that repetition *per se* influences how well we remember something. Further research has now indicated the conditions under which repetition is most effective. A typical experiment was carried out by Madigan (1969), in which subjects were presented with

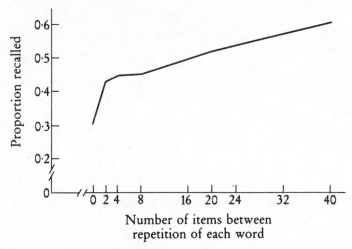

Figure 4.3 The effects of spacing repetition on recall. (Note that recall increases as the time between repetitions lengthens.)
(*After Madigan, 1969, p. 829, and Melton, 1967.*)

a long series of individual words and required to learn them. Each word was repeated, but the interval between repetitions was varied from immediate up to 40 different intervening items. Figure 4.3 shows how well the subjects subsequently recalled the words as a function of the interval between repetitions. Two effects are clearly shown. First, recall of items repeated immediately (the 0 condition) is far worse than spaced repetitions *per se*. This is called the **spacing effect**. Second, the recall of items given spaced repetition increases as the interval between repetitions increases. This is known as the **lag effect**.

To some, it seems counter-intuitive that, within certain limits, repetitions should be more effective the further they are apart. However, the spacing effect is extremely strong, and can be found in many different situations. Unfortunately, explaining it has proved a much more difficult matter, and no definite conclusion has been reached. One theory is that immediate and spaced repetition produce differently encoded memory traces. With immediate repetition, the recency of the first presentation may lead subjects to perform exactly the same encoding operations when the information is repeated, whereas, when the repetition is delayed, the first presentation is less accessible, and the second encoding is likely to be different. This is known as the **encoding variability hypothesis**, and has much in common with the elaboration hypothesis discussed in chapter 2. Both these theories stress that the more variably information is encoded, the more easily it can be remembered, because there are more potential ways in which it can be contacted in the retrieval process.

A variant of the lag effect has been applied in a practical setting by Landauer and Bjork (1978). They investigated how the interval between learning and testing affected memory for names. Subjects were presented with a continuous series of names to learn. At various intervals, these learning trials were replaced by a test trial in which the first name of a previous target was presented and the subject was asked to recall the appropriate surname. Retention of all the names was tested a number of times, but the intervals between these tests were varied systematically. At the end of the experiment subjects were given a final recall test. Of most interest was the comparison between 'uniform' testing, in which the interval between successive tests was constant, and 'expanding' testing, in which the intervals were gradually lengthened. The results showed that the expanding pattern produced much better retention of the names. What this suggests in practice is that learning will be facilitated if the interval between successful recall trials is extended gradually.

Many extravagant claims have been made about methods for improving memory, but there are a number of proven methods which do positively enhance memory ability. Most effective, perhaps, are mnemonics based on mental imagery, but techniques using other factors such as rhyme and key words can also be effective. Practice is another important variable in memory improvement, with distributed practice giving better results than massed practice.

Part 2
Memory Disorders

5 Assessment of Memory Disorders

The assessment, study and treatment of memory disorders is part of **neuropsychology**, the subdiscipline of psychology concerned with the relationship between brain damage and psychological processes. The term is sometimes used more broadly to include any scientific investigation of the nervous system's role in controlling behaviour. In this book, however, the term will be used in its more restrictive sense.

Neuropsychological assessment was first used as a means of distinguishing between patients whose abnormal behaviour stemmed from brain dysfunction and those whose illness was caused by psychological factors. Disorders due to brain dysfunction are described as **organic**, those with no apparent physical cause as **functional**, or **psychogenic**. Early tests were based on the assumption that there was some common element in all organic impairments. These procedures gave only a general assessment of 'organicity', rather than information about the status of different mental functions (Walsh, 1985). The concept of organicity lingers on in some circles, but the vast majority of neuropsychologists recognize that a patient's status can be assessed accurately only by examining specific psychological functions such as memory, language and perception. In this chapter, we will focus on the various tests and procedures that can be used to evaluate memory impairments.

Presented with a patient with a memory disorder, the neuropsychologist's first task is to establish whether the disorder is organic or psychogenic in nature. This can usually be inferred from the patient's medical record. Thus, there would be little doubt that a concussion victim's poor memory had an organic basis. Similarly, a psychogenic loss of memory would be suspected if the patient had no history of brain injury. Unfortunately, distinguishing between these two kinds of memory loss is not always as easy as this, because psychogenic factors may 'overlay' an organic impairment, making accurate assessment of the disorder problematic. Similarly, a psychogenic disorder may be complicated by disorders such as epilepsy.

Case reports of memory disorders have employed many different descriptive terms. Thus a patient may be described as having an impaired 'short-term' or 'recent' memory, or as having difficulty in accessing 'remote memory'. These terms are confusing, because they lack specificity. Take 'short-term' memory, for instance; does this refer to information retained for a few seconds, minutes, hours or days? Similarly, 'recent' memory might refer to events that have occurred subsequent to some injury, but could also include events prior to this. It is therefore necessary to adopt a terminology that can be interpreted unambiguously. The following two terms are now used by most workers: **anterograde amnesia**, which refers to difficulty in acquiring new information after some trauma or illness, and **retrograde amnesia** (RA), in which the patient cannot remember things he or she knew prior to the precipitating illness or trauma. Note also that the period of the patient's life before the onset of amnesia is referred to as the **pre-morbid** and that following it as the **post-morbid** period.

Clinical Assessment

Isolated defects of memory following brain damage are relatively uncommon, and most patients with memory disorders are likely to exhibit other psychological deficits as well. Prior to making any detailed assessment of memory, it is essential to get information about the patient's general neuropsychological status. Many disabilities can be associated with a memory disorder. There may be motivational problems, personality disturbance or attentional problems, all of which would impair memory performance. There may also be perceptual and motor impairments, as well as both receptive and expressive language disorders – some guidance concerning these matters is given at the end of the chapter.

When assessing a patient with memory problems, the clinician's first aim is to find out how extensive the deficit is. In chapters 1–4 we have considered a number of different memory tests, but these are not suitable for clinical assessment, because they were devised to test particular theories, rather than to measure differences between individual people. What we require is a standardized **psychometric** test in which the score achieved by the patient can be compared with a norm for the population, so as to provide an accurate description of the extent of impairment.

The psychometric measurement of memory is dominated by one individual, David Wechsler. In 1945 he devised the **Wechsler Memory Scale** (WMS) as a means of assessing different aspects of memory function (Wechsler, 1945). Wechsler was also one of the pioneers of intelligence testing, and in addition devised the **Wechsler Adult Intelligence Scale** (WAIS) as a means of evaluating human intelligence (Wechsler, 1955). This test and its updated version, which we shall consider in more detail later, comprise various subtests whose scores can be combined to give an **Intelligence Quotient (IQ)**. By reference to normative data, an individual's IQ can then be related to the average IQ for their particular group. Wechsler had the same aim with WMS, and constructed the test so that the various test scores could be combined to give a **Memory Quotient (MQ)**.

The notion of an MQ was driven by the idea that memory was in some sense a single entity whose function could be tested in a number of different ways. However, the preceding chapters have shown that this idea is not tenable, and that there are a number of different components to memory. Thus there can be no single test of memory; rather, a range of tests, each addressing different aspects of memory performance, must be administered, in order to get an overall picture of memory function. This principle is embodied in Wechsler's re-designed test, the **Wechsler Memory Scale – Revised** (WMS-R; Wechsler, 1987). The WMS-R is outlined in table 5.1, which also shows how various combinations of test scores are used to produce memory indices. Like their predecessor, MQ, each of these indices has a mean of 100 in the normal population and a standard deviation of 15.

The WMS-R is a major advance on the WMS, because it involves a more balanced assessment of both verbal and non-verbal memory. In the WMS short-term store was tested by means of digit span only, whereas WMS-R also includes the non-verbal block-tapping task. In this way selective deficits in verbal versus non-verbal short-term storage can be measured. Another advance is the inclusion of delayed memory indices. Very often memory deficits are only apparent with delayed testing; hence the original WMS, which looked only at immediate recall, may have led to underestimation of memory deficits in those with milder impairments.

The WMS-R does have the disadvantage of taking much longer to administer. Also, for patients with severe memory problems, the persistent failure associated with more extensive testing may be counterproductive. There is a shortened version of the test prescribed, but this leaves out the all-important delayed testing component. For this reason some clinicians choose not to use WMS-R, although, without a doubt, it is the major psychometric test of memory reported in the neuropsychological literature. One option is to use the 'Russell' revision of the WMS, which includes a delayed testing component similar to WMS-R (Russell, 1975). However, this lacks the more extensive non-verbal testing of WMS-R.

A major drawback of WMS, which was only partly dealt with in WMS-R, is that no measures of recognition memory are included. As a result, most clinicians include an additional measure of recognition memory. A commonly used test is the **Recognition Memory Test** (RMT; Warrington, 1984), which involves two subtests, one involving words, the other a non-verbal test using unfamiliar male faces. Subjects are shown each item for 3 seconds, and are asked to make a 'pleasant or unpleasant' judgement about each one (you will recall from chapter 2 that this is a semantic orienting task designed to enhance memory – something

Table 5.1 Wechsler Memory Scale – Revised

Test	Procedure
Personal and current information	Question about age, date of birth, name of Prime Minister.
Orientation	Questions about date and where patient is.
Mental control	Count backwards in 1s from 20. Recite the alphabet. Count forwards in 3s.
Figural Memory	Patient shown a series of abstract designs and then given a recognition test.
Logical memory	Patient is read a story (approx. 60 words) and must recall as much as possible. Two stories are given. Immediate and delayed test.
Visual paired associates	Patient is shown six pairs, each comprising an abstract figure and a colour and must learn the associations. Immediate and delayed test.
Verbal paired associates	Patient is read 10 pairs of words: 6 are 'easy' associations (e.g. metal–iron), and 4 are difficult (e.g. crush–dark). Patient is then given the first word of each pair and asked to recall the second. Patient has up to six trials to learn associations. Immediate and delayed test.
Visual reproduction	Patient is shown a figure and asked to draw it from memory. Four figures are given. Immediate and delayed test.
Digit span	Patient is read a short sequence of numbers and asked to repeat them back in correct order. Size of sequence is increased until subject fails or maximum of 8 is reached. Procedure is then repeated, but patient must report numbers in the reverse order to that read out.
Visual memory span	Examiner taps a series of coloured squares in a pre-defined order, and patient must repeat back the sequence. Size of sequence is increased until subject fails or a maximum of 8 is reached. Procedure is then repeated, but patient must repeat the sequence in reverse.

that is very useful when dealing with severely impaired subjects). Recognition is then tested by a 'forced choice' method, in which pairs of items are presented, and the subject is required to state which one is the target. Age-related norms are available for each subtest, and it is also possible to decide whether a discrepancy between scores on the two subtests is significant or not. When a discrepancy is significant, it suggests that the patient's memory for verbal information is poorer than for non-verbal information, or vice versa. RMT is quick to administer, and not oppressive for patients. It has been criticized, however, as relatively insensitive to impairment, particularly in younger subjects, and with older subjects, it often produces chance levels of performance.

There is a large and ever growing range of psychometric memory tests available, and only a small fraction of them can be considered here (see Parkin and Leng, 1993; Hodges, 1995, for reviews). Rey (1964) devised a number of memory tests, of which the most well-known is his **Complex Figure** (see figure 5.1). This comprises a detailed but meaningless figure which the subject is instructed to copy. Although meaningless, the figure does have some inherent geometric structure, being comprised, for example, of a central rectangle traversed by horizontal, vertical and diagonal lines. By monitoring how the patient copies the figure, it is possible to see whether he or she takes advantage of this structure. Failure to do so can be a consequence of many factors, such as frontal lobe damage (see chapter 7), and will also help to explain why some patients subsequently recall the figure badly when attempting to draw it from memory. However, a patient who copies the figure normally but still forgets it must have a different problem, unrelated to the way the picture was perceived in the encoding phase.

Earlier we noted that time is an important constraint on testing procedures; clinicians are often very pressed for time, and tests that require an hour or so for administration are likely to be used only for a small number of special patients. This has led to the development of screening tests which are both quick to administer and capable of being used by a range of professionals other than trained psychologists (e.g. occupational therapists, speech therapists, physiotherapists and nursing staff). The best known of these screening tests is the **Rivermead Behavioural Memory Test** (Wilson et al., 1985) which provides a relatively quick means of deciding whether or not a patient has a severe memory problem. The test is illustrated in table 5.2, and failure on any component is usually indicative of notable memory impairment. However, it may not detect some more subtle disorders of memory, such as those due to frontal lobe dysfunction. The test elements were derived from a survey of the memory difficulties experienced by closed head injury victims – a fact that may explain why it correlates particularly well with relatives' observations of patients and why

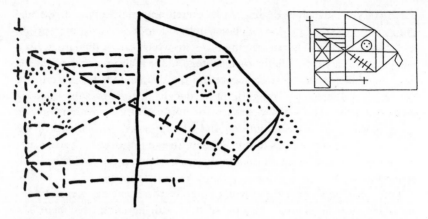

Figure 5.1 Copying of the Rey figure (*right*) by a patient with frontal lobe damage. Copying illustration indicates the order in which various parts of the figure were copied: solid line first, broken line second, dotted line third, broken/dotted line fourth. Note how the patient makes little use of the overall organization of the picture when copying.

it acts as a valid predictor of a patient's potential to return to work. The test has also been developed as a means of assessing memory impairment in young children (Wilson et al., 1991).

Measuring Retrograde Amnesia (RA)

The development of clinical memory tests has centred on measuring anterograde memory difficulties, with little attention being paid to possible retrograde deficits. This bias stems, in part, from the fact that RA, although disturbing, has less impact on the day-to-day life of a patient than does anterograde amnesia. Another problem is that retrograde amnesia is much harder to assess, because it involves testing the patient for memories they once possessed – something that is obviously problematic because one simply cannot know with any certainty what someone had in their memories prior to their brain injury. Another complicating factor is that remote memory loss tends to be uneven, with memories for events immediately prior to the onset of brain injury being more disrupted than those formed early in life. This **temporal gradient** has been known since the last century, and, in honour of its discoverer, is said to reflect **Ribot's law** (Ribot, 1882). This law, stated briefly, is that the vulnerability of memory to damage is an inverse function of its age. The mechanism responsible for this temporal gradient is still a puzzle. However, it is an empirical fact, and measures of remote memory performance have to take it into account.

Perhaps the most obvious way of measuring retrograde amnesia is to take a personal history. However, this apparently simple procedure is fraught with difficulty. Most problematic, aside from the time involved, is the tendency of patients to fabricate memories (this is known as 'confabulation', and will be discussed in more detail in chapter 7). An interview of this kind can be made more focused by using an **autobiographical cueing procedure**, in which the patient must recollect specific experiences when cued with single-word cues like 'flower' (Robinson, 1976). This procedure does not take into account the problem of fabrication unless independent verification of recollections is undertaken. However, the results of this initial assessment can be clinically informative. A patient may, for example, offer only very vague memories, or may tend to offer memories always from a restricted period of time. This would suggest different types of problems and thus be a valuable guide to further investigation.

Autobiographical cueing is useful, but it is difficult to make generalizations across individuals, because each person's autobiographical memory is different. Thus one patient might have a better autobiographical memory because their life has been richer. However, Kopelman and his colleagues

Table 5.2 Outline of the Rivermead Behavioural Memory Test

Test	Procedure
Remembering a name	Patient is shown photograph of a named person and told to remember it. Retention is tested 20–5 mins later.
Remembering a hidden belonging	One of the patient's possessions is hidden. Retention of location is tested 20–5 mins later.
Remembering an appointment	Alarm clock is set to ring 20 mins later. Patient has to ask a specified question when bell rings.
Picture recognition	10 line-drawings of common objects are shown to patient. 5 mins later, patient must pick out target pictures from sequence of 20 pictures.
Immediate prose recall[a]	Similar to logical memory component of WMS.
Face recognition	Patient views 5 faces. 5 mins later, subjects pick out targets from sequence of 10 faces.
Remembering a route and delivering a message[a]	Interviewer traces a route around a room and leaves a message at one particular point. Patient then tries to repeat the route.
Orientation	Similar to WMS.

[a] A delayed test for these items also given.

have recently attempted a standardized procedure known as the **Auto-biographical Memory Interview** (AMI; Kopelman et al., 1990). The procedure acknowledges the distinction between personal semantic memory (i.e. general facts we know about ourselves such as where we went to school) and autobiographical memory (recollections of specific incidents). Sets of questions relating to each type of memory are asked about three time periods: childhood, young adulthood and recent. In order to impose a common structure, particular questions are asked (e.g. 'Where was your secondary school?'), and recommendations are made for prompting autobiographical memory (e.g. 'Describe an incident involving you and a school friend'). A scoring procedure has been devised so that a patient's score can be compared with the normal range, and the problem of fabrication is avoided by establishing a brief personal history from relatives and checking responses against this.

An alternative way to measure remote memory is to examine an individual's memory of public events – these constitute events in the individual's society that most people can be assumed to know about. Sadly, these events are more often than not tragedies of various kinds, such as the death of John Lennon and the bombing of the trade centre in New York. Alternatively, remote memory can be assessed by asking an individual to identify the faces of people who were well known at different times. The most well-developed test of remote memory based on this type of knowledge is the **Boston Remote Memory Test** (BRMT; Albert et al., 1979), which is illustrated in table 5.3. The test has both 'easy' and 'hard' items. The latter entail not just a manipulation of difficulty, but also reflect whether or not an item is decade-specific or not. A difficult or decade-specific item is one which was current news only for a specific, relatively short period of time (e.g. Kurt Coobain, eruption of Mount St Helens), whereas an easy item is one that has remained well known and discussed until the present day (e.g. Marilyn Monroe, the Gulf War). This distinction is considered important, because it is thought that only responses to decade-specific items can give a true picture of an individual's memory for that decade. Response to easy items could, in theory, be based much more on later learning. However, it is notable that both easy and hard items appear to give similar temporal gradients in testing (Albert et al., 1979; Parkin et al., 1990a) – see figure 5.2.

Other tests of a similar nature have been developed, although none is commercially available or related to a substantial body of normative data. A number of tests based on recalling events and personalities have been reported (e.g. Parkin et al., 1993; Parkin and Hunkin, 1991). Kapur and colleagues (1989) describe their 'Dead or Alive Test', in which individuals are asked whether a given individual (e.g. Anwar Sadat) is alive or dead, and, if dead, whether the death was natural or not and when it occurred. This test is an effective means of establishing temporal gradients in

Table 5.3 Outline of the Boston Remote Memory Battery

Test	Procedure
Faces	Patient shown a series of faces of people famous in different decades (e.g. Charlie Chaplin, Mussolini, Lyndon Johnson). If patient cannot identify them, cues are then given (e.g. starred in *The Gold Rush*).
Recall	Patient asked questions about events in different decades (e.g. Kermit the Frog, Miss Piggy, and Fozzie Bear are characters in what popular TV show? Answer: The Muppet Show). Cues are given if patient cannot answer (e.g. creator was Jim Henson).
Recognition	Patient asked questions about events in different decades. Has to select one of three alternatives as the answer (e.g. Bernard Montgomery: a) wrote *For Whom the Bell Tolls*, b) was a British general (correct), c) was president of the AFL).

amnesics, and is of additional interest because the dating component may be dissociated from the other measures (Parkin et al., 1993).

Memory Questionnaires

Assessment of memory using psychometric procedures is essential in any investigation of memory impairment. However, there has long been concern that this sort of testing does not tell us all we need to know about a patient's difficulties. In particular, such procedures tell us little about the impact of a patient's disorder on their everyday life. To provide this sort of information, a number of memory questionnaires have been developed which enable investigators to get an impression of how a patient's memory disorder affects them on a day-to-day basis. Typically the patient's response is compared with that of a relative they live with, so as to get a measure of accuracy. This can be particularly important when trying to assess the degree of insight that a patient has into their memory disorder. It is not uncommon, for example, for memory-impaired patients to claim that their memory is entirely normal. Thus, on a questionnaire, they might erroneously report that they have no memory difficulties. Questionnaires also enable the social impact of memory disorder on patients and their families to be assessed. The following is an extract from the records of an amnesic patient and his wife who filled in the questionnaire designed by Sunderland and co-workers (see below). Both were asked if there had been any problems lately.

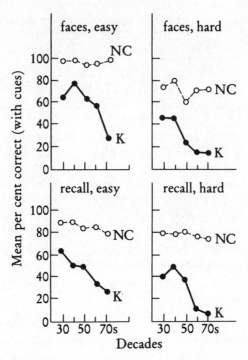

Figure 5.2 Performance of Korsakoff patients (K) and normal controls (NC) on components of the Boston Remote Memory Test.
(*From Albert et al., 1979.*)

Q.　　　　Have you been unable to pick up a new skill such as a game, or work some new gadget after you have practised it once or twice.

Patient.　Never.

Wife.　　Got very angry with a new game over Christmas. Very pedantic that we were not playing the rules right. Stormed out when he lost. Then made sure he beat Clare next time he played her. Hasn't played since.

Sunderland and colleagues (1983) have produced a widely used questionnaire which is outlined in table 5.4. It asks a range of questions about different types of forgetting, and it is easy to compare the responses of patients and relatives. Experiments have shown that the severity of memory disorder as measured by this questionnaire correlates with patients' performance on components of the WMS such as paired-associate learning and logical memory. The **Cognitive Failures Questionnaire** (CFQ; Broadbent et al., 1982) was designed to measure various mental lapses, including those involving memory. Thus it would record instances such as leaving things on the stove to burn, forgetting appointments, and putting empty milk bottles back in the refrigerator. This test has proved very useful in a variety of contexts, such as measuring the effects of drug therapy and exposure to harmful environmental agents such as lead.

Parkin and colleagues (1988) report a different kind of questionnaire which is specifically aimed at measuring **metamemory**. This can be defined as our knowledge about our memory, and asks questions such as the following:

Imagine that George and Alf (same age and IQ) place a bet that they will be able to learn the names of all cheeses sold in England by the following week. However, George has forgotten that he has already

Table 5.4 The Memory Questionnaire of Sunderland and co-workers (sample)

Speech
Forgetting the names of friends or relatives or calling them by the wrong names.
Feeling that a word is on the tip of your tongue.

Reading and writing
Forgetting the meanings of unusual words.
Unable to follow a story.

Faces and places
Forgetting where you put something. Losing things around the house.
Failing to recognize friends.

Actions
Discovering that you have done a routine thing twice by mistake.
Being absent-minded.

Learning new things
Unable to pick up a new skill or game.
Unable to cope with a change in routine.

Instruction: Please indicate how often you do these things by circling the appropriate numbers:

4	several times a day
3	about once each day
2	once or twice a week
1	less than once a week
0	never.

For instance, if you find that you are forgetting the names of friends and relatives very frequently, circle 4. If, on the other hand, you do so only rarely, circle 1.

learnt them, albeit the previous year, whereas Alf is starting from scratch. Who will learn quickest?

Here the answer is obviously George, and a correct answer indicates that the subject knows that prior learning can lead to subsequent savings in relearning (see chapter 3).

You've been invited to a wedding. How do you make sure you remember to go?

In this case subjects are offered options such as writing a note or relying on themselves or others for a reminder. Here the answer can be revealing about insight. Thus someone with a severe memory disorder who states that they just rely on themselves might be considered to lack insight into the impact of memory loss on their life.

Assessment of Other Neuropsychological Functions

Neuropsychological disorders of memory rarely, if ever, present themselves in isolation, and the clinician faced with a memory-impaired individual must also attempt to evaluate other aspects of cognitive function. If this is not done, then false conclusions may be drawn about why a patient fails on a particular memory test. The range of neuropsychological tests available is huge, and all that can be attempted here is to describe some of the more commonly used tests of cognitive function (for an overview of tests available for neuropsychological disorders, see Crawford et al., 1992).

Visuo-perceptual function

Brain injury can often cause field defects – the loss of vision in part of the visual field – and if undetected, these can cause havoc in evaluating a patient's visual memory. The presence of **field defects** is formally tested using **perimetry**. This can be done using specialized equipment or, more informally, using a method where the subject fixates on the examiner's nose. The examiner then extends his or her outstretched hand at a particular place in the visual field, and moves it in until the subject says they can see it. By doing this from positions in each quadrant of the visual field, it is possible to get a reasonable idea about the presence of any defect.

Normal performance on perimetry is no guarantee of normal perceptual ability, and a patient may exhibit a range of higher-order visuo-perceptual deficits known collectively as **agnosias**. There are many different tests for these, which aim to assess the existence of deficits at different levels of the

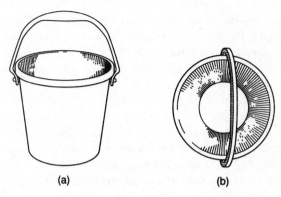

(a)   (b)

Figure 5.3 Example of items from an unusual views test. The item is presented in (a) conventional view and (b) unconventional view, and the subject must decide whether the items are the same or different.
(*From Beaumont and Davidoff, 1992.*)

perceptual process. One approach to this is to use a screening procedure such as the **Rivermead Perceptual Assessment Battery** (Whiting et al., 1985). This involves a number of subtests that address different levels of perceptual function. At the simplest level there are tests involving the copying of shapes and the matching of colours. Perceptual constancy is measured in a number of ways, such as asking subjects to pair up different-sized pictures of the same object. Higher-level tests involve cube copying and object matching and a test in which halves of animals are presented and have to be matched up. An alternative is the **Visual Object and Space Perception Test** (VOSP; Warrington and James, 1991).

At a more complex level there are a number of tests that are used to measure **figure–ground discrimination** – the ability to separate a stimulus from its background. Another very useful test of organizational ability is the incomplete figures or closure test. This can be done using a variety of different stimuli, and the patient's task is to name the object depicted in the incomplete representation. Warrington and her colleagues have devised a number of perceptual tests addressing the later stages of perceptual function. These include the **unusual views test** (see figure 5.3). This tests the ability to recognize the same object depicted from two different perspectives. Finally, there is the **matching to function test**, in which the subject has to match two objects by function rather than physical appearance (**Birmingham Object Recognition Battery**, BORB; Riddoch and Humphreys, 1995).

Attentional impairments

'Attention' is a broad term, and there are many ways of assessing it. An important deficit to look for, particularly if a patient's injuries have affected the right side of the brain, is **unilateral neglect**. This is a curious attentional disorder in which the patient fails to attend to the left side of the world due to damage on the right side of the brain (much more rarely the reverse occurs, with left-sided damage causing right-sided neglect). This may be seen on a global scale, when the patient ignores everything on the right, or in a more subtle way, when the patient ignores the left side of things wherever they are presented. Neglect is a variable disorder, but one quick means of detecting it reasonably reliably is the **line bisection task**. Here the person is presented with lines of varying length and asked to bisect them. Typically, the neglect patient bisects lines towards the right, as if the left half of the line did not exist. If neglect is detected, care must be taken not to address the patient on the neglected side.

Distractibility is often a problem, and this can be evaluated using the **Stroop Test**. The task, which has recently been standardized (Trennery et al., 1989), involves three conditions: reading out a list of colour-names given in black ink, naming the colour of a series of colour-patches, and naming the colour of the ink in which a series of colour-names are written. In the latter test the colour-name and the colour of the ink are never the same, so to perform the task, the subject must ignore the colour-name and concentrate on the ink. Difficulty on this task is indicated when the subject takes longer than when dealing with the same colour-names in the first two conditions. The third, 'colour incongruent' condition is often very difficult for people with brain injury, and failure on this test is a very sensitive indicator of brain damage. It can, for example, indicate impairment when other tests show no sign of a deficit.

Wechsler Adult Intelligence Scale (WAIS)

The WAIS and its more recent updated form, WAIS-R (Wechsler, 1981), are widely used in neuropsychological investigation, although it should be stressed that it was not devised specifically for the study of brain damage. It is used to derive an intelligence quotient (IQ) which itself is calculated from performance on a range of subtests addressing different mental abilities. The various subtests fall into two subsets: verbal and performance. Each of these tests yields a raw score which is converted into a scaled score. The scores for verbal and performance subsets are then aggregated to provide separate measures of **verbal** and **performance IQ**, which, in turn, can be used to calculate a **full-scale IQ**.

Performance on WAIS can reveal a number of interesting facts about a patient. First, the measure of full-scale IQ, when combined with a measure of pre-morbid IQ, provides the best basis for assessing whether a patient has undergone any generalized intellectual decline. Another important feature concerns any obvious discrepancy between the verbal and performance

IQs. In a normal individual the two scores are about the same, so any significant discrepancy between them indicates that brain damage has been selective. In a normally lateralized person a high verbal IQ and a low performance IQ would indicate predominantly right-hemisphere damage, whereas the reverse result would be indicative of left-hemisphere lesions. Deciding when a VIQ–PIQ discrepancy is significant has turned out to be a difficult methodological exercise, but, as a rule of thumb, a discrepancy of around 20 points should be taken seriously.

At a finer level, analysis of performance on different subtests may have particular significance. There is an extensive literature on this (see e.g. Lezak, 1995), but care must be taken because of difficulties in being sure that poor performance on a given test has not arisen by chance. Finally, because WAIS tests so many different abilities, it is time-consuming, and the time spent evaluating a patient provides an opportunity to observe a patient's all-round ability. One should also note that WAIS appears to be easier than WAIS-R (although this might be partly due to the gradual world-wide increase in IQ). Because both WAIS and WAIS-R take quite a time to administer, it is sometimes useful to consider short forms which enable a reliable estimate of overall performance (see Crawford et al., 1992).

Estimating pre-morbid intelligence

One of the most important things an investigator needs is some estimate of a patient's pre-morbid intellectual ability. Factors such as previous career obviously provide us with a good indication, but objective measures are needed if we are to be certain (with the current high unemployment situation, one often finds people with high IQs doing quite menial jobs!). The most widely used means of estimating pre-morbid intelligence is the **National Adult Reading Test** (NART; Nelson, 1991). The test is based on demonstrations that language ability is a relatively robust function, in that it can remain constant when other cognitive abilities are in decline due to illnesses such as Alzheimer's Disease.

The test comprises a list of words which are all irregular in the sense that they do not obey English spelling rules (e.g. ACHE, GAUGE). The subject is asked to read out the words, and a note is made of any errors that are made. Performance on NART has been standardized against performance on WAIS, so a simple equation allows an estimate of WAIS IQ to be derived from the NART score. More recently, NART has been adapted to provide an estimate of pre-morbid WAIS-R IQ. NART is considered reasonably reliable except when dealing with patients who have specific reading difficulties, known as **acquired dyslexias**, or visual acuity problems.

Language

Following Walker (1992) assessment procedures for language disorders can be divided into two broad types: **batteries**, comprising a range of subtests each addressing a specific component of language function, and **task-specific tests**, a range of tests each concerned with a specific language ability.

Perhaps the most well-known test battery is the **Boston Diagnostic Aphasia Examination** (BDAE; Goodglass and Kaplan, 1983). This tests the entire range of language abilities, including oral expression, writing, and oral and written comprehension. Testing is done at the level of both single words and more complex language material. The BDAE also allows assessment of deficits often found in association with language disability: in arithmetic, apraxia, and visuo-spatial disturbance. Among the most commonly used task-specific tests are the **Graded Naming Test** (McKenna and Warrington, 1983) and the **Boston Naming Test** (Kaplan et al., 1983), which can both be used to assess the ability to name objects; the **Token Test** (McNeil and Prescott, 1978), which can be used to detect less obvious loss of receptive language; and the **Pyramids and Palm Trees Test** (Howard and Orchard-Lisle, 1984), which assesses the ability to understand the meaning of pictures and words. For more details on task-specific tests and language assessment more generally, consult Walker (1992).

Frontal lobe function

Perhaps the most complex problem in neuropsychological testing concerns the assessment of frontal lobe function. As we shall see later, the frontal cortex is considered, among other things, to be the seat of executive processes; so it is unlikely that there is a single 'frontal function'. Hence the assessment of frontal function requires a range of tests to be given. However, the likelihood of two neuropsychologists agreeing on the same set of tests is highly unlikely. What follows, therefore, is my personal selection.

One way to divide up tests of frontal function is to use Eslinger and Grattan's (1993) recent distinction between reactive and spontaneous flexibility. Reactive flexibility refers to the readiness to shift cognition and behaviour freely, according to the changing demands of a situation. Spontaneous flexibility describes the ready flow of ideas and answers in response to a question.

The most commonly used test of reactive flexibility is the **Wisconsin Card Sorting Test** (WCST; see figure 5.4; Nelson and O'Connell, 1978).

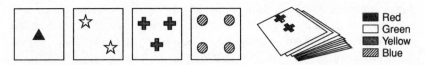

Figure 5.4 The Wisconsin Card Sorting Test.
(*Reproduced from Lezak, 1995.*)

The subject is presented with four reference cards and a pack of exemplar cards. The task is to sort the cards according to a rule (e.g. grouping cards together by shape). After a number of correct sorts, the patient is asked to think of a different rule. There are three rules, and usually these have to be discovered twice each. Patients can make a variety of errors, but of most interest are **perseverative errors**, where the patient persists with a response that has just been deemed wrong. There are a number of different procedures for this test (see Parker and Crawford, 1992).

One way to measure spontaneous flexibility is to use fluency tasks. These measure the ability to generate exemplars of particular categories. The simplest fluency tasks are the letter-based ones such as **FAS** (Spreen and Strauss, 1991). Here the patient generates as many different words as possible in 1 minute, beginning with each of the three letters. More complex fluency tasks involving generating words from semantic categories or alternating with examples from different categories. A more complex fluency task is the **Alternate Uses Test** in which subjects must think up alternative uses for everyday objects (Eslinger and Grattan, 1993).

The frontal cortex is also implicated in planning, and one way of assessing this is the **Tower of Hanoi** test. There is also a simpler variant of this known as the **Tower of London** (see figure 5.5). Here the subject must achieve the goal of moving all the discs from the left peg to the right peg obeying the rule that a larger disc must never rest on a smaller disc. This test is particularly good at picking up higher-order planning deficits, although not all patients with frontal damage fail this test. For the latter,

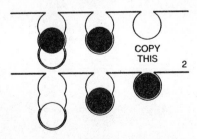

Figure 5.5 A subproblem from the computerized Tower of London test. Two moves (indicated) are required to make the two arrangements identical.
(*From Owen et al., 1990.*)

more complex tasks requiring the scheduling of various concurrent activities are the only way of demonstrating an impairment (recently a test battery aimed at assessing more complex aspects of frontal function has been produced; see Wilson et al., 1996).

Systematic memory assessment is essential for both clinical practice and accurate research. It is important to assess many aspects of memory. Thus, following an assessment using, for example, the Wechsler Memory Scale – Revised, other tests must also be given. These include an assessment of recognition and remote memory. Questionnaires about memory can also yield valuable information that clinical tests do not provide, in particular an insight into the patient's everyday memory problems. Memory impairments rarely occur in isolation, and it is advisable to assess other mental abilities such as perception, attention, intelligence (including a pre-morbid assessment), language, and frontal lobe function.

6 The Amnesic Syndrome

In fiction, amnesics are typically portrayed as wandering the streets, unable
to say who they are or how they came to be there. Amnesia of this sort does
occur (see chapter 10), but in neuropsychology, the term **amnesic** is most
commonly used to describe a patient suffering from what is called the
amnesic syndrome. This can be defined as a permanent global disorder of
memory following brain damage. Historically, interest in the amnesic
syndrome lagged behind interest in other neurological conditions. The
early Egyptians were the first to document neurological problems. Among
the Greeks, Hippocrates (460–370BC) correctly diagnosed epilepsy as a
disease of the brain, and also noted that damage to one side of the brain
produced paralysis and convulsions on the opposite side of the body.
However, neither Hippocrates nor any other Greek scholar appears to have
linked disorders of memory with the brain. Indeed, some Greeks, such as
Aristotle, considered that memory was located in the heart.

Medicine in the first millennium was dominated by the writings of
Galen (AD131–201), who wrote more than 400 different treatises, many of
them on neurological illness, but with no mention of amnesia. This is rather
surprising, given that one of Galen's duties was to attend injured gladiators,
many of whom must have exhibited post-concussional syndrome, including
loss of memory. By the time the first anatomical drawings of the brain
appeared in the Middle Ages, the existence of memory as one of several
specific mental abilities located in the brain had been recognized (see figure
6.1). Recognition of different mental functions led scholars to consider
how these functions might be distributed within the brain. One theory
allocated each mental ability to a different cerebral ventricle. Figure 6.1
shows the famous woodcut by Gregor Reisch (1467–1525), in which
the faculty of 'memorativa' is located in the fourth ventricle. The alternative, correct view that functions are localized within the tissue of the
brain itself also had its proponents. Notable among them was Descartes,

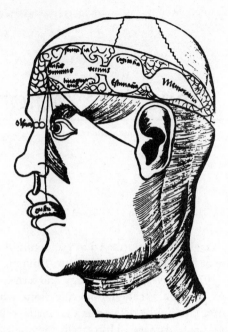

Figure 6.1 Woodcut by Gregor Reisch illustrating the ventricular localization theory of brain function. Note that the fourth ventricle appears to be the location of memory. A curiosity of this diagram is that the ventricular system shown is that of a cow, not a human, because in medieval times depiction of the internal organs of the human body was forbidden.

although he suggested erroneously that the pineal gland was the centre of memory.

Further developments concerning the relationship between memory and the brain did not occur until the latter part of the nineteenth century, when a number of neurologists began to take an interest in memory disorders. This, coupled with improved anatomical accounts of the brain and neuro-pathological techniques, provided the starting-point for modern interest in the amnesic syndrome. A number of important figures can be identified, including Ribot (see chapter 5) and Hughlings Jackson. However, present-day interest in the amnesic syndrome stems most directly from the work of Carl Wernicke and Sergei Korsakoff.

In 1881 Wernicke described an acute neurological condition which included among its symptoms ataxia, optic abnormalities and gross confusion. According to the tradition of naming in neurology, this condition was termed **Wernicke's Encephalopathy**. At the same time, Korsakoff was studying the long-term recovery of patients who had survived a neuro-logical illness usually associated with long-term alcohol abuse. Korsakoff noted that the major symptom of his patients was a profound memory disorder, in which they seemed almost totally incapable of learning any new information. It is now established that what Korsakoff was studying was the long-term effects of Wernicke's Encephalopathy; patients in this condition are diagnosed as having the **Wernicke–Korsakoff Syndrome**, but we will follow common practice and abbreviate this to **Korsakoff's Syndrome**.

Because of the enduring prevalence of alcoholism, Korsakoff patients have been the most readily available subjects for students of the amnesic syndrome, and most of the literature has been concerned with them. Talland's notable monograph *Deranged Memory* (1965), for example, is exclusively devoted to patients with Korsakoff's Syndrome. However, the amnesic syndrome can arise from a number of causes, and interest in patients in whom the syndrome has developed for other reasons is growing. Thus, Korsakoff's Syndrome must not be considered synonymous with the amnesic syndrome.

General Characteristics of the Amnesic Syndrome

Although no two patients are ever exactly the same, patients presenting the amnesic syndrome consistently show the same pattern of deficits and preserved abilities – indeed, it is the consistency of this pattern that allows the term 'syndrome' to be used. Briefly we can define the amnesic syndrome as comprising the following features:

1 No evidence of impaired short-term storage as measured by tasks such as digit span on WMS-R.
2 Semantic memory, and other intellectual functions, as measured by tests such as WAIS-R, generally intact. Thus, to be classed amnesic, a patient would have an average IQ, but his or her scores on the WMS-R (especially the delayed memory index) would be well below normal levels.
3 A severe and permanent anterograde amnesia is present. On tests of recall, such as free recall, and WMS-R hard-paired associate learning, performance will be exceptionally poor. WMS-R logical memory and visual reproduction scores will also be very low. Recognition will also be poor, with chance performance often observed on tests such as RMT.
4 Retrograde amnesia will inevitably be present, but its extent can be extremely variable, with some patients having extensive deficits and others lacking memory only for recent parts of the pre-morbid period.

5   Procedural memory, as measured by skill learning, conditioning, per-
    ceptual learning and priming will also be relatively intact.

The Neuropathology of the Amnesic Syndrome

One reason why the amnesic syndrome is important is that it provides an
opportunity to learn more about the neuroanatomy of memory. The oldest
form of neuropathology is the post-mortem, in which the brain of a
deceased person is examined at either a macroscopic or a microscopic level.
In some cases post-mortem analyses are the only conclusive basis for
establishing which brain structures were damaged in a particular patient.
Increasingly, however, researchers are making use of *in vivo* imaging
techniques, where it is possible to investigate the structure and function of
the living brain.

A commonplace method, now used routinely in neurological investigation, is **computerized axial tomography** (CAT) scanning. CAT is a
sophisticated form of X-ray procedure which assesses the density of brain
tissue at numerous points, and from this constructs a three-dimensional
image. On CAT scans areas of damage show up as darker regions (see figure
6.2a). CAT was the first method to be developed in the imaging revolution,
but it was soon followed by a procedure known as **Magnetic Resonance
Imaging** (MRI). This technique involves momentarily aligning atoms in a
particular direction within a magnetic field using radio waves. When these
waves are turned off, the atoms produce a voltage (magnetic resonance),
and this is used to construct an image. Figure 6.2b shows the greater degree
of structural detail available from an MRI scan. More recently, MRI
techniques have been adapted in order to measure physiological changes
in the brain, a technique known as **functional magnetic resonance
imaging** (fMRI); see Moonen, 1995, for a recent review of this technique
and its applications.

A further important development has been **positron emission tomography** (PET). PET exploits a procedure known as autoradiography, in
which radioactive compounds (radioisotopes) are injected into the blood-
stream and the distribution of the substances is measured using X-ray
techniques. When applied to the brain, PET techniques provide a map of
how the radioisotope has been absorbed in different parts of the brain. PET
not only provides a basic picture of the brain, but, by measuring the extent
to which the isotope is present in any brain region, it can also provide
information about the physiological status of different brain regions. Thus
an area shown to have a high level of radioisotope is one that is obviously
very active, whereas a region with little or no radioisotope may be
dysfunctional in some way (see figure 6.2c). As we shall see later, PET is a
useful way of measuring the activity of different brain regions when

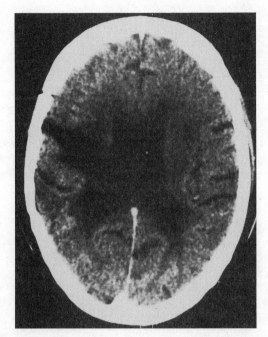

Figure 6.2a Computerized axial tomography (CAT) scan showing damage to the right hemisphere of the cortex.
(*From Halligan et al., 1996.*)

subjects are actually carrying out tasks, thus enabling the relationship between different mental activities and various brain regions to be mapped.

The amnesic syndrome can arise from lesions in a number of different parts of the brain, either singly or in combination. Figure 6.3 illustrates the various brain structures which, when damaged, can give rise to the amnesic syndrome. These structures occur in two distinct areas of the brain: the **medial diencephalon** and the **medial temporal lobe** of the cortex. As we noted earlier, much of what we know about the amnesic syndrome has stemmed from investigations of patients with Korsakoff's Syndrome. Neuropathological studies indicate that these patients suffer damage to a variety of diencephalic structures, most notably the dorsomedial thalamic nucleus, the **mamillary bodies**, the **mamillothalamic tract** and certain areas adjacent to the third ventricle. However, there is also a degree of cortical involvement, especially in the frontal cortex; and more recently it has been pointed out that Korsakoff patients may have significant damage in the medial temporal lobe.

The cause of Korsakoff's Syndrome is Wernicke's Encephalopathy, and there is now overwhelming evidence that the primary cause of this illness

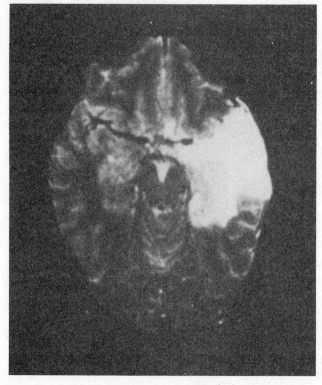

Figure 6.2b MRI (magnetic resonance imaging) scan of the brain of someone who suffered herpes simplex encephalitis, a viral infection of the brain. The light area indicates damage to the left temporal lobe.
(*Photograph courtesy of Narinder Kapur.*)

is thiamine deficiency, which results in haemorrhaging in the diencephalic region (see figure 6.4). Evidence for the involvement of thiamine in human memory came from studies showing that thiamine therapy could relieve some of the deficits shown by Korsakoff patients. Thiamine deficiency was also implicated in a unique study carried out by De Wardener and Lennox (1947). These army doctors were among British soldiers held captive by the Japanese. They lived on 'a grossly unbalanced diet consisting mainly of polished rice', under appalling conditions in which diseases such as dysentery were endemic. This created severe malnutrition, and the authors noted the occurrence of Wernicke's Encephalopathy in more than 50 men, many of whom reported memory problems. Although conditions were extremely primitive, some post-mortem investigations were carried out, and these confirmed diencephalic brain damage.

A number of issues regarding Korsakoff's Syndrome remain unresolved. First, there have been claims that a persistent form of the disorder depends

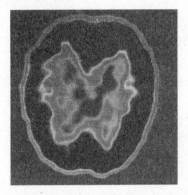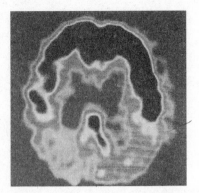

Figure 6.2c PET scans of (a) a normal brain and (b) someone with Alzheimer's Disease. Lighter regions at the front of the Alzheimer brain indicate malfunctioning. PET scans are normally coloured.
(*From Davison and Neale, 1994.*)

on both thiamine deficiency and alcoholism; but there are now a number of instances of the disorder in the absence of alcoholism. Parkin and colleagues (1991), for example, described a dense Korsakoff state in a woman who developed thiamine deficiency as a consequence of inadequate intravenous feeding. Another puzzle is to explain why only a small number of heavy drinkers develop the disorder. Here it has been suggested that Korsakoff's Syndrome is linked to a hereditary deficiency in a certain enzyme (see also Kopelman, 1995b, for a review of this issue and other aspects of Korsakoff's Syndrome).

While Korsakoff's Syndrome remains the primary cause of diencephalic amnesia, other causes can also give rise to it. The thalamic region is prone to vascular disorders, and many instances of amnesia can arise as a consequence of this. Figure 6.5 shows an MRI scan of a patient known as JR, who suffered a small stroke in the thalamus. Although the lesion is small, it had a major disruptive effect on his memory, which in many respects was as severe as that seen in Korsakoff's Syndrome. The reason why JR's lesion had such an impact was because it damaged both the dorso-medial thalamic nucleus and the mamillothalamic tract.

Diencephalic amnesia can also arise from the presence of tumours. The floor of the third ventricle is adjacent to diencephalic structures, and tumours here can exert local pressure on those structures and cause memory loss. Recently we reported the case of RK, a man who had a tumour pressing on the mamillary bodies (Parkin and Hunkin, 1993). The tumour was treated with radiotherapy, and gradually shrank. As this happened, we were able to plot the steady improvement in RK's memory.

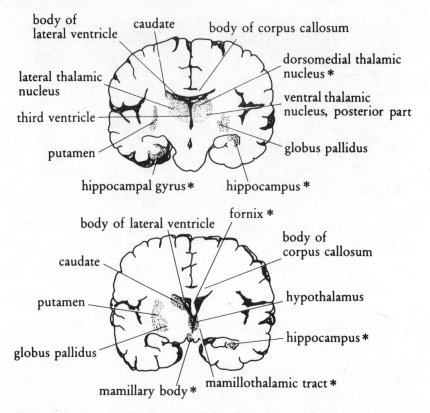

Figure 6.3 Cross-sections of the human brain. Those areas marked with an asterisk are known to be damaged in patients with the amnesic syndrome. (*From Butters and Cermak, 1980, p. 12.*)

As long ago as 1880 it was recognized that damage to the temporal lobe region of the brain could cause significant loss of memory. However, it was not until the 1950s that this relationship was fully appreciated. At that time neurosurgeons were using a technique known as lobectomy as a means of treating temporal lobe epilepsy. In this technique, which we considered briefly in chapter 3, the areas of the temporal lobe responsible for the seizures are identified and then removed. Scoville and Milner (1957) reported the results of using this technique on a group of patients which included the now famous amnesic case, HM. As a treatment for epilepsy, the technique worked well, but for some of the patients there was a devastating side-effect: they were left with an extremely dense amnesic syndrome.

On the basis of notes taken during the operations, the surgeons were able to understand why only some of the patients developed amnesia. The

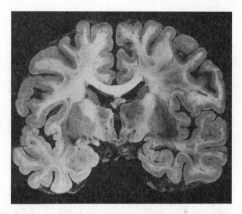

Figure 6.4 Cross-section of the brain of someone who suffered from Korsakoff's Syndrome. Note the severe damage to the mamillary bodies and the lesioned tissue in and around the third ventricle.
(*From Victor et al., 1971.*)

medial temporal lobe contains within it structures known as the **hippocampus** and the **amygdala**, and it was noted that only subjects who had both of these removed bilaterally developed an amnesic state. Initially it was thought that removal of both structures was necessary to produce an amnesic state, but more recent research has shown that damage to the hippocampus alone has far more implications for memory than damage to the amygdala. Zola-Morgan and co-workers (1986), for example, reported a man known as RB who suffered a small stroke which selectively damaged a part of the hippocampus known as the CA1 field. Although showing little evidence of retrograde amnesia, RB exhibited anterograde amnesia. By contrast, damage to the amygdala appears to affect the processing of emotion rather than memory (Young et al., 1995).

The amnesia shown by case CB, although disabling, was less severe than that found in HM and other patients with temporal lobe lesions. Squire and Knowlton (1994) have accounted for this by arguing that a severe amnesic state will develop only if the hippocampus is damaged along with adjacent areas of cortex. This was the case with HM, hence his dense amnesia; it also explains why the amnesia associated with **herpes simplex encephalitis** (HSE) is so devastating. This is a viral infection of the brain that rapidly causes extensive brain damage centred on the temporal lobes. MRI scans of patients who have had this illness shown that the lesions are extensive, and are not restricted to the hippocampus (see figure 6.2b). Wilson and colleagues (1995), for example, describe the case of C, who, following HSE, developed a profound amnesic state. On the logical memory component of WMS, for example, he remembered only one item of information immediately, and nothing after a delay, even with considerable

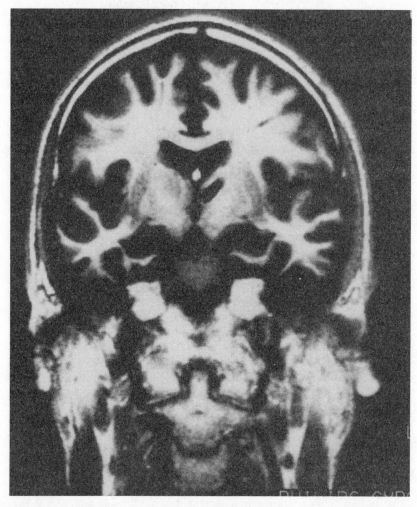

Figure 6.5 MRI scan of patient JR showing lesion in the region of the left thalamus.
(*Parkin et al., 1994, p. 44.*)

prompting. He was also severely impaired on tests of retrograde amnesia, saying that he had never heard of people like John Lennon or John F. Kennedy.

There are many other ways in which the temporal lobes can become damaged and give rise to amnesia. Most common is **closed head injury** –

so-called because it involves a blow to the head which does not penetrate the skull. When a closed head injury occurs, the brain tends to twist on its axis, and the temporal lobes are particularly vulnerable to the effects of this. Closed head injury is sadly a widespread occurrence, but patients with this problem have not featured much in the investigation of amnesia because, along with the memory difficulties, they often have many other deficits which make interpretation of their impairment problematic. The other common cause of temporal lobe amnesia is a **cerebro-vascular accident** (CVA), or **stroke**. Here disruption of the blood supply to the temporal lobes results in a rapid and irreversible deterioration of brain tissue known as an **infarction**.

Recently, the *New England Journal of Medicine* described a man who arrived at a casualty room highly intoxicated. He was given a precautionary scan, which revealed, quite extraordinarily, the presence of a large nail in the rear of his brain. Questioned about this, he remembered a suicide attempt some years previously, in which he had fired a nail gun up his nose. This may sound bizarre, but the neurological literature reveals many instances where, either through accidents or suicide attempts, people have introduced into their brains an astonishing variety of objects, including sewing needles, nails, paintbrushes, parts of a gun, iron bars, keys, knives, strips of wire and even chopsticks. These cases of 'unusual low-velocity intracranial injuries' have generally been of purely medical interest, often because the injuries, despite their horrendous nature, appear to cause surprisingly small impairments. However, as the following account shows, these relatively good outcomes all depend on where the object goes:

> I was working at my desk. . . . My room-mate had come in [and] he had taken one of my small fencing foils off the wall and I guess he was making like Cyrano de Bergerac behind me. . . . I just felt a tap on the back . . . I swung around . . . at the same time he was making the lunge. I took it right in the left nostril, went up and punctured the cribiform area of my brain.

This account of an accident comes from a man known as NA, who, as a result of the fencing foil injury, now has a severe amnesia. While his memory problems have been of considerable interest, the case is perhaps best-known for the debate over where his brain is actually damaged. Early descriptions located the damage in the diencephalon centred on the left dorsomedial thalamic nucleus, thereby suggesting a pure 'diencephalic amnesia' (Squire, 1982). However, Weiskrantz (1985) made the point that it was not possible to insert a fencing foil into the brain via the nose and reach the thalamic area without passing through some other brain regions on the way. In a macabre, if not heroic, attempt to resolve the debate, Zola-Morgan and Squire (1985) obtained an intact cadaver, and attempted to simulate NA's injury with a surgical instrument. Three attempts failed to produce a lesion in the mamillary bodies, but came close to the presumed site of NA's lesion. Modern research has now vindicated Weiskrantz's claim, in that MRI scans of NA's brain show that he has lesions in a number of brain regions, including parts of the temporal lobe (Squire et al., 1989). Recently, however, Dusoir and colleagues (1990) have described a man who, during an assault, had a snooker cue rammed up his nose. This left him densely amnesic, and an MRI scan revealed that the cue has principally damaged the mamillary bodies.

Describing the Amnesic Syndrome

The general characteristics of the amnesic syndrome indicate that it is not some general deterioration of memory function, but a selective impairment in which some functions, such as learning novel information, are severely impaired, while others, including memory span and language, remain normal. This has two important implications. First, the consistent nature of the amnesic syndrome means that our models of memory must be structured so as to account for the pattern of impairment it produces. Second, the pattern of impairment may provide important evidence about the organization of memory – the assumption being that amnesia is not some random decay of the memory system, but a selective impairment of some component(s), leaving others intact.

In chapter 1 we noted a major conceptual distinction in memory models between STS and LTS. STS is assumed to rely on temporary active storage processes which initiate, but are none the less independent of, those processes underlying the formation of permanent memory traces in LTS. This allows for the possibility that STS might continue functioning normally even if the processes responsible for permanent trace formation were defective. A defining feature of the amnesic syndrome is a normal memory span, indicating that STS function is preserved. From this it follows that the amnesic syndrome must be a deficit in the function of LTS.

The apparent sparing of STS in the amnesic syndrome is well illustrated by an observation of HM reported by Milner (1971). She noticed that he 'was able to retain the number 584 for at least 15 minutes, by continuously working out elaborate mnemonic schemes. When asked how, he replied: "It's easy. You just remember 8. You see 5, 8 and 4 add to 17. You remember 8, subtract it from 17 and it leaves 9. Divide 9 in half and you get 5 and 4, and there you are: 584. Easy." A minute or so later, HM could not remember the number or any of his complex mnemonic and did not even know that he had been asked to remember a number.'

Having localized the deficit to LTS, it is now necessary to be more specific about how this structure has been impaired. As we saw in chapter 2, LTS is considered to be a tripartite structure composed of episodic, semantic and procedural memory. The pattern of impairment in the amnesic syndrome, as we defined it earlier, seems to fit nicely with this division of LTS. First, the ability to make use of previously acquired skills indicates that procedural memory is unaffected. Second, preservation of language and general intellectual function suggests an intact semantic memory. By contrast, the almost complete failure to recall or recognize novel information and the difficulty in remembering past personal events suggests a selective failure of episodic memory. We will first deal with those functions that appear intact in the amnesic syndrome.

Procedural and Implicit Memory in Amnesia

Studies of HM showed that he was able to learn a number of motor skills. One of these was the pursuit rotor task, a test of hand–eye co-ordination. HM consistently improved on the task, although not as much as controls (Corkin, 1968). Figure 6.6 shows HM's performance on the mirror drawing task. Here the subject must trace between the two lines of the star while looking at their hand in the mirror. From the graph it is clear that HM learned this task, but in this and all other tasks which he succeeded in doing, he consistently denied knowledge of having done them before. Pursuit rotor was one of a number of new motor skills that HM was able to acquire normally, and this gave rise to the suggestion that 'motor memory' was selectively preserved in amnesia. However, more recent research has shown that amnesic patients also show residual learning capability on non-motor tasks.

Amnesic patients also show **perceptual learning**. In a typical experiment the patient is first presented with a stimulus and then asked to make some kind of response to it. Following an interval, the stimulus is presented again, and the subject is asked to make the same response. In addition, the patient is asked whether he has ever seen the stimulus before. Crovitz and colleagues (1981) showed amnesic subjects 'picture puzzles' such as that shown in figure 6.7, and measured the time they took to identify them correctly. The pictures were presented again the next day, and the patients were asked to identify them. On the second presentation, the patients' ability to remember seeing the pictures was very unreliable, but they identified them more quickly than on day 1. The picture shown in figure 6.7, for example, took an average of 163 seconds to identify on day 1, but only 17 seconds on day 2. This was not due to a 'practice effect', because new pictures presented on day 2 were identified much more slowly. This result, along with results of many similar studies (e.g. Meudell and Mayes,

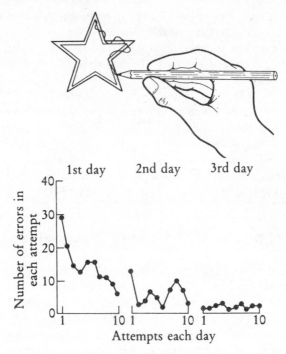

Figure 6.6 The mirror drawing task and HM's performance on three consecutive days. Note that by day 3 HM's performance is virtually error free, even though he had no recollection of having done the task before.
(*From Blakemore, 1977.*)

1981), shows that amnesics can retain information about the perceptual organization of a stimulus, even though they have no conscious recollection of it. Other perceptual learning skills have been found to be intact in amnesia, including reading mirror-reversed words, speeded reading of normal text, and resolving random dot stereograms (see Squire et al., 1993).

There seems little doubt that procedural memory is intact in amnesia, and there is also evidence on a range of tasks used to demonstrate implicit memory in normal subjects. Korsakoff patients, for example, show normal repetition priming using the stem completion procedure (see chapter 3), despite extremely poor explicit memory when the same stems are used as recall cues (e.g. Graf and Schacter, 1985). Cermak and colleagues (1985) showed that Korsakoff patients had lowered recognition thresholds for previously exposed words and that this effect has also been extended to non-words (Musen and Squire, 1991). In chapter 3 we considered the object decision task as a means of measuring implicit memory for structural information. This paradigm has been used with amnesics, and they also

Figure 6.7 One of the 'picture puzzles' used by Crovitz and co-workers. (*Crovitz et al., 1981, p. 273.*)

show a structural priming effect. Other studies have shown picture priming, in which subjects correctly identify fragmented pictures more accurately if the picture has been pre-exposed.

From our previous discussion of implicit memory you will recall that a distinction is drawn between pre-semantic and semantically mediated implicit memory. The former, which is considered to be a function of various perceptual representation systems, does not involve the acquisition of meaning, whereas the latter does. Our brief review indicates that pre-semantic implicit memory operates well in amnesic subjects, but can new semantic memory be retrieved under implicit conditions in amnesia?

McAndrews and co-workers (1987) showed amnesic subjects puzzle sentences such as 'The haystack was important because the cloth ripped', and asked them to think of the concept that made sense of it ('parachute'). This task was then re-presented at intervals of up to a week, and the solution time was compared with that for similar novel sentences. At all intervals a semantic or conceptual priming effect was obtained, with previously exposed sentences being understood more quickly than novel sentences. The study compared severely amnesic subjects with moderately amnesic subjects, and showed that, despite far better recognition memory for the sentences in the moderately impaired group, the extent of conceptual priming for the two patient groups was indistinguishable. This shows that the priming effect obtained could not be attributed to some of the amnesics having explicit memory available.

Even greater retention of semantically based implicit memory comes from the study of KC, the man who became densely amnesic following a closed head injury. He was shown pictures, each accompanied by a sentence which was vaguely related to the picture (e.g. a picture of a man in a hospital setting with the sentence 'MEDICINE cured HICCUP'). Even after an interval of one year KC could still reliably produce the final word of many of the sentences he had been shown, despite having no explicit recollection of having been shown the sentences before.

A particular problem has been whether amnesic patients can show **novel association priming**, an issue that has considerable significance when we come to consider options for remediation based on preserved implicit memory (see chapter 11). Graf and Schacter (1985) initially exposed amnesics to pairs of unrelated words (e.g. WINDOW–REASON), and then gave a stem completion test for the second member of each pair. When completion was attempted, the second of the pair was paired either with its original partner (e.g. WINDOW–REA___?) or with a different word (OFFICER–REA___?). In this way priming could be compared as a function of same or different **semantic context**.

The logic of this experiment is that higher levels of priming in the same versus different conditions indicates that a semantic association between the previously unrelated word-pairs has been established, and that this contributes to the priming effect. Graf and Schacter (1985) obtained an ambiguous result, in that better priming was observed in the same context condition only for less memory-impaired patients. Shimamura and Squire (1989) followed up the Graf and Schacter study by presenting amnesic subjects with sentences in which two words were highlighted (e.g. 'A BELL was hanging over the baby's CRADLE'). The same manipulation of context was then undertaken, but no evidence of enhanced priming with the same context was found. Mayes and Gooding (1989) used a similar type of task, and found that only a proportion of their amnesic subjects showed semantic context effects in priming.

Other studies, however, suggest that implicit memory for novel associations does occur. Musen and Squire (1993) presented pairs of unrelated words for study, and then tested implicit memory by measuring the speed at which these words could be read. In order to test for the influence of novel association learning, reading speed for 'old' word-pairs (i.e. pairs presented during learning) was contrasted with that for new pairings of words. In this task novel association learning is demonstrated by faster reading of old word-pairs. Two experiments using a single trial did not show any evidence of novel association learning, but when multiple learning trials were used, evidence for novel association learning was obtained.

A key factor determining novel association learning in amnesics is the nature of the initial learning phase. Graf and Schacter (1985) showed that novel associations were acquired quite readily by amnesic subjects, provided the pairs were presented in an elaborative context. This involved presenting each word-pair and asking subjects to decide how easily the two words could be related to each other, and then requiring them to form a sentence using the two words. In a recent study, Valerie Jenkins and I have confirmed that severely amnesic patients can acquire novel associations if they are given elaborative encoding instructions (Jenkins and Parkin, submitted).

Recently there has also been interest in the possibility that amnesic subjects might show implicit learning – that is, learning that occurs without the subject being able to explain what it is they are learning (see chapter 3). Experiments have now shown unequivocally that amnesic patients can show considerable learning on tasks such as artificial grammars and the sugar production task (see chapter 3; Knowlton et al., 1992; Squire and Frambach, 1990).

Knowlton and colleagues (1994) examined probabilistic learning in normal and amnesic subjects. In one experiment subjects attempted to learn which of two fictitious diseases ('nermitis' or 'caldosis') was most reliably predicted by combinations of between one and four different symptoms (headache, fatigue, rash and sneezing). For any combination of symptoms the probabilities associated with each disease could vary. Thus headache and fatigue predicted nermitis with a 90 per cent probability, whereas rash and sneezing predicted the illness with only a 43 per cent probability. On each trial subjects were presented with between one and four symptoms and required to indicate which disease they thought the hypothetical patient was suffering from. Feedback about accuracy was given on each trial. In this and other similar tasks the amnesics learned the probability of different outcomes at rates similar to controls.

Semantic Memory in Amnesia

In my account I have proposed that semantic memory may be spared in amnesia. If this is true, then it should be possible for amnesics to acquire new general knowledge. This possibility was investigated by asking HM to define common words and phrases that had come into use only since his operation. He did show some ability to do this, correctly defining 'rock and roll', for example, but his success was relatively slight. In one experiment, HM tried to learn the meaning of ten unfamiliar words. After extensive training, he was hardly able to match any of the words with their definitions (Gabrieli et al., 1983). Similarly Grossman (1987) attempted to teach Korsakoff patients the meaning of a low-frequency colour-adjective 'bice'. They were initially taught the meaning of the word by associating it with a pen of a particular colour. They achieved this somewhat laboriously, but failed to generalize the knowledge to other objects with the same colour.

While there are some counter-examples (e.g. Hirst and Volpe, 1988), the general failure of amnesic patients to acquire new semantic memory might reflect an episodic impairment, in that episodic memory is needed in the early stages of acquiring new knowledge. As a result, it is perhaps more instructive to examine how amnesia disrupts pre-existing knowledge. If semantic memory is spared in amnesics, we should find evidence of good general knowledge. A key line of evidence usually cited in support of separable semantic memory in amnesia is patients' standard levels of performance on intelligence tests. However, it has been pointed out that tests like WAIS-R deal primarily with information acquired by early adult life. We have already seen that remote episodic memories tend to be spared, so this apparently normal intelligence might just reflect a similar advantage for knowledge laid down early.

The case of PZ, a university professor who became a Korsakoff patient shortly after writing his autobiography, is instructive (Butters, 1984). As one would expect, his ability to recall events from his life showed a marked temporal gradient, with only those from the 1920s intact. However, when his knowledge of scientific terms was assessed, he showed a similar retrograde amnesia, and was only able to define those acquired earlier in his career. This parallel loss of event memory and general knowledge has been demonstrated elsewhere. Verfaellie and Roth (1996), for example, have shown that Korsakoff patients are poor at defining words that came into use during the decades for which they have a dense amnesia for events.

Another difficulty revolves around the tasks on which amnesic patients show retrograde amnesia. In chapter 5 we saw that amnesic subjects not only show poor autobiographical (i.e. episodic) recall, but, in addition, fail on tests involving general knowledge of past events and the identification of famous people. Try answering the question 'Who commanded the allied forces in the Gulf War?' Hopefully you will remember 'Norman Schwarz-koff', but in doing so, are you recollecting an event from that time? It would seem not, and, similarly, identifying a picture of him would not require any episodic recollection. Thus, when amnesics fail on tasks such as this, we cannot say that they are failing a test of episodic memory. Rather, it seems that they have lost some aspect of semantic memory.

In chapter 2 we noted an alternative proposal, in which LTS was divided into procedural and declarative memory, the latter referring to any memory that is consciously accessible. This solves some of the problems raised above for the episodic–semantic distinction, but it is not without its faults. RFR became densely amnesic as a result of herpes simplex encephalitis (Warrington and McCarthy, 1988). Thus he could retain little information on standard memory tests, and could not even identify close friends and family. It was thus surprising to discover that he had none the less learned the meaning of new words and abbreviations (e.g. AIDS) that had come into use during the period for which he was now amnesic. In addition, he retained a remarkable ability to describe his friends in a general way, even though he could not remember any event involving that person. Thus, describing a colleague, he said: 'He is a rather chunky individual. Everything is large except for his height which is about 5'10". I'm not sure if he has ginger hair ... He is an outgoing character of Scottish descent. I vaguely remember joking references towards his Scottish ancestry and his love of whisky. He does have a very attractive wife with the very apt first name of Eve.' There are now other instances of remote memory breaking up in selective ways. Kapur and co-workers (1989), for example, describe a dense amnesia for public events with intact personal event memory, and the converse is described by O'Connor and colleagues (1992).

At present, therefore, it remains unclear as to what is the best way of describing the amnesic deficit. There is general agreement that procedural and implicit memory is intact, but the best way to describe the deficit is still an issue. When venturing further into the amnesic literature, it is important to be aware of this difference of opinion and its consequent effect on the terminology employed by different writers.

Explaining the Amnesic Deficit

Attempts to provide an explanatory theory of amnesia have concentrated on amnesic patients' low scores on tests measuring the explicit recollection of new information. Perhaps the first modern theory of amnesia was the **consolidation theory** (Milner, 1966) which proposed that amnesics lack the fundamental ability to form new permanent memory traces. Soon after its proposal, this theory was discounted on the grounds that the amnesic deficit was not total, because amnesic patients were clearly able to learn under certain conditions.

One of the conditions was demonstrated in a classic study by Warrington and Weiskrantz (1970), in which amnesic patients were first shown individual words. When memory was tested using conventional methods, the amnesics performed poorly. However, when asked to identify degraded word forms (see figure 6.8), the amnesic patients did as well as controls when the degraded words corresponded to target words they had studied. From our earlier considerations, we can see that this is just one more example of preserved procedural memory in amnesia, and, as such, is irrelevant to understanding the amnesic deficit. However, at the time a different interpretation was placed on the results. It was argued that amnesic patients suffered from high levels of proactive interference, in that recall was contaminated by large numbers of additional irrelevant responses. However, the degraded words acted as 'surrogate' retrieval cues, in that they restricted recall to only those words that would map on to the degraded form.

Figure 6.8 Degraded words of the type used by Warrington and Weiskrantz (1970).
(*From Bradshaw and Mattingly, 1995.*)

Warrington and Weiskrantz (1970) thus proposed a **retrieval deficit** theory of amnesia, in which the deficit was localized entirely at the output stage. However, the theory failed to provide an adequate account of amnesia. It was difficult, for example, to explain why amnesic patients varied in their ability to retrieve their pre-morbid memories if amnesia was due to a generalized retrieval impairment. One could, rather awkwardly, restrict the theory to explaining anterograde amnesia, but here the authors themselves produced additional data dismissing the retrieval deficit theory.

The Context Deficit Theory of Amnesia

One theory that has gained substantial support argues that amnesia represents a deficit in the use of **contextual information** (Mayes, 1988). Context can be defined as information associated with a specific memory that allows differentiation of that memory from other memories. As we saw in chapter 3, it is usual to distinguish between two forms of context: intrinsic and extrinsic. To remind you, intrinsic context refers to features that are an integral part of the stimulus itself, such as the particular meaning extracted from the word at the time of learning. Extrinsic context corresponds to those features that are associated merely incidentally with the stimulus itself, such as time of encounter and surroundings (often referred to as temporo-spatial attributes). Studies of amnesia have concentrated on memory for extrinsic context, but, more recently, possible deficits in memory for intrinsic context have also been explored.

Before going any further with the contextual deficit theory, it is necessary to remind ourselves that recognition can be based on either **familiarity** or **recollection** (see chapter 3). Thus a target might be recognized because the context of its previous occurrence comes to mind, or it is recognized as something previously encountered without any context being evoked. Returning to amnesia and a possible contextual deficit, there are a number of studies consistent with this theory. Winocur and Kinsbourne (1978) examined how Korsakoff amnesics performed on the A → B, A → C paired-associate paradigm. Here patients are first asked to learn one response to a stimulus (e.g. ELEPHANT → 'cigar') and then, on a second list, to associate the original stimulus with a new response (ELEPHANT → 'telephone'). Typically amnesics show many 'intrusions' on this test, in that on the A → C phase, they tend to recall many of the A → B associations. However, when the A → C phase took place in an environment that was very distinct from that used in the A → B phase, the number of A → B intrusions was significantly lower. It was presumed that the distinctive context provided in the A → C phase enabled the associations to become interwoven with sufficient contextual information to discriminate them more effectively from those learned in the A → B phase. Amnesics may therefore be poor at encoding extrinsic context under normal conditions, but be able to utilize it provided it is sufficiently distinctive.

Huppert and Piercy (1978b) investigated the performance of Korsakoff amnesics and normal people on a task involving temporal discrimination. The subjects saw 80 pictures on one day, followed by a different set of 80 pictures on the following day. Within each set, half the pictures were shown once, and the remainder were shown three times. Ten minutes after the day 2 presentation ended, subjects were shown a sample of pictures from days 1 and 2. Subjects were asked to decide whether or not each picture had been seen 'today' (i.e. on day 2 as opposed to day 1). As figure 6.9 shows, both groups usually placed pictures seen three times on day 2 in the 'today' category, whereas pictures shown once on day 1 were least often placed in this category. However, the groups differed in that amnesics were just as likely to categorize as 'today' pictures those seen three times on day 1 as those seen once on day 2. By contrast, control subjects placed very few of the repeated day 1 pictures in the 'today' category, but correctly categorized over two-thirds of the pictures seen only once on day 2.

On the assumption that familiarity fades with time, the performance of amnesics indicates that their decisions about context were determined by the overall familiarity of each picture. Thus pictures presented three times on day 1 seemed as recent to amnesics as those presented once on day 2,

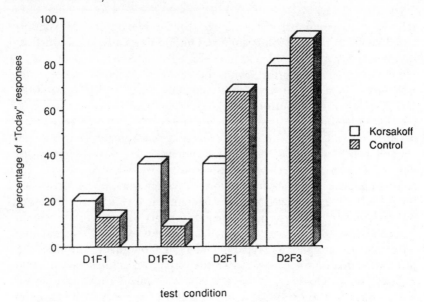

Figure 6.9 *Data from Huppert and Piercy, 1978, p. 349.*
Key: D1 = day 1; D2 = day 2; F1 = pictures presented once, F3 = pictures presented three times.

because both were associated with similar amounts of familiarity. By contrast, the performance of normal subjects seems determined by both factors. The more accurate identification of pictures presented three times on day 2 compared with those presented once suggests that familiarity plays a role. However, the fact that normals accurately distinguished pictures presented once on day 2 from those presented three times on day 1 indicates that their responses involved an additional search stage in which each picture was linked to a specific temporal context – that is, 'day 1' or 'day 2'. The fact that the amnesics could not do this implies that they had no record of temporal context.

One problem with Huppert and Piercy's study was that amnesic and normal subjects were tested over the same retention interval. Thus, not only were amnesics poorer on temporal discrimination, they also performed worse overall. This allows for the possibility that the temporal discrimination deficit might characterize poor memory in general, rather than reflect a specific impairment in the amnesic syndrome. To test for this, Meudell and co-workers (1985) replicated Huppert and Piercy's finding, but also repeated the experiment on normal subjects using much longer retention intervals. The effect of this was to make the normal people's memory as poor as the Korsakoffs in the study. Despite this, the normal subjects were far more able to discriminate events in time, thereby suggesting that Korsakoff amnesia is qualitatively different from poor normal memory.

Amnesia – More than One Syndrome

Unlike most neuropsychological impairments, the amnesic syndrome can arise from damage to two very distinct regions of the brain: the mid-line diencephalon and the medial temporal lobe region. Some theorists (e.g. Warrington and Weiskrantz, 1982) have argued that this is not problematic, because, although distinct, these two brain regions are linked together as parts of the **limbic system**. Thus it is not surprising that similar deficits arise when each of the regions is damaged independently.

A problem with this unitary view of amnesia is that it presupposes that the limbic system comprises a memory circuit in which all the structures play the same role in memory formation. Unfortunately it is not easy to take this further and explain exactly what this circuit is achieving. The only formal proposal was that of Warrington and Weiskrantz (1982), who suggested that normal memory depends on the moderation of semantic memory in the temporal lobes by cognitive mediational mechanisms located in the front cortex. Cognitive mediation was defined as those processes which enable the use of **imagery, elaboration** and other means of embellishment known to enhance memory. In experimental terms, the existence of cognitive mediation might be manifest in experiments where instructions to use imagery exert a beneficial effect on performance.

Warrington and Weiskrantz argued on the basis both of their own work and that of others (e.g. Jones, 1974) that imagery instructions did not enhance the memory performance of amnesics. However, Leng and Parkin (1988) pointed out that some of these studies involved very poor levels of performance, which would make any effects difficult to detect. They went on to show, in line with several other studies, that imagery does improve amnesics' memory quite considerably. Thus, using the only operational definition of cognitive mediation, there was no evidence of a deficit in amnesics.

An alternative to the 'circuit' view of amnesia is that different components of the limbic system undertake different functions with regard to memory. The major corollary of this view is that damage to different limbic sites should produce qualitatively different impairments of memory. Work in this area is in its infancy, but, as we shall see, there is emerging evidence of important differences between patients whose amnesia arises from damage centred on the temporal lobes and that due to damage in the mid-line diencephalon.

L'Hermitte and Signoret (1972) carried out the first study purporting to show a difference between temporal lobe (TL) and diencephalic amnesia. They compared patients with Korsakoff's Syndrome with three patients who suffered extensive temporal lobe damage following herpes simplex encephalitis. A number of tasks were used, but the basic finding was that the

TL patients learned less effectively and forgot more rapidly than the Korsakoffs.

There are problems, however, with studies that compare forgetting rates in different groups of patients. Amnesic patients vary in the severity of their deficit, just as patients with other neuropsychological disorders do. As a result, any difference in forgetting rate might be spurious, because the groups being compared might differ in the severity of their amnesia. To get around this, a number of researchers have advocated a 'titration procedure' to equate initial learning and thus try and circumvent differences in severity. A good example is a study by Huppert and Piercy (1978a), who compared the forgetting rate of controls, a group of Korsakoffs and the temporal lobe amnesic HM. They presented 120 pictures, memory for which was tested after 10 minutes, 1 day and 7 days. Acquisition was equated at 10 minutes by using variable exposure during learning. Controls saw each picture once for only 1 second, Korsakoffs each picture for 8 seconds, and HM saw each picture for 10 seconds.

At 10 minutes HM's score fell just within the Korsakoff range, thereby allowing, it was claimed, a comparison of forgetting given similar levels of acquisition. HM appeared to forget more rapidly, but this result has been challenged. Weiskrantz (1985) points out that if HM's performance is replotted in terms of retention as a proportion of initial acquisition (rather than just raw recognition rate), his forgetting curve is similar to the Korsakoffs. Another problem is that although matched at 10 minutes after the end of the learning sequence, there are big differences in the amount of time that elapsed since the start of learning. For controls the retention interval starts only 2 minutes after the learning sequence started, whereas for HM retention starts 20 minutes after learning commenced.

Context Memory in Diencephalic and Temporal Lobe Amnesia

Most work in this area has been carried out in my own laboratory in conjunction with Nick Leng and, most recently, Nikki Hunkin. Our starting-point was the fact that the various experiments described earlier, in which amnesic patients showed very poor memory for context, relied almost exclusively on Korsakoff patients. As a result, these experiments were more appropriately described as demonstrations that diencephalic amnesia could be attributed to a contextual memory deficit. We set out to discover whether a contextual impairment might also explain the memory impairment experienced by survivors of herpes simplex encephalitis and other patients in whom amnesia arose as a consequence of primary temporal lobe damage – the argument being that if the context deficit

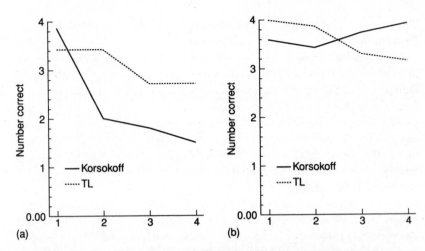

Figure 6.10a,b Performance of Korsakoff patients and temporal lobe (TL) patients on two versions of the recency judgement task (see text for details). (*Data from Hunkin and Parkin, 1993, and figure from Parkin, 1992.*)

theory also accounts for temporal lobe amnesia, then it would be reasonable to consider amnesia as a single syndrome.

To investigate this, a recency judgement task was devised. On trial 1 a 2 × 2 array of pictures was presented, and the subject was instructed to try and remember them. Following a 60-second interval involving distracting activity the subject was required to pick the four target pictures from an array of 16 pictures. This procedure was then repeated three times, except that pictures that had been targets became distractors, and vice versa. Three more trials were given, and the subject's task was to indicate which four pictures they had been asked to identify *most recently*. By the fourth trial each picture had been a target once and a distractor three times. The effect of this was that, after trial 1, all items were familiar, and some record of temporal context was required for correct recognition. Korsakoff patients showed a marked drop in performance from trial 1, whereas the TL group did not show a reliable drop in performance until trial 4 (see figure 6.10a). A possible problem with these findings is that Korsakoff patients are known to be very sensitive to proactive interference (see chapter 3). To check that this was not the explanation, the experiment was repeated using completely different items on each trial and, as figure 6.10b shows, both groups performed similarly under these conditions (Hunkin and Parkin, 1993).

As we saw earlier, it has been suggested that temporal lobe amnesics forget more rapidly. It was therefore possible that the good performance of the temporal lobe patients on the recency judgement task was due to the fact that they simply forgot the pictures used on each trial very quickly. To test this possibility, we repeated the original recency experiment, varying the retention interval from 30 to 120 seconds (Hunkin and Parkin, 1993). If rapid forgetting were contributing to the good performance of the temporal lobe group, one would expect poorer performance with 30-second intervals compared with 120. However, the results showed no difference in performance across retention intervals, thereby suggesting that rate of forgetting was not important.

In a further study (Hunkin et al., 1994) we compared diencephalic and temporal lobe amnesics on the list discrimination task devised by Squire and colleagues (1981a). In this task subjects are presented with two lists of sentences separated by 3 minutes of conversation. Subjects are then presented with a single list of sentences containing both targets and distractors, and are asked to identify the sentences they saw in the learning sequence. Further, contingent on identifying a target, they are required to say whether it occurred in the first or second list.

The list discrimination task provides measures of both recognition and memory for temporal order. The two groups did not differ in terms of recognition. However, there was a marked difference in memory for temporal order. In line with an earlier study by Squire (1982), the diencephalic group were at chance on discrimination, but the temporal lobe group performed significantly above chance. Moreover, the latter also showed a strong correlation between recognition and correct list discrimination.

These studies suggest that a common explanation for diencephalic and temporal lobe amnesia is not possible. The former is accommodated by the context deficit theory, but temporal lobe amnesia requires a different explanation. At present it is not clear what this might be, but one possibility is that it represents a deficit in consolidation.

Focal Retrograde Amnesia

Kapur (1992) has identified what he has termed **focal retrograde amnesia** (FRA). This refers to a memory impairment in which the primary deficit is a loss of remote memory, with performance on anterograde tests only mildly impaired. A problem with this type of disorder is that some of the patients may be suffering from psychogenic disorders (see chapter 10) or they may be **malingering** – in some way faking or dissimulating memory impairment. However, once these possibilities are discounted, a range of case histories remains in which focal retrograde amnesia is presented within the context of identifiable brain injury (Kapur, 1992). A typical case is presented by Kapur and colleagues (1994). This man performed within normal limits on tests of anterograde memory, but his retrograde amnesia was severe.

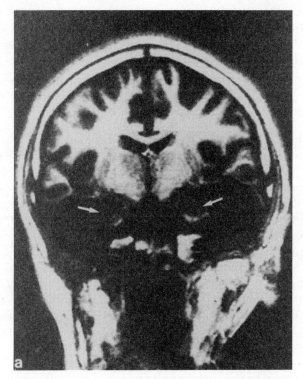

Figure 6.11 Cross-section of patient TJ's brain. Arrows indicate intact hippo-campal regions. Large dark areas adjacent to arrows correspond to temporal lobe lesions.
(*From Kapur et al., 1994.*)

How might we explain FRA? In order to do this, it is important to look more carefully at the patients. First, we notice that there are essentially two types of patient showing this unusual deficit: those with identifiable brain lesions and those who appear to have developed the disorder from extremely minor injuries (Parkin, 1996b). Examining the former group, two important points emerge: they almost all have lesions in the temporal lobes, but the hippocampus has been spared (see figure 6.11; but see Hunkin et al., 1995); their performance on tests of anterograde memory is not normal, but is far better than that found in amnesics.

With these two points in mind, it is relatively easy to explain what is going on. As we have seen, the hippocampus is crucial for memory function, and the general view is that it in some way moderates the process of consolidation. However, because the hippocampus is small, it cannot be the storage site of memory. For storage to occur, the hippocampus must in some way recruit sites in the temporal cortex. The former group of patients thus have an intact consolidation mechanism, but lack the normal availability of storage sites because of temporal lobe damage. As a result, they do not learn new information normally, because the storage areas are damaged – a state of affairs which also explains why remote memory is disrupted. It should also be borne in mind that the assessments of anterograde amnesia made in these cases usually involve relatively short retention intervals, thereby maximizing the possibility that the patient will perform normally.

Cases where FRA has been reported following minor brain injury (often not even involving unconsciousness) are more problematic. De Renzi and colleagues (1995), for example, report the case of a man who, following a road accident, presented with a dense retrograde memory loss, even though there was no evidence of head trauma. In addition, he also reported loss of procedural memory such as how to shave. This case is rather similar to others that have been reported (see Parkin, 1996b), and there is some disagreement as to how these cases should be interpreted. Some, such as Luchelli and co-workers (1995), have suggested that these impairments have an organic basis. However, it is also the case that these disorders could be of psychogenic origin. Loss of procedural memory, for example, is frequently considered a sign of psychogenic or malingered amnesia (see chapter 11). In connection with this it is notable that most of these cases recover their lost memories.

Patients with the amnesic syndrome exhibit a severe anterograde amnesia and a degree of retrograde amnesia. Their intelligence, language and immediate apprehension appear to be normal. The syndrome can arise from lesions in the mid-line diencephalon or damage to the medial temporal lobes. Evidence shows that amnesic patients have intact STS but impaired LTS. The nature of the LTS impairment is a matter of some debate, with some arguing that it represents a selective loss of episodic memory, and others arguing for a broader deficit in what is termed 'declarative memory'. It is well established that the presence of amnesia has little effect on existing procedural memory, and new procedural memory can also be formed. Amnesics perform normally or near normally on a wide range of implicit memory tasks. Various explanations of the amnesic deficit have been put forward, of which the most popular is the context deficit theory. However, this appears to account only for diencephalic amnesia, and an alternative theory, such as of a consolidation deficit, may be needed to explain temporal lobe amnesia. Focal retrograde amnesia represents a memory disturbance primarily affecting pre-morbid memory.

7 Memory and the Frontal Lobes

The history of medicine contains many bizarre incidents, but none more so than the extraordinary case of Phineas Gage. On 13 September 1848 Phineas Gage was working as a railroad engineer in New England, his job being to lay explosive and then detonate it. The procedure involved boring a hole, placing the explosive in the hole, and then covering it over with sand. After this a fuse and a tamping iron were used to set off the explosive. By mistake, Gage placed the tamping iron directly on the explosive, at which point it exploded, sending the tamping iron right through his skull and then 20 or so feet into the air (see figure 7.1). Remarkably, Gage did not lose consciousness, and was able to walk to the cart that took him to hospital. Gage's body was exhumed in 1866, and the skull, along with the offending tamping iron, have been preserved for posterity. This enabled Damasio and colleagues (1994) to examine Gage's skull with modern neuro-imaging techniques. Using a reconstructed brain similar to that of Gage and an estimate of the tamping iron's most likely trajectory, they concluded that his lesion would have involved several parts of the left and right frontal lobes, but no other brain region.

Gage did not die from this terrible injury, and lived for a considerable number of years. Moreover, in some ways the injury seems to have had remarkably few consequences. He had little difficulty with language, and no obvious intellectual problems. However, there were changes. Gage had previously been considered an outstanding employee, with excellent prospects, but now he was unreliable, disrespectful and lacked the ability to plan his life effectively: to his friends he was 'no longer Gage'. Gage's case is usually cited as evidence for the involvement of the frontal lobes in determining personality. However, although often overlooked, Gage also appeared to have a certain type of memory problem. Thus in a rare account it was noted that Gage 'was accustomed to entertain his little nephews and nieces with the most fabulous recitals of wonderful feats and hairbreadth escapes, without any foundation except in his fancy' (Harlow, 1993, p. 277). From our modern perspective we can identify these fabrications as

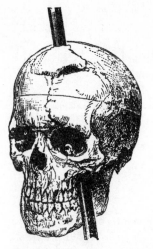

Horrible Accident. Phineas P. Gage, a foreman on the Rutland Railroad at Cavendish, Vt., was preparing for a blast on Wednesday last, when the powder exploded, carrying through his head an iron instrument, an inch and a fourth in circumference, and three feet and eight inches in length. The iron entered on the side of his face, shattering the upper jaw, and passing back of the left eye, and out the top of his head. Singularly enough, he was alive at two o'clock the next afternoon, in full possession of his reason, and free from pain.

Figure 7.1 Phineas Gage's skull showing the trajectory of the tamping iron. Text insert is a copy of the newspaper report at the time. (*From MacMillan, 1986.*)

a memory disorder known as 'confabulation'; this is just one of the memory deficits associated with damage to the frontal lobes.

Frontal Lobe Damage and Memory: Some Phenomena

The frontal lobes comprise one-third of the cerebral cortex, so it is not surprising that they have many functions, or that many different theories have been put forward to explain how they operate. However, our concern in this chapter will be quite specific, and will examine how the frontal lobes are implicated in memory function.

At a clinical level, the most commonly reported memory impairment following frontal lobe damage is **confabulation**. At a basic level, this means simply the production of a false memory; but to be used effectively, it has to be refined somewhat. Most patients with memory disorders will, if pressed hard enough, attempt to answer questions even though they cannot remember. Thus, if asked what they had for dinner, they might say 'fish and chips', when the answer should be 'spaghetti bolognese'. These **momentary** confabulations are characterized as responses that could be correct, given the patient's circumstances, but just happen not to be. By contrast with these are **fantastic** confabulations, in which the patient's recollections are clearly fictional in the view of everyone but the patient.

A good example is given by this personal account of a doctor who sustained frontal lobe damage during the Gulf War.

That month was a dim dark nightmare. Blankness was interspersed with bizarre and uneasy happenings. I remember mad things, uncharacteristic reactions to things, recollections seemingly lasting for hours instead of seconds. I was unable to distinguish between fact and fiction, imagination and reality. Consequently I made up utterly believable stories, and related these with such conviction that no one knew whether they were coming or going. I was convinced that my parents had moved house and that people on the television were my friends. (Anonymous, 1996, p. 1485)

There are now a large number of studies documenting fantastic confabulation, and these link the disorder, incontrovertibly, to frontal lobe dysfunction (Moscovitch, 1989).

Source Amnesia

Laboratory studies have identified a number of other memory impairments which seem to be tied specifically to frontal lobe damage. **Source amnesia** occurs when a person remembers an event or fact correctly, but fails to remember the source of their knowledge. To demonstrate this, Schacter and colleagues (1984) presented amnesic patients with fictitious facts (e.g. 'Bob Hope's father was a fireman'), spoken by either of two experimenters. Recall tests showed that the facts could often be recalled, but that the patients rarely remembered who they were spoken by. A link with defective frontal lobe function was established by showing that subjects with the greatest source amnesia performed most poorly on tests of frontal lobe function. Subsequent studies have confirmed a link between frontal dysfunction and source amnesia. Janowsky and colleagues (1989b) asked frontal patients and controls to learn a series of 'Trivial Pursuit' type facts. After about a week subjects were tested for their memory of the facts and, if correct, how they knew the facts. Frontal patients had normal memory for the facts, but poor memory for their source, often claiming that they had heard the fact somewhere else.

Memory of Temporal Order

There is now considerable evidence that the frontal lobes play a critical role in memory of temporal order. This was nicely demonstrated in an early study by Corsi, in which subjects were presented with pairs of stimuli (see Milner et al., 1991). At various intervals a test card appeared with a question mark between the stimuli, and subjects had to decide which of the two stimuli had been seen most recently. On some trials both stimuli would have been seen previously, but different intervals would have elapsed (e.g. 8 versus 16 trials ago), thus making the judgement one of relative recency. However, when one of the stimuli was novel, the task was effectively one of plain recognition. The key result, obtained using words, pictures and abstract designs, was that the frontal patients were impaired on recency discrimination but not on recognition; thus they had specific problems remembering the temporal order in which two stimuli had been presented. Shimamura and co-workers (1990) presented frontal patients and controls with a 15-word list and then, after providing the words again in random order, required the subjects to reconstruct the original list. Frontal patients found this task much more difficult, even though their memory for the words, as assessed by recognition, was normal. The same study also showed that frontal lesions affect the ability to correctly sequence facts about the past, even when general knowledge of those facts is intact.

Metamemory

Metamemory describes our ability to know whether or not our memories contain a particular piece of information. An example of this might be failing to recall the capital of Peru (Lima) but knowing that you would recognize it if it were shown to you – an ability usually described as **feeling of knowing**. Janowsky and colleagues (1989a) presented frontal patients and controls with sentences, and then asked them to recall key words. Thus, shown the sentence 'At the museum we saw some ancient relics made of clay' they would subsequently be presented with 'At the museum we saw some ancient relics made of __?' and asked to recall the last word. If they could not, they were asked to rate their ability to recognize the word when presented. When tested after a substantial delay, frontal patients' metamemory was found to be impaired relative to controls.

False Recognition

In a recognition test subjects are typically shown a random sequence of previously seen items (**targets**) and novel stimuli (**distractors**). In **yes–no** recognition the subject examines each item serially, and decides whether or not it was a stimulus they were asked to remember. Yes–no recognition can be tested either by presenting all the stimuli in a single array or by means of a **single probe** technique in which each stimulus appears individually and a response is required. In a **forced choice** recognition test a target stimulus is presented along with one or more alternatives, and the subject has to choose which item was the target. In recognition testing a correct response is usually referred to as a **hit**, failure to identify a target as a **miss**, and incorrect identification of a distractor as a **false alarm**.

Studies of patients with frontal lobe damage have begun to identify patients who make abnormal numbers of false alarms in recognition memory. Delbecq-Derousne and co-workers (1990) report that RW made large numbers of false alarms on a forced choice test. RW's manner indicated that he was as sure about these false alarms as he was about hits. On recall he performed reasonably well, although it was notable that he tended to include far more false information in his recall (**intrusions**) than did control subjects.

JB (Parkin et al., 1996) is known to produce high rates of false alarms on a variety of recognition memory tests. Combined across a range of tests, his hit rate averages about 80 per cent (within normal range), but his false alarm rate, around 40 per cent, is extremely high. JB also tends to be very sure about his incorrect responses, and, like RW, he produces large numbers of recall intrusions amongst the correct information. Sometimes these intrusions are random, but on other occasions they clearly come from other events. In one instance he was asked to recall the instructions for the experiment. The first part was correct, but he then effortlessly introduced extra information involving instructions from an experiment he had participated in several days before. Schacter and colleagues (1996a) describe BG, who also had circumscribed damage to the frontal lobes (see figure 7.2). On a variety of tasks BG made excessive numbers of false alarms, even though, like JB, his hit rate remained normal. Again BG was very confident about his false alarms. Using the recognition and conscious awareness paradigm (RCA; see chapter 3), it was shown that BG frequently associated his false alarms with specific recollections.

Defective Recall

There are many indications that recall is badly disrupted by frontal lobe damage even when recognition performance is within normal limits (Shimamura, 1994). Impairment is particularly evident in autobiographical recall (see chapter 8), in that frontal patients can produce vague memories and require a lot of prompting before producing something specific. CB (Parkin et al., 1994), for example, was particularly poor when asked to retrieve specific memories in response to cue words such as 'flowers'. Thus he would spontaneously give responses such as 'I like flowers', although when prompted, he was able to recollect a specific memory.

If normal subjects are given a word list to remember and are then given cues for half the words in the list, their memory for the uncued words is impaired. The explanation of this is that the cues provided get in the way of generating retrieval cues for the uncued words. Incisa della Rocchetta

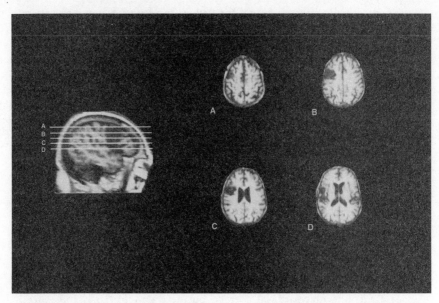

Figure 7.2 MRI scan of BG's brain at four different levels demonstrating presence of a large lesion in the right frontal lobe.
(*Photograph courtesy of Dan Schacter.*)

and Milner (1993) examined how frontal patients responded to this cueing effect and found that the effect was much more dramatic. Recently Stuss and colleagues (1994) have shown that poor organization may also contribute to impaired recall following frontal lobe damage. Typically a word list will be recalled more easily if it has some inherent structure (e.g. comprising words from obvious categories). Stuss and co-workers found that frontal patients failed to make as much use of this factor as did controls. However, they concluded that poor organization was not the sole explanation, and that other factors, such as an inability to inhibit repetitions, also contributed to the deficit.

The above studies indicate that a variety of memory impairments seem directly related to frontal lobe function. In the next section we consider how theories of frontal lobe function might account for how these deficits arise.

The Frontal Lobes as Executive

While many theories of frontal lobe function have been put forward, the most widely accepted idea is that the frontal lobes constitute the centre of an 'executive' which governs the more complex and deliberate aspects of behaviour. This executive concept provides a plausible basis for explaining the case of Phineas Gage, for example, since most of what happened to him can be attributed in one way or another to poor decision making and personal control.

The executive theory has been most extensively developed by Norman and Shallice (1986). They suggest that, at any particular time, most of an individual's ongoing activity comprises routine automatic responses which require no conscious intervention. Routine activities are those like driving, in which the actions can be performed even though our thoughts may be on very different things. However, when a plan needs to be formulated in response to a novel situation, or a decision made about various options, routine operations are inadequate, and control passes to the **Supervisory Activating System** (SAS). Returning to driving, the SAS would be invoked to deal with the problem of driving abroad. Routine responses would be geared to driving on the left, but, in order to drive safely in France, these responses would have to be suppressed, and the new pattern of driving on the right imposed by the SAS.

Shallice (1988) has proposed that the SAS could be involved in memory in two specific ways. First, the SAS is considered responsible for setting up descriptions which provide the basis for accessing particular events in memory. Initially these descriptions may be rather vague, but, via inter-action with the stored contents of memory, they become more specific until a particular memory is located. In addition, the SAS is also directly involved in assessing whether a retrieved memory is appropriate, thus allowing, for example, memory of a real event to be distinguished from a figment of the imagination. On the basis of these two roles, Shallice has suggested that patients with impairments to the SAS could have problems in either formulating the description of memories or in deciding whether retrieved memories are appropriate.

Hanley and colleagues (1994; see also Hanley and Davies, 1997) have argued that these two types of impairment can be observed. They studied ROB, a woman who suffered damage to the left caudate nucleus, a structure closely related to the frontal lobes. She was examined on a range of recall and recognition tests, including some which were matched for difficulty. In every case her recognition memory appeared normal, but her recall memory was very poor. They suggested that ROB had a problem in formulating descriptions at retrieval; this had a dramatic effect on recall, but no effect on recognition, because a description of the to-be-retrieved information is not needed, only a decision about appropriateness.

In order to illustrate the opposite deficit, Hanley and co-workers point to patient RW, who, it will be recalled, produced high levels of false alarms in recognition and many intrusions in free recall. Here it could be argued that the verification stage has been disrupted, thereby allowing many false alarms and intrusions. Moreover, fantastic confabulation could be seen as an extreme example of this deficit, where the assessment of appropriateness is so disrupted that wildly implausible memories are accepted as true.

While this account is neat, it does not fit all the available evidence. As we saw earlier, our patient JB produces high levels of false alarms and abnormal levels of intrusions. He thus resembles RW, and might be considered to have a verification deficit. If this were correct, then we would expect JB's recognition memory to improve if we gave him instructions to perform more accurately. We have tried two approaches to this: the use of a monetary incentive and placing a ceiling on the number of responses he is allowed to make. Incentives were found to either increase his false alarm rate or make no difference. Similarly, being told to be as accurate as possible and respond only when he was sure had no effect on the proportion of false responses (Parkin et al., in preparation).

Norman and Schacter (in press) have provided an alternative explanation of how frontal lobe damage affects memory. They argue that their patient BG, and by implication JB, have a poorly focused retrieval system. This theory is closely linked to Shallice's idea of retrieval descriptions, and proposes that effective retrieval depends on the setting up of a proper set of criteria whereby to evaluate any retrieved memories. They argue that the distinction between description and verification cannot be sustained, because the information providing the description cannot be operationally distinguished from that underlying verification.

Instead, Norman and Schacter argue that high rates of false alarm arise because the patient sets a very weak criterion for accepting an item as a target. Thus, when shown a list of words, the resulting event description is 'I saw a bunch of words' without much additional detail. Armed with a description of this kind, it is easy to see why most words presented in a recognition test might be accepted as targets. However, a large number of false alarms in this test might arise because subjects are generally familiar with the words. To counter this, it has been shown that both BG and JB show just as many false alarms when the stimuli used are totally unfamiliar (e.g. non-words). Schacter and colleagues (1996b) illustrate this point further by showing that BG performs normally on recognition when targets and distractors are drawn from different categories (e.g. furniture and animals). Here even the poorly focused description 'I saw a bunch of animals' is sufficient for normal recognition.

Norman and Schacter's theory is attractive, not only because of its explanation of false recognition, but also because it explains why frontal patients typically have poor recall, the argument being that a focused retrieval context is just as important for deciding what to recall as it is for recognition decisions. However, what about ROB, in whom recognition was entirely normal? Here the theory is less successful, because it is argued that normal recognition in the presence of poor recall is due to a complete inability to focus retrieval and a consequent reliance on familiarity to guide recognition. As we have seen in a number of places, recognition can be mediated by familiarity, but it is difficult to see how it could provide a level of performance similar to controls who presumably have recollective information available as well.

Defective Retrieval or Defective Encoding?

Whether we accept Shallice's theory or that of Norman and Schacter, it is important to observe that both theories locate the role of frontal lobe function at retrieval. Thus both theories argue that frontal lobe damage in some ways impairs access to memory by producing vague descriptions of what is being sought. A problem with this approach is that it appears to suggest that the event description arises independently of the memory that is being sought, but this cannot be so. In order to produce a description of event X, no matter how vague, you need some information about event X in order to start the process. It therefore follows that the generation of a description will depend, in part, on the quality of representation of the target event. This allows for the possibility that encoding factors could influence the quality of event descriptions. Frontal structures might, for example, be implicated in deciding which aspects of a stimulus are encoded, and, in turn, these could influence the ease with which an event description evolves.

We have recently examined this issue with regard to JB (Parkin, 1997), who was given a series of recognition tests. For half of these he was left to his own devices, and produced very high levels of false alarms. For the other half of the tests, he was instructed to carry out a semantic orienting task on each word as he attempted to learn it (see chapter 2). The results were quite striking, in that false alarms were significantly reduced.

The reduction of false alarms following instructions to use an orienting task indicates that JB's high false alarm rates may stem from faulty encoding processes. This explanation is also consistent with recent *in vivo* neuro-imaging studies of the frontal lobes. In these experiments, normal subjects participate in memory experiments while being PET scanned (see chapter 6) at the same time. The scanning procedure is able to identify those brain regions that are most active at any point during the performance of a task. Shallice and co-workers (1994) devised experiments which enabled them to distinguish between encoding and retrieval operations, and examined the pattern of brain activity resulting from each. The results showed that the left frontal lobe was associated with encoding operations, and the right frontal lobe with retrieval. Findings similar to these have now been reported by Tulving and colleagues (1994) and also by Fletcher and co-workers (1995). Returning to JB, he has his left frontal damage, so his sensitivity to encoding manipulations would be expected from the PET scanning studies.

Interestingly, BG (Schacter et al., 1996b) has right frontal damage, but, to date, there is no evidence that his deficit is primarily one of retrieval.

Recently Schacter and co-workers (1996b) have provided important new evidence concerning differences between true and false memory. In their experiment, subjects first studied lists of words that were connected to various theme words. Thus subjects might hear candy, sour, sugar, bitter, good, taste, tooth, nice, honey, soda, chocolate, heart, cake, eat, and pie – all of which revolve around the theme word 'sweet', which itself did not appear in the list. In the next phase subjects were given a recognition test while undergoing a PET scan which enabled the pattern of brain activity accompanying recognition responses to be accurately measured. The recognition sequence contained both true targets (e.g. honey) and 'illusory targets' such as 'sweet'. Areas of the left hippocampus were active during the recognition of true targets and false recognition of illusory targets. However, for true targets only, there was also activation in the areas of the temporal lobes that store information about the sound of words. This finding suggests that true and false memories are distinguishable in that only true memories contain information about the perceptual features of an event (in this case the sound of the word).

Frontal Lobes and Memory: An Integration

In this chapter we have reviewed a variety of memory phenomena associated with frontal lobe damage. We must now attempt to integrate them into the explanatory framework we have just considered. While the exact nature of frontal lobe memory impairment remains to be explained, it seems reasonable to conclude that frontal patients suffer from an inability to specify memories in any great detail. This may be because of faulty encoding, faulty retrieval, or both. A deficit of this kind can go a long way towards explaining many of the above phenomena. Poor recall relative to recognition can easily be attributed to poorly focused retrieval, as can enhanced sensitivity to part-list cueing effects. Both source amnesia and impaired memory for temporal order and frequency might also arise from an inability either to encode or to retrieve the relevant attributes for those decisions. High levels of false recognition also seem amenable to an explanation of this kind, but what about confabulation? At a stretch one could argue that it represents poorly focused retrieval *in extremis*, in that the retrieval context lacks any link with reality. However, it is likely that confabulation requires a more complex explanation, in that poor memory processes are only part of the story.

It is now well known that damage to the frontal lobes affects memory in various ways. The phenomena of confabulation is by far the most striking deficit, but many other impairments have been noted. These include source amnesia, impaired memory for temporal order, deficits in metamemory, a tendency to make false identifications, and defective recall. These deficits have been related to the idea that the frontal lobes serve as an executive system which guides retrieval and confirms the status of retrieved memories.

8 Ageing and Dementia

So far we have considered memory disorders which only an unfortunate few of us are likely to experience at first hand. In this chapter I will consider a form of memory disorder that we will all expect to experience: that due to the normal processes of ageing. Although a decline in memory is evident from a relatively early point, it becomes far more noticeable once we reach retirement age. Considering his own memory, the author John Mortimer noted:

> The distant past, when I was acting my solo version of Hamlet before the blind eyes of my father, duelling with myself and drinking my own poisoned chalice or, further back, when I was starting an English education, with huge balloons of boxing gloves lashed to the end of white matchstick arms, grunting, stifled with the sour smell of hot plimsolls which is, to me, always the smell of fear, seems as clear as yesterday. What are lost in the mists of vanishing memory are the events of ten years ago.

While there is a slight irony in Mortimer having constructed such a complex sentence to make his point, his observations on ageing are accurate. As we get older, it is not our early memories we forget; it is the things that have happened more recently. We have, of course, encountered this pattern earlier in the book when we were considering retrograde amnesia, and it is of great interest that normal loss of memory should show a similar pattern. We will return to this point at a later stage.

Measuring Age-related Changes in Memory

Designing experiments to measure how memory changes with age is not as simple as it might seem. The commonest approach is the **cross-sectional** one, in which a comparison is made between groups of older and younger subjects. However, a demonstration of poorer memory in older subjects using this approach may be misleading, because other factors could be responsible: Some of the older subjects could be in the early stages of dementing illnesses such as Alzheimer's Disease. This problem can be avoided by giving the subjects various screening tests such as the *Mini-Mental State Examination*. (Folstein et al., 1975)

The longer you have been alive, the more exposed your brain has been to various factors that could damage it. This has led to the view that many age differences may be exaggerated, because the older subject groups contain a higher proportion of 'non-optimum performers' – people performing badly, not because of age, but due to some other 'risk factor', such as alcoholic brain injury, late-onset diabetes, minor head injury, depression or the residual effects of earlier psychiatric treatment (e.g. a course of electroconvulsive therapy). The importance of risk factors is illustrated in a study of memory scanning by Houx and colleagues (1991). Old and young subjects had to memorize a set of numbers, and then decide as quickly as possible whether individually presented probe numbers were part of the set. As one might expect, older subjects took longer to respond, but when the presence of risk factors was taken into account, the effect of age on response was relatively small. Thus, as well as excluding people with dementing illness, a good study of ageing and memory must also rule out the contaminating influence of increased risk factors in the elderly group.

Educational level is also a crucial factor. Older subjects are far more likely to have left school early compared with their younger counterparts. Educational level, as measured by tests such as Verbal IQ (Wechsler, 1981), is known to be correlated with memory ability. In making age-related comparisons of memory performance, it is therefore essential to include some control for educational level; otherwise, the observed differences may merely reflect different levels of education. Matching for educational level, however, creates a different problem. Typically, the goal of experiments is to be able to use results derived from representative samples to make inferences about the population as a whole. However, if our young and old populations differ significantly in terms of educational background, any comparison of age differences that controls for educational differences lacks **external validity**.

Problems with cross-sectional designs have led some researchers to use **longitudinal** designs, in which the same individuals are tested at different points in their lives. This type of design also has its problems. First, there is the obvious difficulty of keeping track of the same subject group across a span of 50 years or more. Second, there is the 'drop-out' problem, in that successive test sessions will comprise fewer subjects, with those remaining tending to be the ones who do well. As a result, the group average at the end of the study will be based on better performing subjects than it was at the start. One answer is to analyse only data from non-drop-outs, but this introduces a more subtle difficulty. Owens (1959, 1966) began by testing 363 college freshmen in 1919 on an army intelligence test. Testing occurred twice more, in 1950 and 1961, by which time the sample had been reduced to 96. Surprisingly, Owens found that these 96 men had actually *improved* with age. This highlights the possibility that **practice effects** can contaminate longitudinal designs, even when test sessions are separated by years.

Finally, whatever design we use, there is the simple problem of confidence. In his book *A Good Age*, Alex Comfort (1976) wrote: 'Although perfectly able to learn . . . older people get upset and anxious because of fear of failure. They may in fact appear not to learn because they would rather risk not answering than to give a wrong answer which confirms their own fears and other people's prejudices' (p. 120). Self-doubt is thus one factor that could adversely affect memory performance in the elderly. Another is task interest. Young subjects may, for various reasons, be more willing than the elderly to engage in the often meaningless and trivial memory tasks set up by experimental psychologists. Age-related studies of memory must therefore ensure that the elderly are not underperforming because of poor confidence or lack of motivation.

The study of ageing and memory is therefore methodologically complex, but within these limitations, investigations of age-related memory loss have produced many interesting findings and genuine progress towards understanding a problem that is of relevance to us all (see Kausler, 1991, for an excellent overview of these issues).

Experimental Studies of Ageing

The investigation of age-related memory impairment has been very much influenced by the theoretical constructs we considered in chapters 1–4. Thus researchers have attempted to examine how STS and LTS are differentially affected by age, and whether young and old people show similar patterns of recognition memory. Many studies have shown that STS, as measured by tasks such as digit span, does not decline significantly with age (e.g. Botwinick and Storandt, 1974). Interestingly, this finding cannot be attributed to flaws in cross-sectional designs, because age-based comparisons of digit span have been conducted for many years, and the results are remarkably consistent (Kausler, 1991). However, the elderly do not do well on all tests of immediate memory. Wingfield and co-workers (1988) compared young and elderly on three tests of short-term storage: digit span, word span and **loaded word span**. In the latter, subjects read sentences and had to decide whether they made sense or not, and at various points repeat back the last word of each sentence they had read. Age differences on the two simple span tasks were minimal, but the elderly showed much poorer performance on the loaded span task.

Despite showing very large declines in free recall ability, elderly subjects show relatively little change in recognition memory (e.g. White and Cunningham, 1982). Recently Micco and Masson (1992) have provided interesting evidence concerning the poor ability of older subjects on recall. Young and old subjects were presented with a target word and a context cue word that was either a strong or a weak associate (e.g. CROWD – people; CROWD – riot), and were required to generate a set of one-word clues that would enable another person to produce the target. A second group of young and old subjects were then given the clues in the presence of either the strong or the weak associate, and were asked to try to generate the target word. Clues generated by older people were less effective in facilitating target production, particularly in the presence of a weak associate. In addition, older subjects found it more difficult to work out what the target word was, especially when clues were presented alongside weak associates. The authors concluded that these data indicate an age-related decline in the ability to encode and retrieve context-specific information, and that this deficit is particularly evident when the context formed does not reflect information typically associated with the stimulus. Given that generative strategies may play an important role in retrieval (see chapter 3), the elderly might show recall impairments because they are less efficient at using cues.

Recognition is, of course, a much easier task, so the absence of any great age effect could simply reflect insensitivity of the test. This point is nicely countered in a study by Craik and McDowd (1987), who devised a recognition test that was more difficult than a recall test. Age-related differences were still not found on the recognition test, although the easier recall test did elicit better performance by the young.

It would seem, therefore, that recognition memory does not deteriorate significantly with age. However, more refined analysis does indicate some deterioration. In an experimental task known as **multiple item recognition memory** (MIRM) subjects are shown an array of items in which one is designated as the target word they should try to remember and the others as incorrect items (e.g. *parrot*, fern, pliers, tissue). At a later point the array is re-presented minus the target indicator, and the subject tries to identify the target item. Figure 8.1 shows data obtained by Kausler and Kleim (1978), in which performance of young and old was compared under conditions where the array contained either one or three incorrect items. Young subjects made far fewer errors overall, and were not influenced by the number of incorrect items in the array. Older subjects performed more poorly, and made substantially more errors when three incorrect items were present.

To understand why the elderly do so poorly on MIRM, compared with other tests of recognition memory, we must first examine the recognition tasks more closely. In the Craik and McDowd study a yes–no recognition

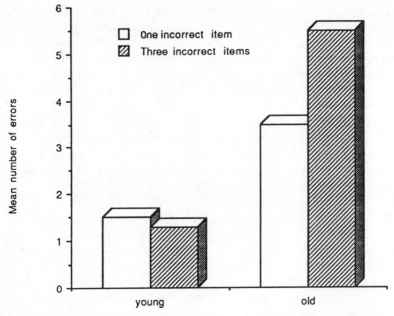

Figure 8.1 Performance of young and old subjects on the multiple-item recognition test.
(*Data from Kausler and Kleim, 1978.*)

task was used, in which target items had to be distinguished from distractors that had not been pre-exposed. In chapter 3 we noted that recognition memory is not a single process, but the joint product of two processes: a context-free assessment of familiarity and a context-dependent explicit recollection. The standard yes–no recognition task maximizes the possibility of familiarity-based responding, because the distractors, unlike the targets, have not been exposed prior to the recognition test, and do not have any enhanced familiarity. MIRM is different, because both targets and distractors have been pre-exposed, and correct recognition of targets depends critically on the retrieval of explicit contextual information (i.e. in that particular array it was 'parrot' that was the target). Given the poor encoding of context implied by the study of Micco and Masson (1992), the age deficit on MIRM is perhaps to be expected.

Our interim conclusions about ageing and recognition memory can therefore be revised by stating that ageing interferes little with the use of familiarity as a basis for recognition, but has a substantial effect on any recognition task that demands the retrieval of context. This account of ageing and recognition memory gains further support from a study conducted by Parkin and Walter (1992) in which age differences in recognition memory were explored using the recognition and conscious

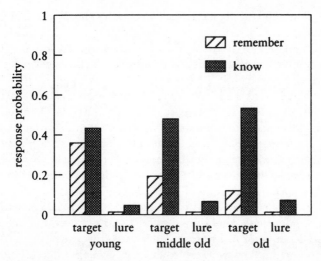

Figure 8.2 The effects of age on the experiential nature of recognition memory. 'Target' refers to words which subjects were instructed to try and learn. Lures are items subjects did not study that are present in the recognition test. (*Data from Parkin and Walter, 1992, p. 295.*)

awareness paradigm (described in chapter 3). Two groups of older subjects (one averaging 67 years, the other 81 years) were compared with a group of young subjects, and the results are shown in figure 8.2. As you can see, there is a dramatic change in the subjective nature of recognition memory as we get older, with the number of 'remember' (R) responses declining and the number of 'know' (K) responses increasing. K responses are an indication that the subject's recognition response is based on familiarity rather than any contextual recollection, so the age-related increase in K supports our contention that older subjects rely more on familiarity information for recognizing something.

The substantial age-related impairments shown on episodic memory tasks are not mirrored in tests of semantic memory. Comparison of young and old subjects on standardized vocabulary tests indicates little effect of age (e.g. Berkowitz, 1953; Salthouse, 1982). Indeed, it is not unusual in ageing research to find that older subjects have a slightly higher vocabulary score than younger subjects. However, reliance purely on vocabulary scores may itself be misleading. Botwinick and Storandt (1974), for example, found that younger subjects produced qualitatively better definitions of words than older subjects, even though vocabulary scores in the two age-groups did not differ. Also, in a study by Bowles and Poon (1985) older subjects performed more poorly on a 'reverse' vocabulary test which required them to give a word in response to a definition – a finding that probably derives from the same kind of deficit as that revealed in the Micco and Masson study discussed earlier.

Vocabulary test data thus suggest a small age-related loss of semantic memory. An alternative approach is to look at whether ageing leads to a slowing down of semantic memory processes, as opposed to a loss of information. Howard and colleagues (1986) examined the nature of **associative priming** in young and elderly subjects. Subjects were presented with single words known as a **primes**, each followed by a string of letters (the target) which varied randomly as to whether they constituted a real English word or not. Furthermore, when it was a word, it could either be related to the prime (e.g. BIRD → 'eagle') or unrelated (e.g. BIRD → 'sock'). Subjects were required to decide as quickly as possible whether each string of letters was or was not a word – a task known as **lexical decision**. Under these conditions a **priming effect** is typically found, in that lexical decision for real words is faster when the prime is related to the target. Howard and co-workers found that young subjects showed a priming effect even when the time elapsing between the prime and the target was as little as 150 msec. Older subjects also showed a priming effect, but only when the time between prime and target was increased to around half a second or more. Older subjects therefore understand associations as well as younger people, but take longer to activate them.

Procedural and Implicit Memory in Ageing

Motor skills acquired early in life certainly remain intact as we get older. For example, ballroom dancing is a frequent activity of retired people, which they perform without any difficulty whatsoever. Hill (1957), then aged 30, measured how quickly he could type a 100-word passage. Without any intervening practice he then retested himself on this passage when aged 55 and 80, and found that his ability was remarkably preserved. Salthouse (1984) examined Hill's claim more formally by comparing typing speeds of typists of different ages. The subjects copy-typed a passage displayed on a screen, and the time between each successive key stroke was recorded. Somewhat surprisingly, there was no age difference in the average time between key strokes. This did not reflect a general absence of response slowing in the older group, because, on a simple reaction time task, the older subjects were much slower. Further investigations by Salthouse showed that the absence of any slowing down in typing with age arose because older subjects had evolved more sophisticated strategies (e.g. looking further ahead) which compensated for their more general slowness.

Light and Singh (1987) examined possible age differences in cued recall and stem completion tasks. The results showed a marked age effect on cued recall, but only a small, non-significant age difference on stem completion. This finding was in keeping with an earlier study by Light and colleagues (1986) in which fragment completion priming also failed to reveal a significant age difference, even though young subjects again showed a small advantage. Other studies, however, have found poorer performance by elderly subjects on implicit memory tasks (e.g. Chiarello and Hoyer, 1988), and it has been suggested that sample size might be the critical factor determining age effects in implicit memory.

A recent study offers an alternative explanation of why age deficits in implicit memory might emerge. Russo and Parkin (1993) made age-based comparisons of implicit memory using the **picture completion paradigm**. Subjects were first shown degraded picture sequences, which became systematically more informative until the subject identified the depicted object. Twenty-four hours later, subjects were reshown the original sequences plus an equal number of new sequences. Both young and old subjects identified the previously exposed picture sequences more quickly than the new sequences, but this priming effect was much greater in younger subjects. This suggested that the older subjects had poorer implicit memory; however, further analysis suggested a different explanation. At the testing phase subjects were also asked to recall the names of the objects depicted in the sequences used in the original learning episode. As you would expect, the elderly performed more poorly on this explicit measure. More interestingly, this measure allowed the picture completion data to be re-analysed, distinguishing between picture sequences that were also recalled and those that were not. Confirming earlier studies (Parkin and Streete, 1988; Parkin and Russo, 1990), young subjects showed much greater priming for pictures they were able to recall, but the elderly showed no such difference. Furthermore, when analysis was restricted to non-recalled sequences, no significant age differences in picture completion priming were found. These results suggest that the poorer implicit memory performance by the elderly arose simply because they made less use of explicit memory to help them with the task.

Recently, Howard and Howard (1992) have demonstrated another interesting age difference using an implicit learning task. Subjects were asked to watch for an asterisk to be shown in one of four boxes, and when it appeared, to push the key underneath the box as quickly as possible. Trials were given in blocks, in which a particular sequence was repeated ten times. Implicit learning was measured in terms of the increased speed with which subjects pressed the buttons in repeated trials, as compared with random sequences. Explicit memory is assessed by asking subjects to try to predict which box the next asterisk will appear in. Howard and Howard found no difference between young and old on the implicit test, but that older subjects were significantly poorer on the prediction task.

Metamemory

As we saw in chapter 7, metamemory partly involves our ability to monitor the contents of our memory so that we can, for example, predict whether or not we will recognize something we are unable to recall. Butterfield and colleagues (1988) compared 18- and 70-year-olds on the feeling of knowing task (FOK), and found no age difference; but a subsequent study by Anooshian and co-workers (1989) did find a reliable decrease in the FOK accuracy of older people. Earlier, Bruce and colleagues (1982) compared old and young subjects on their ability to predict how well they would recall a word list. The age-groups did not differ in their predictions, but, as one might expect, the older subjects recalled less. Older subjects thus seem over-optimistic about their memory ability. This phenomenon is further illustrated in a study by Lovelace and Marsh (1985) in which old and young subjects were presented with individual word-pairs and asked to rate how easily they would be able to recall them later. Both groups were accurate in so far as more pairs rated as easy to recall were recalled successfully, but there was still a big age difference in that, even for those word-pairs considered easy, the younger subjects recalled substantially more. However, older subjects do not always overrate their memory. Hertzog and co-workers (1990), for example, asked old and young subjects to predict their performance on recall of both a categorized list and a narrative text. Older subjects recalled less on both tasks, and accurately predicted this.

Rabbitt and Abson (1991) assigned older subjects four laboratory memory tasks (recognition, memory span, recall and cumulative learning) and asked them to fill in two questionnaires that probed their subjective knowledge of their mental efficiency in everyday life. Memory performance was found to be uncorrelated with subjects' own estimates of their memory ability. However, significant relationships were found between memory ability and the extent of self-rated depression, age and intelligence. Findings of other studies of the relation between memory self-assessment questionnaires and objective memory ability are inconsistent, some showing positive relationships (e.g. Dixon and Hultsch, 1983), others negative relationships (West, 1986).

Metamemory also relates to our understanding of how memory operates. Investigating this, Loewen and colleagues (1990) asked young and old subjects to answer questions about their memory capacity, their knowledge of the demands that different tasks make on memory, and the extent to which they employed strategies. Older subjects reported having poorer memories, and were less likely to employ encoding strategies. However, no age differences were found in the subjects' knowledge about memory task demands.

Key Features of Age-related Memory Impairment

A summary of the key features of age-related memory loss will help us understand why this occurs.

- Performance on tests of short-term storage is largely unaffected, unless the task has a working memory component (e.g. loaded memory span).
- Age produces a marked impairment in recall ability, as shown on the free recall.
- Although recognition memory does not decline dramatically with age, it changes qualitatively, with responding becoming increasingly reliant on familiarity.
- There is little evidence of a decline in semantic memory, although the speed at which older people can access their knowledge declines notably.
- There is some evidence of a decline in metamemory performance.
- Implicit memory ability is largely intact.

Theoretical Explanations of Age-related Memory Decline

Perhaps the most popular explanation of age-related memory loss is that it arises from a decline in some general 'resource'. Thus, age decrements on a variety of tests can all be attributed to the same resource deficit. The most widely explored resource in this context is **processing speed**; thus Salthouse (1980) states that 'mental operation time may be the principal mechanism behind age differences in nearly all cognitive functioning' (p. 61). Slower processing speed would have a number of obvious consequences for memory, such as poorer encoding, slower retrieval and less efficient organization. Processing speed is also an attractive hypothesis because it relates neatly to physiological evidence that neuronal activity slows down with age (e.g. Cremer and Zeef, 1987).

Experimentally, the processing speed hypothesis gains support from studies in which age-related changes in memory are shown to be reduced when processing speed, as measured by simple tests of clerical speed, is taken into account. Using a method like this, Salthouse (1985), for example, found that the relationship between age and a decline in free recall ability was substantially reduced, although, importantly, not eliminated. Salthouse (1994) examined the relationship between processing speed, age and associative learning. Subjects were required to learn associations between abstract symbols, and, as predicted, reliable age differences were found. Further analysis indicated that the ageing effect was largely due to forgetting information about previously correct responses. However, this forgetting was itself attributable to poorer encoding by older subjects, which in turn was significantly related to processing speed. Salthouse thus concluded that age-related deficits in associative learning were largely due to the consequences of slower processing speed, although, as before, this factor did not explain all age-related change.

A second resource-based approach suggests that ageing leads to a decline in **attentional resources**. One prediction of this theory is that young subjects will behave like older subjects if they are asked to perform two tasks simultaneously. A number of studies have shown that such divided attention manipulation does reduce the memory performance of younger subjects to a level resembling that of older subjects. A related prediction is that older subjects, because of their reduced attention, will be affected more by divided attention. Studies exploring these possibilities have been reviewed by both Hartley (1993) and Salthouse (1991), but their conclusions differ. Hartley views the data as consistent with the attentional theory, whereas Salthouse considers that there are too many studies producing contradictory results.

Evidence for the attentional resource hypothesis varies for a number of reasons. First, there is considerable variation as to which tasks are used. For example, Gick and colleagues (1988) and Morris and colleagues (1988) failed to find that divided attention caused larger deficits in older subjects, whereas Craik and McDowd (1987) did find this effect. The two studies showing no effect used a working memory task, while those showing an effect used free recall. Results of this kind suggest that it will not be easy to explain age-related memory effects in terms of the decline of a single attentional resource. Indeed, some theorists believe that the concept of a unitary attentional system is now invalid, and that different attentional mechanisms must be specified according to the task being performed. Attempts to link age-related memory change to these revised ideas about attention may still be possible, provided the picture does not become too complex. However, if the data start to suggest that each memory task is identified with its own kind of attentional resource, the approach will lose any generality.

Another approach is to consider age-related memory loss in terms of changes in working memory ability. As we saw in chapter 2, working memory comprises a central executive plus associated slave systems. A number of studies have shown that tasks which predominantly tap the storage component of working memory (e.g. digit span) show little influence of age (e.g. Wingfield et al., 1988), whereas those that are thought to implicate the central executive more directly (e.g. sentence span) do show an effect (e.g. Hayslip and Kenelly, 1982), thereby suggesting that age results in a decline in central executive function.

Despite results of this kind, this working memory account suffers from requiring assumptions to be made about which tasks are tapping which components of the system. In addition, Salthouse and his colleagues have shown that age differences in measures of working memory can be reduced considerably if basic processing speed is taken into account (e.g. Salthouse and Kersten, 1993).

Hasher and Zacks (1988) have suggested that increased age brings with it higher degrees of **disinhibition**. This can be defined as inability to suppress information which is not relevant to the task in hand, allowing it to remain in working memory once it has become activated. In terms of memory function, disinhibition might cause deficits by allowing too much irrelevant information to be encoded or by allowing increased competition from irrelevant information at retrieval.

Support for the disinhibition account of ageing comes from a paradigm known as **negative priming**. In a typical study two words are presented simultaneously, but only one, the target, must be attended to. On subsequent trials either the target or the other word will be represented. The key finding is that subjects take longer to name the non-target word, and it is assumed that, in some way, a response to that word has been inhibited. Hasher and Zacks found that elderly subjects showed evidence of reduced negative priming compared with controls, and suggested that this represented increased disinhibition with age.

Inhibition is known to be a function of the frontal lobes, which, as we have seen in chapter 7, are known to be implicated in memory function. The phenomenon of age-related disinhibition might therefore be one aspect of a more general relationship between ageing, memory and frontal lobe function.

Ageing, Memory and Frontal Lobe Function

As we get older, our brains lose neurons, and this loss is most prominent in the frontal cortex. This has led to the idea that normal age-related memory loss might, in part at least, be related to a loss of memory abilities specifically associated with the frontal lobes. Earlier we noted the Parkin and Walter study showing that ageing results in recognition memory becoming more familiarity-based. This study also examined how the change related to measures of frontal lobe function, and it was found that increased familiarity-based responding was associated with evidence of greater frontal lobe impairment.

I and my colleagues (Parkin et al., 1995) compared young and elderly subjects on the list discrimination task (LDT), which measures both recognition and the ability of subjects to recollect the temporal or context information about a target's prior presentation (e.g. 'Which list was a target in?' 'Was the target presented to your left or your right?'). No age differences on recognition were found, but the elderly performed much worse on memory for temporal context. The extent of the deficit in temporal context memory again correlated with measures of frontal lobe function, although the pattern was different to that found by Parkin and Walter, thus suggesting that different aspects of memory might be related to different aspects of frontal lobe function (see also Parkin and Lawrence, 1994). Recently, Glisky and co-workers (1995) have also illustrated a link between age-related memory loss and frontal lobe function.

Overview of Theories of Memory and Ageing

As the above account shows, there are many approaches to the study of memory and ageing, and no definitive account has yet emerged. A deficit of attention, while plausible at an intuitive level, is difficult to sustain, because memory tasks do not uniformly interact with age and divided attention. A decline in working memory capability also seems a reasonable idea, but suffers because the working memory model lacks specificity, especially in terms of which memory tasks directly tap the central processor. There is also evidence for disinhibition increasing with age, but this phenomenon has not been widely investigated in relation to memory.

At the time of writing (1996) the two most popular theories relate to processing speed and frontal lobe dysfunction. However, it is possible that these theories may come together somewhat. For example, Salthouse and Fristoe (1995) have shown that age differences on a frontal lobe test called the **Trail Making Test** revealed that most observed age differences were attributable to differences in processing speed. Since most frontal lobe tasks can be considered measures of speed in some way or another, it may be that the processing speed explanation lies at the heart of age-related differences. However, it is important to remember that processing speed has never been able to account for age differences entirely. In addition, there are studies showing that different aspects of memory correlate with different measures of frontal function (e.g. Parkin and Lawrence, 1994) – a finding that is hard to reconcile with a single deficit in processing speed. Finally, recent work by Rosalind Java and me (submitted) has shown that substantial age effects in recall and recognition remain even when differences in processing speed are taken into account. The explanation of age-related memory loss in terms of a single factor thus seems unlikely.

Temporal Gradients and the 'Reminiscence Bump'

Earlier we noted John Mortimer's observation that his memory of the more recent past was inferior to that of the more distant past. In this section we will examine evidence confirming this fact, and also try to understand why the memory of older people shows this characteristic pattern.

One means of addressing a person's memory for the past is to use the **autobiographical cueing** procedure first suggested by the British psychologist Francis Galton. In this procedure subjects are given individual words (e.g. 'river') and required to recollect a specific personal episode that the word reminds them of. Figure 8.3 shows data from an experiment by Jansari and Parkin (1996) in which this procedure was carried out on two groups of subjects, one aged between 56 and 60, the other between 36 and 40. Look first at the data shown by the solid lines on the graphs. You will notice that, in both groups, there is very little recall of events from the period 0–5 years. This is the phenomenon of **infantile amnesia** – our almost complete inability to recollect any events from the earliest years of our life (see chapter 10). Returning to figure 8.3, there are two important differences overall. First, it is clear that the young subjects recall far more events from the very recent past than do the older subjects. Second, older subjects show a 'bump' in their recall for the early part of their lives, with poorer memory for events occurring in the middle of their lives. By a contrast, younger subjects show little evidence of a 'bump' in their recall.

In his autobiography Beverley Nichols concludes that 'Twenty-five seems to me the latest age at which anybody should write an autobiography. It has an air of finality about it, as though one had clambered to the summit of a great hill, and were waving goodbye to some very distant country which can never be revisited' (Nichols, 1926, p. 9). Nichols is implying that there is something very special about our youth, which sets it apart from more mundane later life. Interestingly, a view of this type underlies one attempt to explain why older adults show a bump in their recall of early memories. It has been suggested that in later life we undergo a life-review process, and that, because of their significance, we concentrate on adolescent and early adulthood events. Why this should occur is not that well specified, but one suggestion is that this period of life includes many of the defining moments from which our sense of personal identity has developed (e.g. Fitzgerald, 1992; Romaniuk, 1981).

The above explanation has led to the term 'reminiscence bump' being used to describe this period of enhanced memory. However, recent evidence suggests that this bump may have a less interesting origin. You will recall from figure 8.3 that younger subjects have a strong bias towards recalling events from the most recent period of their lives, whereas older subjects do not. Because with the experimental procedure used, there is a

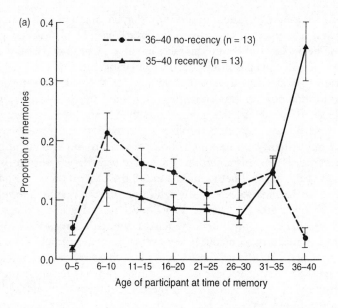

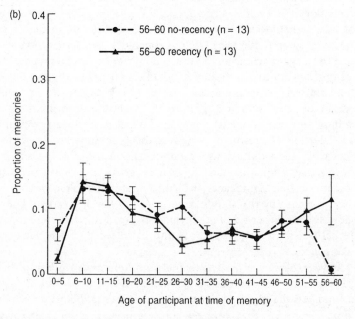

Figure 8.3a,b Data from Jansari and Parkin, 1996.

fixed number of cue words and only one memory per cue is allowed, it follows that young subjects have far fewer opportunities to recall events from earlier parts of their lives than do older subjects. The absence of a reminiscence bump in the younger subjects could therefore be simply an artefact of sampling in that younger subjects choose not to retrieve earlier memories very frequently.

To test this idea, Jansari and I repeated the experiment, but this time subjects were not allowed to recall events from the most recent time period. These data are represented by broken lines on the graphs. Predictably, blocking recency had little effect on the older subjects, but it resulted in a substantial reminiscence bump emerging in the recall pattern of the younger subjects. This latter result is inconsistent with a 'life review' explanation of the bump, because this ties the phenomenon to increasing age. Instead, it supports the less interesting explanation that the bump tends to be restricted to old age simply because younger subjects have a bias to recall from the most recent past.

What we still have to explain, however, is why these early life memories are retained, by both young and old alike. It might be, for example, that early memories have specific components which make them particularly amenable to retrieval (e.g. first serious relationship, going to college), but in absolute terms, these memories are no more distinctive than those for later periods of life. This possibility was tested by Jansari (1995) in an experiment in which subjects were asked to retrieve memories about the same type of event (e.g. a wedding) from different times. He found that the early memories were still the strongest being retrieved more quickly and in more detail than those from later times.

At the moment it is not clear why earlier memories should be more accessible, but one view is that their status is different from that of memories of later life. One idea is that older memories have become more 'semantic' in nature; that is, our recollections are more like general knowledge about ourselves rather than memories of specific events. This idea gains some support from a study by Nigro and Neisser (1983) who got subjects to distinguish between two types of event memory: **observer** and **field**. An observer memory is one in which you can 'see yourself' doing something, whereas in a field memory the event is experienced as if you were seeing it again. Interestingly, Nigro and Neisser reported that more recent experiences tend to be recalled as field memories, suggesting that, with age, memories may well change their form.

Ageing and Memory: Use or Lose it?

One question older people frequently ask is whether or not it does them good to keep their minds active. What they are worried about is the possibility that frequent use of their mind will somehow 'wear their brain out' and that they will, among other things, start to lose their memory more quickly. Alternatively, is it a case of use it or lose it?

We can begin to answer this question by looking at the animal literature. A number of studies have examined the effect that enriched versus impoverished environments have on brain development. In one study rats lived either in an environment where there was plenty of stimulation or in one where stimulation was minimal. It was found that animals reared in an enriched environment had more neurons than those who lived in the impoverished environment, thereby suggesting that richer environments slow down loss of neurons in the later stages of life (e.g. Cohen, 1990).

It has, of course, proved impossible to test the 'use it or lose it' hypothesis rigorously in the human population. However, our varying treatment of retired people does provide some insights. For many older people retirement is a rich experience, involving activities such as the University of the Third Age along with more traditional roles such as being a grandparent. Others are not so lucky, and may well end up in nursing homes where there is an emphasis on routine and little in the way of stimulation beyond TV and bingo. Many of the latter will be people with dementing illness, but there is a significant group who remain mentally active but enter homes because of physical infirmity.

The relationship between residential environment and the development of memory impairment has begun to receive some attention. Winocur (1982) provided a number of demonstrations that institutionalized elderly performed more poorly on memory tests than elderly people living at home. Craik and McDowd (1987) examined memory performance in elderly subjects who were either living actively in the community, living in a residential facility that encouraged activities, or living in a standard institution where activity was minimal. The results showed no difference between the first two groups, but those living in the standard institution showed poorer memory performance. Cockburn and Smith (1993) examined the prospective memory (remembering to do things) in people admitted to care at different points in their lives. Interestingly, they found poorer prospective memory in people admitted to care earlier in their lives. Institutions rely heavily on routines, so perhaps it is not surprising that longer-serving inmates should have the poorest prospective memory. The idea that institutionalization inhibits the use of certain memory functions is backed up by Holland and Rabbitt (1991), who found that institutionalized old people tended to spend much more of their time dwelling on the past.

The evidence seems clear. Older people are best advised to keep mentally active.

Memory in Dementia

The name **dementia** refers to a class of degenerative brain disorders, all of which produce a gradual decline in mental function. Dementia is usually assessed using tools such as the **Clinical Dementia Rating** (CDR) scale (Hughes et al., 1982). This is based on interviewing both the patient and a carer, and obtaining ratings of such things as memory, orientation, judgement and personal care. On this scale 0 equals no dementia and 3 equals severe dementia.

The commonest form of dementia is known as **Alzheimer's Disease** (AD). This is characterized by the presence of senile plaques and neurofibrillary tangles throughout the brain. The time course of AD varies considerably, but the disorder is first noticed when the person becomes forgetful and has problems finding words (this is typically defined as CDR 0.5). As the disease progresses to CDR 2.0, patients become unable to manage on their own, and need help with many basic activities such as getting dressed. Finally, in CDR 3.0 memory is so severely affected that they are unable to recognize close relatives or even their own reflection in a mirror.

The memory impairment in AD is particularly noticeable on any test of episodic memory, and provides a good way of discriminating AD patients from unaffected individuals. Knopman and Ryberg (1989) asked AD patients and healthy controls to generate a sentence based on each of ten words they would subsequently have to remember as means of promoting deeper encoding (see chapter 2). The procedure was then repeated, and 5 minutes later the subjects attempted recall. The scores on this test reliably distinguished AD patients from controls with a probability of 0.95. There have also been a number of studies suggesting that even when AD patients do learn new episodic information they forget it very rapidly (e.g. Hart et al., 1988). However, this claim is a matter of some controversy (see Brandt and Rich, 1995).

What is less disputed is that AD patients show abnormal levels of 'intrusions' in memory (e.g. Fuld et al., 1982; Jacobs et al., 1990). The term 'intrusion' is used rather loosely in this context, and refers to the generation of false information during recall or the false identification of distractors as targets in a recognition test (so-called false alarms). Interestingly, these high levels of intrusion error are thought to be 'pathognomic' for AD, in that they distinguish the disease from other forms of dementia – we will return to this point later.

In chapter 6 we saw that memory span was largely unaffected in human amnesia, thereby suggesting a selective preservation of STS. Unfortunately, the same situation does not prevail with AD. Corkin (1982), for example, found that patients with more severe dementia also had poorer memory span. In chapter 2 we briefly considered the working memory approach, in which primary memory was seen as a central executive associated with two slave systems. Baddeley and colleagues (1991) first found a task, pursuit rotor tracking (see chapter 6), which both AD patients and controls could perform at similar levels. They then found another task, digit span, and also equated performance on this task. The AD patients and controls were then required to perform both tasks simultaneously. Under these conditions the AD patients fared badly, whereas the controls had little difficulty performing the two tasks together. Interpreting this result, Baddeley and co-workers suggest that the AD deficit arises because the central executive is impaired, and is thus unable to co-ordinate responses on the two tasks. This finding is supported by a study by Becker (1988), who found that the memory deficit in AD appeared to have two components: one involving central executive function and the other episodic memory.

Another area in which memory loss in AD differs from amnesia is semantic memory. As we saw amnesic patients tend not to have significant deficits in this area, whereas AD patients do. Their deficit is particularly marked on tasks such as picture naming. Shown pictures of animals, for example, they will frequently fail, and just give a general response such as 'animal' or an associated animal name. This has led some to suggest that semantic memory is degraded in AD, with only higher-level, coarser information left intact. However, in a series of studies Nebes and his associates (e.g. Nebes, 1989; Nebes et al., 1986) have suggested that AD patients are just slower, thus echoing Salthouse's interpretation of normal age-related change in cognitive function. On one test, subjects were shown a 'prime' word and then asked to decide whether a string of letters was a real word or not. Normal subjects, given this task, show faster response times for identifying real words if the prime is related (e.g. 'table' → CHAIR). Nebes and colleagues (1986) found that these associative priming effects can occur with AD patients, provided a longer interval elapses between the prime and the letter string. Thus it is not the association in semantic memory that is lacking. The deficit lies in the time taken to activate the association.

However, the work of Chan and co-workers (1993a, b) suggests disorganization in the semantic memories of AD patients. These researchers were interested in how AD patients and controls represented similarities and differences between animals. To find out, subjects were asked direct questions (such as which two of three animals are most alike), and indirect measures were made from the proximity of animal names in a verbal fluency task (i.e. the tendency to recall similar types of animals in succession). Using this technique, it was found that AD patients had less accurate representations of animals because they relied heavily on perceptual features, as opposed to abstract features such as domesticity (see also Chan et al., 1995).

On balance, it would appear that semantic memory is disorganized in AD patients, and this also affects episodic memory performance. Typically, if normal subjects are presented with word lists containing items from a number of categories, they will exploit this fact to improve their memory. However, Weingartner and co-workers (1982) failed to find this tactic in AD patients, thus suggesting that they were unable to make effective use of the categorical relations in the lists.

The enormous interest in implicit memory has led, inevitably, to experiments exploring this form of memory in AD sufferers. Again, there appear to be important differences between AD patients and typical amnesics. Stem completion is an implicit task we considered in chapter 3. To recap, this involves presentation of a word (e.g. REASON), followed by a test phrase in which the subject sees REA__? and is asked to produce the first word that springs to mind. Repetition priming is said to occur if 'reason' is produced as a response at more than the chance rate. In chapter 6 we saw that amnesic patients perform well on this task (e.g. Graf and Schacter, 1985) but a number of studies have shown that AD patients do not (e.g. Shimamura and Squire, 1987). Some studies have suggested that this is because AD patients do not engage in sufficient elaborative processing during learning (e.g. Grosse et al., 1990); another recent study has demonstrated that reading the words aloud allows AD patients to show normal priming (Downes et al., 1996). By contrast with these deficits, other measures of implicit memory indicate normal performance in AD patients. Bondi and Kaszniak (1991), for example, showed that AD patients impaired on stem completion priming performed normally on the pursuit rotor task. If subjects are presented with an unusual member of a category (e.g. a tuba) and are then asked to generate examples of it (musical instruments), they will tend to produce the unusual name more often than if it had not been exposed – the phenomenon of **conceptual priming**. Monti and colleagues (1996) examined the extent of conceptual priming in AD patients, and found that it was impaired by comparison with controls.

AD also produces a profound retrograde amnesia, which usually exhibits a temporal gradient. Beatty and co-workers (1988), for example, found that AD patients performed much better on the earlier decade questions of the BRMT than on questions dealing with the 1970s and 1980s. Similarly, Kopelman (1989) found evidence of temporal gradients on various measures of remote memory. However, not all studies have indicated a temporal gradient in AD (e.g. Wilson et al., 1981). It is not clear why this should be, but differences in the form of testing or severity of dementia seem likely explanations.

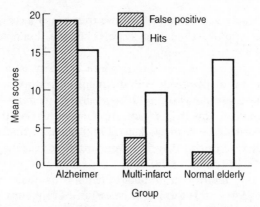

Figure 8.4 Mean number of false alarms and hits on a recognition test made by patients with Alzheimer's Disease, multi-infarct dementia, and normal elderly controls.
(*Data from Judge and Parkin, submitted.*)

Other Forms of Dementia

Although the term 'dementia' is often used synonymously with AD, it is important to remember that dementia can take many other forms. The next most common is **multi-infarct dementia** (MID), or **vascular dementia** which is caused by circulatory disturbance in the brain. It is not always easy to distinguish between this form of dementia and AD, but recent studies of memory have revealed an important difference. We saw earlier that AD patients' recognition memory was characterized by the production of high levels of false alarms. It has been suggested that this may be a means of distinguishing MID from AD. My colleague Elizabeth Judge and I set out to test this possibility by comparing false alarm rates in AD patients, MID patients and controls. Figure 8.4 shows that there is a dramatic difference between the patient groups. AD patients, as expected, show a very liberal attitude to recognition, making lots of hits but also a high number of false alarms. By contrast, MID patients appear very conservative, and show the reverse pattern. We saw in chapter 7 that high levels of false alarms are also characteristic of patients with frontal lobe problems, so it is possible that the two patient groups have the same underlying deficit.

The diagnosis of dementia is often complicated by a disorder known as **pseudo-dementia**. This term refers to behaviour that can be seen as an attempt to mimic the symptoms of dementia by people suffering from depression. It can be very hard to distinguish from real dementia, with between 5 and 15 per cent of 'demented' patients turning out, rather, to be depressed. Interestingly, research has shown that patients with pseudo-dementia can be distinguished from AD patients in that they do not make high levels of false alarms but, instead, respond very conservatively on recognition tests (Gainotti and Marra, 1994). However, as we have seen, this conservative mode of responding is also seen in MID. Recognition performance cannot, therefore, unambiguously distinguish any form of dementia from pseudo-dementia.

Dementia can also occur in other disorders, such as multiple sclerosis, progressive supranuclear palsy, Huntingdon's chorea (HC), Parkinson's disease (PD) and HIV infection. Collectively these disorders are known as **sub-cortical dementias** (SCD), because they are thought to arise from malfunctions in areas outside the cerebral cortex. Brandt and Rich (1995) have recently compared the nature of these dementias, and noted a number of important differences. Most striking, perhaps, are the differences found between AD and HC patients. As we have seen, AD patients typically show impairments on stem completion priming, but perform normally on other forms of implicit learning such as the pursuit rotor task. Exactly the opposite appears to prevail with HC, with normal stem completion but considerable impairments on procedural memory tasks. This emphasizes the point that we cannot consider implicit memory to be a single entity.

Memory declines inevitably with age, but in an uneven manner. Age has little effect on short-term storage, semantic memory and implicit memory, but there is a marked decline of explicit memory. Recall is the most affected. Recognition does not decline greatly with age, but changes qualitatively by becoming more familiarity-based. Age-related memory loss has been variously attributed to a decline in various resources, particularly processing speed, or to the decline in frontal lobe function that also characterizes ageing. Memory is severely affected in AD and other forms of dementia. Unlike those suffering from the amnesic syndrome, AD patients appear impaired on tests of explicit and implicit memory. Most dementias have the same general character as AD, but there are some important differences.

9 Transient Disorders of Memory

So far, we have been concerned with impairments of memory that are permanent. However, there are a number of memory disorders which are temporary, and these can be divided into those that arise from organic brain dysfunction and those that have a psychological origin. The latter are known as **psychogenic amnesias**, and we will deal with them in chapter 10. Our concern in the present chapter is with those which have an organic cause.

Transient Global Amnesia

Regard and Landis (1984) reported the case of a healthy 40-year-old policeman who, whilst exercising in a gymnasium, suddenly became confused. Returning to work, he repeated the same question many times in an attempt to orient himself. His doctor could find no signs of neurological illness, but, convinced that something was wrong, the patient drove through heavy traffic to hospital. CAT scans and other neurological tests showed no signs of abnormality, but psychological testing revealed a profound memory impairment. The patient knew who he was and his location, but was completely confused about the time, and had a retrograde amnesia (RA) for the previous few months of his life. He showed concern about his disorder, and did not confabulate. Formal testing revealed a dense anterograde amnesia. He was unable to remember anything about a 15-word list 40 minutes after hearing it, and performed little better on a similar test of visual memory. By contrast, his digit span was within the normal range, and all other mental abilities were normal. Nine hours after onset, his RA had receded, in that only his memory for the last two days was impaired, but there was little improvement in his anterograde deficit. However, this subsequently improved, and after 72 hours his performance on memory tests was within the normal range. One month after the episode there was no sign of memory impairment.

This case is typical of a disorder known as **transient global amnesia** (TGA). Its major features can be defined as:

- A sudden onset of anterograde amnesia coupled with RA for more recent events in the patient's life.
- Disorientation in time but no loss of personal identity.
- Patients usually have insight into their memory disorder, although not always.
- Repetitive questioning and stereotyped responding.
- No impairment of any other psychological function.
- Duration of attack is usually short-ranging, from minutes to days, although the average duration is about five hours.
  (Goldenberg, 1995)

A considerable amount is known about the aetiology of TGA. Victims usually have a healthy background, and are typically between 50 and 70 (e.g. Hodges, 1991). Its incidence, which seems equally frequent in men and women, is low, being less than 2 per cent of a typical population of neurological patients – that is, 4 per 100,000 of the population. TGA can be precipitated in many ways, including sudden changes of temperature (e.g. taking a cold shower), physical stress, eating a large meal and even sexual intercourse. Several toxins have been associated with TGA, most notably clioquinol, an active component of many anti-diarrhoea drugs until it was banned. In 1966 widespread flooding in Japan led to extensive distribution of clioquinol to combat dysentery. Following this, more than 100 people reported symptoms similar to those of TGA. Mumenthaler and co-workers (1979) reported several European cases, including a student who developed diarrhoea during a trip to Paris. She took only the prescribed dose of clioquinol-containing tablets, but, on return home, found that she could remember nothing about her holiday.

The cause of TGA is still unknown, although two types of theory have been put forward. The first of these is known as **spreading depression** (SD) – a phenomenon in which neurons become depolarized and thus non-functional. While there is no direct evidence for SD causing TGA, there is circumstantial evidence to support the idea. There is known to be a strong association between migraine and TGA, with about 20 per cent of sufferers experiencing both disorders (e.g. Hodges and Warlow, 1990). Studies of people having migraine attacks show that there are some similarities between the brain dysfunction they experience and that recorded in animals in whom SD has been experimentally induced. However, a problem for this theory is that factors known to precipitate TGA (e.g. physical exercise) are not typically associated with migraine, and vice versa (Goldenberg, 1995).

The second theory is that TGA is a form of **transient cerebral ischemia**, which leads to a temporary reduction in the blood supply to regions of the brain concerned with memory function. A problem with this theory, however, is that you would expect TGA to increase in parallel with other diseases of the brain's vascular system. However, as we have seen, it appears to decline after 70, when diseases such as atherosclerosis actually start to increase dramatically. Also, whichever theory is correct, it is also unclear which of the brain structures concerned with memory is affected during TGA. Recent neuro-imaging studies of TGA point to the involvement of the temporal lobes; but other studies have suggested that either the thalamus is primarily affected (Hodges, 1994) or the frontal lobes (Baron et al., 1994).

Epilepsy and Memory Disorder

Epilepsy is an illness in which the patient suffers recurrent fits of seizures. There are a number of forms of seizure. In a **grand mal** seizure the patient falls to the ground and becomes unconscious, and initially the body becomes rigid and the mouth clenched. In the second phase there are jerking movements, which gradually slow down until the person becomes relaxed. Following a grand mal seizure, consciousness gradually returns and there is often a feeling of confusion. Patients who suffer such a seizure do not remember events during the seizure (the **ictal** period), and also have a poor memory for events occurring after the seizure (**post-ictal** period). During the post-ictal period it is possible to observe the phenomenon of **automatism**, in which the person is able to carry out quite complex actions without any apparent volition and has no record of these events once they have recovered. In a **petit mal** seizure the person experiences what are known as 'absences', which may last from a few seconds to around half a minute. In this form of seizure the patient, most commonly a child, appears oblivious to their surroundings, and gives the impression of daydreaming.

Grand mal and petit mal are classified as generalized seizures, because the epileptic activity occurs across a wide area of the brain. In a **partial**, or **focal**, seizure the epilepsy is limited to a particular region of the brain, and such seizures may either be **simple**, if there is no disturbance of consciousness, or complex, if the person's consciousness is affected. Recently it has been recognized that **complex** partial seizures can give rise to a form of temporary memory impairment rather similar to TGA; this has been termed **transient epileptic amnesia** (TEA; Kapur, 1993).

Although TEA has only recently been identified, it was first reported by Hughlings-Jackson (1889), who described the case of a Dr Z. The latter was examining a patient and correctly diagnosed pneumonia; but after the examination he could remember nothing, but realized he had examined the patient because he had written down the diagnosis. More recently, Palmini and colleagues (1992) described a series of epileptic patients who experienced brief amnesic periods in the absence of any other epileptic signs. One man, for example, proposed to his fiancé during an amnesic episode, but could not remember anything about it! Kapur (1993) also reports a series of patients who experienced similar episodes. These include a woman who awoke in the night, and was unable to recognize her family or her home.

Although similar to TGA, Kapur (1993) has emphasized some important differences between the two disorders. Thus TEA patients do not usually ask repetitive questions, and are rarely anxious. There are also instances of TEA causing greater retrograde than anterograde amnesia. In addition, TEA can occur many times, whereas multiple episodes of TGA are uncommon. The cause of TEA is not fully understood, but it is thought to arise from the partial seizures interfering with parts of the medial temporal lobe (Palmini et al., 1992).

Post-traumatic Amnesia

Closed head injuries involve a blow to the skull that does not expose the brain. Severe memory loss occurs in about 10 per cent of patients admitted to hospital following closed head injury, but our concern here will be with those for whom there is a complete or near-complete recovery. Concussion has dramatic and usually immediate effects on an individual. If the blow is sufficiently powerful, the person will collapse, and respiration may even cease for a moment or two. As consciousness is regained, the victim will start to move, make noises, and eventually speak. There will be signs of restlessness, and the victim may be irritable or even abusive. Although fully conscious, the patient will be confused, disoriented and show marked anterograde and retrograde memory deficits. This period of memory loss is termed **post-traumatic amnesia** (PTA), and varies in length from a few seconds to several months (Russell, 1971).

Assessment of PTA and its duration are of considerable importance, because the length of time a patient experiences PTA appears to be related to whether or not their memory will recover (see below). The usual means of measuring PTA is subjective, with patients being asked to recall their first memory after their accident and to estimate when they thought their memory had returned to normal. However, this method is unreliable, because it relies directly on the patient's memory. A more reliable altern-ative is to use questionnaires, observational strategies and formal testing. To this end, a number of procedures have been developed for monitoring patients with PTA (Goldstein and Levin, 1995).

Memory function during PTA is very much like that found in the amnesic syndrome. Thus the learning of word lists will be very poor (e.g. Gasquoine, 1991), and there will also be very rapid forgetting (Levin et al., 1985). However, as one might expect, there is evidence of preserved learning on tests of procedural memory. Levin and colleagues (1985) showed that PTA patients performed normally on the pursuit rotor task and other procedural tasks (see also Wilson et al., 1992). Gasquoine (1991) also found that patients suffering from PTA showed a good ability to recall the location of rooms in a floor plan.

The inability of PTA victims to remember events immediately preceding their trauma is consistent with the existence of an STS in which information is retained in a temporary and labile trace, the assumption being that the trauma has interfered in some way with the normal process of transfer. This disruption could occur in two ways: concussion could disrupt maintenance of the temporary trace or interfere with the consolidation process itself. Two lines of evidence support the latter possibility. First, Regard and Landis (1984), along with other clinicians, report that digit span is normal during the PTA phase. Normal performance of this task reflects an intact STS, so PTA victims would seem to be unimpaired in this respect.

The second, rather unusual source of evidence comes from a study by Yarnell and Lynch (1973). They examined PTA in American footballers immediately after they had been concussed. In this game players have to remember a set of instructions about the 'play' they must follow. At the time of concussion, therefore, a player is keeping in mind a certain amount of information about what he should be doing. In one case a player was concussed whilst being 'gang-tackled' during a '91 curl pattern play'. On immediate questioning, he could name the play, but on removal to the touch-line, he was no longer able to do so. This phenomenon was observed frequently, and suggests that STS continues to function during PTA but that concussion disrupts transfer into LTS.

Levin and co-workers (1985) examined the pattern of RA both during and after PTA. In their first study, young head-injury patients were tested on the 'titles for television programmes' test developed by Squire and Slater (1975). In this test the subject must select from a choice of four titles the one that corresponds to a real TV programme. The programmes are drawn from different time periods (1968–81) in order to detect any temporal gradient that might be present. During the PTA phase victims were equally poor at identifying programmes from all the time periods tested. After the PTA phase, performance improved, but accuracy remained the same across all time periods. The absence of a temporal gradient on the TV programmes test ran contrary to clinical accounts of PTA which suggest that more remote memories are less affected during the PTA phase. Levin and colleagues therefore conducted a second study, in which the patients were questioned about major events in their lives on the basis of information supplied by relatives. Four periods were identified: 'primary school', 'junior high school', 'high school' and 'young adult life'. During PTA there was a clear temporal gradient, with early memories being recalled much better than later ones; but when PTA cleared, this gradient disappeared.

This discrepancy can be accounted for if the two types of RA test address different forms of memory. In chapter 8 it was suggested that the recall of early personal experiences may depend less on the recall of specific experiences than does that of later events. This is because people build up some general reconstruction of their earlier years, which exists independently of memory for the original events. The temporal gradient in recalling personal experiences may reflect patients' reliance on this form of memory. By contrast, knowledge of a TV series may depend more on remembering particular experiences, and the patients' uniform inability to remember them suggests that episodic memory is comprehensively impaired during PTA.

The assessment of RA during PTA can be complicated by a phenomenon known as 'shrinking RA', as demonstrated in the following case (Benson and Geschwind, 1967). A 33-year-old man was admitted to hospital after a head injury which initially rendered him stuporous but not unconscious. He was known to be separated from his wife and family (who lived in Washington), and had lived in Boston for the last two years. In Washington he worked as a bus driver, but in Boston he had held two different jobs, as a messenger and a labourer. During the first week after his accident, a number of mental impairments were apparent; but within a month, these had disappeared except for a severe amnesia. He was very disoriented, and thought he was still living in Washington. This continued for about three months, when suddenly he became concerned about his memory disorder, and his memory for new information showed signs of improvement. His RA also began to lessen; first he remembered the break-up of his marriage, followed by recollection of the first job he had had in Boston. A few days later memory of the second job returned, and by the time the patient was discharged, he had amnesia only for the 24-hour period preceding his injury.

The phenomenon of shrinkage is consistent with the view that earlier memories can be derived from a different source to that needed for the recall of more recent experiences. At the outset a victim of PTA may be wholly reliant on their general knowledge about themselves, which, as we have noted, will be more extensive for earlier periods of life. As recovery occurs, the episodic record becomes increasingly available, and more recent experiences can be recounted. The temporal gradient in this recovery could be explained by suggesting that older experiences are more broadly distributed than newer experiences (this seems reasonable, because older experiences will have been recounted more, and with each retelling, a new memory of that experience is formed). It follows, therefore, that a gradual recovery process will restore some components of older memories before more narrowly distributed newer memories.

An important issue is whether all patients who experience only brief periods of PTA (so-called minor head injuries) recover their memory ability completely. This was certainly the conclusion of many studies. Russell and Smith (1961) found that only 10 per cent of patients with a brief PTA (less than one hour) showed memory difficulties at a later date, compared with 56 per cent whose PTA duration was more than seven days. Similarly, Dikmen and colleagues (1987) reported little evidence of long-term impairment in their sample of survivors. However, a study by Leininger and co-workers (1990) presents a less optimistic view. They studied 53 patients referred for neuropsychological assessment following a minor head injury (all patients had very brief periods of PTA), and found that all of them were significantly impaired on a number of memory tests. Comparing their results with earlier negative studies, they note a number of discrepancies. First, all their patients were referred because they had memory difficulties; thus their sample may represent a subset of mild cases susceptible to long-term impairment. Second, nearly all their cases were victims of motor accidents, and this, because of the greater opportunity for serious injury it provides, may be more likely to cause memory loss. In addition, their subjects were older, thus making them more vulnerable to the effects of brain injury *per se*.

On balance, it seems that a percentage of those who suffer transient episodes of PTA do sustain mild degrees of permanent impairment. However, assuming that any impairment of this kind relates directly to the preceding injury needs to be treated with caution. First, patients showing these deficits may be suffering from illnesses that are adversely affecting their memory (e.g. depression), or they may be taking drugs which impair memory (see later). Second, there is always the possibility that a proportion of these patients are exaggerating their memory impairment for financial gain – so-called malingering (see next chapter). Finally, a person's history should not be overlooked in that the deficit observed might relate to an earlier injury (see e.g. Snoek et al., 1984; Wrightson et al., 1995).

Electro-convulsive Therapy (ECT) and Memory

Few medical treatments have stirred up so much controversy as ECT. Developed in Italy by Cerletti and Bini, ECT is often thought to have been inspired by the Roman tradition of applying electric eels to the head as a cure for madness. In fact, the origins of ECT go back only 70 years, to the Hungarian psychiatrist Meduna. He noted a number of studies reporting that schizophrenia and epilepsy did not occur in the same patient, and speculated that induction of a seizure similar to that experienced in epileptic fits might cure schizophrenia. Meduna induced seizures with camphor and other pharmacological treatments, and claimed success in the treatment of schizophrenia. Cerletti and Bini extended Meduna's work by exploring whether seizures caused by brief electric shocks could achieve similar results. Their first patient was a chronic schizophrenic who received two shocks delivered from electrodes placed either side of his head. The second caused him to burst into song, a sign of apparent therapeutic success. A further seven treatments were given, and a two-year follow-up showed that the patient was leading a normal life.

Because of its simplicity and low cost, the use of ECT spread rapidly, and by the 1950s it was a major form of treatment for depression and other disorders, including schizophrenia. The discovery of psychotropic drugs has since led to a substantial decline in the use of ECT, but it is still a widespread form of treatment. Modern ECT is very different from that used in its heyday. When first developed, ECT was given while the patient was fully conscious. This form of the treatment, which was vividly depicted in the film *One Flew over the Cuckoo's Nest*, produced violent grand mal seizures, which often had unpleasant side-effects. In contemporary ECT, the patient is anaesthetized and then given a muscle relaxant to minimize the physical effects of the seizure. After the seizure, oxygenation is used to facilitate the patient's immediate recovery. The seizure is induced by electrodes placed either bilaterally or unilaterally in the temporal lobe region, and two electrical wave forms can be used: sinusoidal or brief pulse.

Our concern will be with the effects of ECT on memory, the broader issue of its therapeutic effectiveness being beyond the scope of this book. ECT has an obvious, immediate and highly disruptive effect on brain function. On regaining consciousness, the post-ECT patient shows many similarities to a victim of PTA (see above). They are disoriented, confused, unable to respond in a coherent manner, and there is a dense anterograde amnesia. As time progresses, there is a gradual recovery of function, although this is not even, in that orientation in place typically precedes orientation in time.

Testing of memory during the post-ECT recovery phase reveals a substantial impairment. Various forms of recall task, such as paired-associate learning and memory for stories, show a clear anterograde amnesia. In one study Squire et al. (1981b) showed a series of pictures to patients who had received bilateral ECT only 2 hours previously. Their memory for the pictures was then tested 2 hours and 32 hours later. Whilst in the ECT recovery phase, they showed very rapid forgetting, compared with their performance on the same test four months after treatment.

Pre-existing memory is also disrupted by ECT. Squire and colleagues (1981b) gave ECT patients an interview concerning important events in their lives. These answers provided a basis for assessing the patients' episodic memory after ECT. Knowledge of public events was measured using the TV programme test described earlier. One week after ECT there was evidence of considerable RA, but after seven months, all that remained was an amnesia for the days preceding the treatment and a suggestion of some impairment for events in the preceding year – the study was done around the time of 'Watergate', and many of the patients had difficulty recalling these very publicized events. Importantly, memories did not recover with cueing, thus suggesting that they had been permanently lost from memory. More recently, Calev and co-workers (1989) have also shown that remote memory is affected by ECT, using a questionnaire about public events.

Practitioners of ECT agree that treatment results in a small amount of RA for events immediately before the seizure and a degree of amnesia for the treatment period. These deficits are assumed to reflect a transient derangement of memory processes, not any permanent disability. Opponents of ECT claim that it produces more substantial effects on memory. In assessing this argument, one can start by considering the effects of ECT on the physical nature of the brain; if ECT causes permanent memory loss, this might be detected in a neuropathological examination. Since its inception, there has been concern about possible neuropathological changes following ECT. Cerletti himself spent two years investigating the brains of electrically stunned cattle before concluding that ECT was safe to use on humans. The safety of ECT was addressed in a study by Devanand and co-workers (1991), who examined cognitive function and subjective memory complaints of eight people who had each received more than 100 ECT treatments. Despite this intense level of ECT, these patients were found to be no different from eight similar patients who had never received ECT. Following this, a more extensive study by the same authors evaluated whether ECT causes structural brain damage by reviewing the literature on cognitive side-effects, brain imaging, post-mortem data, and the experimental simulation of ECT in animals. In no case was there good evidence that ECT caused any permanent brain damage.

Opponents of ECT place great store by anecdotal reports of permanent loss of memory following treatment. However, these reports usually come from uncontrolled studies based mainly on subjective evidence. The question of whether ECT causes permanent memory failure can only be answered properly by experiments which disentangle the lasting effects of the seizures from other contributory factors. One approach might be to find ECT patients who are complaining about their memory and see if they really show memory impairment. Freeman and colleagues (1980) wrote a newspaper article entitled 'Is there any harm in shock treatment?' It finished with the message 'if YOU have had ECT ... and reckon it has had an adverse effect on you, the group would be grateful if you would help by allowing them to test your memory and ability to think quickly, and see how you compare with other people. It would only take an hour or so . . . and there are no shocks in store. That's a promise!'

The recruits, plus some additional ECT patients, were found to perform worse on memory tests than control subjects. When the influence of residual depression and medication on memory performance was allowed for, the differences between the groups became smaller, but remained significant. Despite this, the authors were unable to conclude that ECT had a lasting effect on memory. First, it was possible that the ECT group may have had a lower than average memory capability before treatment. Before ECT the patients may not have noticed this, but after experiencing the treatment, they may have monitored their memory more carefully in the belief that it might be permanently damaged. Thus a failure of memory prior to ECT would not have raised comment, but subsequent to ECT would be regarded as a sign of impairment, leading them to volunteer for the study. Added to this, recruitment of subjects who believed that their memories were affected might have resulted in poorer levels of task motivation in the ECT group compared with controls.

To avoid these interpretive difficulties, Weeks and colleagues (1980) studied 51 depressed patients who went on to receive ECT, and compared them with two control groups: a group of 51 depressed subjects who did not receive ECT, but were carefully matched to the ECT group in terms of age, sex, class, education and severity of depression, and a group of normal individuals matched in the same way with the exception of depressive symptoms. The ECT group were tested at the outset of the study, and then one week, three months and six months after the termination of treatment (the average was 7.2 treatments). Control subjects were tested at similar intervals except for the test session given one week after ECT. One week after ECT the experimental group showed pronounced impairments, but at three months there was little difference between them and the two control groups. Finally, after six months, the only significant finding was slightly better recall by the ECT group on the logical memory component of the Wechsler Memory Scale (WMS).

The data of Weeks and his co-workers are consistent with a number of other studies in showing no permanent impairment of memory following ECT. However, failure to detect memory impairments may be because standard memory tests are insensitive to the particular impairments produced by ECT. A typical complaint of ECT patients is an inability to remember events occurring in the time period preceding the treatment. Janis (1950) used an autobiographical memory test similar to that used by Squire and colleagues (see above), and found evidence of substantial impairments three months after ECT. However, he concluded that motivational factors may have played a role, because amnesia was most evident for 'experiences which tend to arouse anxiety, guilt, or a lowering or self-esteem'. The strongest evidence for a more extensive, permanent RA following ECT comes from the study by Squire and co-workers described earlier. They found an impairment in the retrieval of both personal memories and public events for the preceding year. If forgetting was determined purely by the personal content of memories, this would not explain the poor performance on the second type of test, since this presumably involves emotionally neutral information.

The controversy surrounding ECT is likely to continue for some time, and the question of whether it affects memory permanently is likely to figure strongly in these arguments. We have considered only a small amount of the evidence, but some interim conclusions can be drawn. Studies which have examined the long-term effects of ECT and have controlled for the influence of extraneous factors indicate that ECT does not have any extensive effect on permanent memory function. All patients show a degree of RA for events immediately preceding ECT and the treatment period itself. The only objective evidence for a more severe impairment is Squire and colleagues' (1981b) finding; but, as Fink (1984) points out, the year preceding ECT represents the height of the patient's morbidity, and this may be the cause of amnesia.

If ECT does not permanently affect memory, why are there so many complaints from patients and individual case histories reporting long-term deficits? We have already noted that experiencing ECT may cause patients to conclude falsely that their memory is impaired. Squire and Slater (1983) examined a group of ECT patients, and found significant differences between patients who complained of memory difficulties and those who did not. Complainers tended to believe that ECT had been an ineffective treatment for their depression; thus their self-assessment of memory might have reflected their continuing illness rather than a true loss of memory. Furthermore, complainers tested three years after ECT maintained that they had memory problems of an 'amnesic type', even though there were no objective signs of such a problem. Squire and Slater suggest that these complaints are 'based on the experience of amnesia initially associated with ECT and reflect a persisting, and perhaps altogether natural, tendency to question whether memory functions have fully recovered' (p. 6).

Although these subjective inaccuracies are likely to be at the root of many complaints following ECT, they seem insufficient to account for all such reports. One problem is that most studies report their results in terms of group averages with little or no information about the performance of particular individuals. Thus within a large number of individuals receiving ECT a few individuals may be susceptible, but their presence is masked by an averaging procedure (Weiner, 1984). However, for a very different view of ECT, see Cameron (1994).

Drug-induced Amnesia

A wide range of drugs are known to influence memory. The most well-known of these is ethanol, whose effects on human memory may be familiar to many of you reading this book! The nature of memory in alcoholics was considered briefly in chapter 6, and there is further discussion in chapter 10. This section will be concerned with some other drugs known to have amnesic effects in humans.

Hallucinogenic drugs often seem to impair memory, but it is not clear whether this is a genuine effect on memory or due to some more general cognitive derangement induced by the drug. Because of its widespread use, there has been considerable interest in the effects of marijuana on memory. Anecdotal reports suggest that there is an impairment of memory whilst under the influence of marijuana. Comments such as 'My memory span for conversation is shortened, so that I may forget what the start of the sentence was about even before the sentence is finished' and 'If I read while stoned, I remember less of what I've read hours later than if I had been straight' are commonplace amongst marijuana-users (Tart, 1972).

Experimental studies generally confirm these subjective views. Abel (1971), for example, examined subjects' performance on the free recall task with and without marijuana intoxication. He measured both immediate and delayed performance, and found that intoxicated subjects recalled less than normal subjects from the early parts of the list, but that there was no difference in the recency effect for the two groups. This suggests that LTS function is disrupted by marijuana intoxication, but in what way? Darley and colleagues (1974) identified two groups of subjects, and gave each subject a series of free recall trials, on which the two groups produced similar levels of recall. One group was then given marijuana, and one hour later both groups were given recall and recognition tests for the first set of lists. The drugged group performed as well as the control group on both kinds of test. While the drugged subjects were still intoxicated, the experimental procedure was repeated with ten new lists. With immediate testing they recalled less from the earlier list positions than the controls, but showed normal recency, and at delayed testing they recalled and recognized fewer words than the controls. Because the marijuana group were able to remember the first set of lists normally, even though they were intoxicated, but in a similar state showed impairments on the second list, indicates that marijuana affects the acquisition of new information rather than its retrieval.

Wetzel and colleagues (1982) examined remote memory during marijuana intoxication using the TV programmes test described earlier. The marijuana group did not differ from a placebo group on this test, but were found to be impaired on their ability to learn a word list. This result concurs with the results of Darley and co-workers by locating the deficit in the storage of new information rather than retrieval of existing memories. We should also note that marijuana can exert state-dependent effects, possibly because it induces subjects to make unusual associations during learning (see page 47). Linked with this is a study by Stacy (1995), who showed that marijuana-users' associations to ambiguous cues were related to their drug habit, thus suggesting that the generation of drug associations may partly underlie addiction to the drug.

Before leaving the topic of marijuana, we should also note that a number of studies now suggest that chronic marijuana use can have effects of extending beyond the period of intoxication. Pope and colleagues (1995) reviewed a number of studies, and found that deficits on tasks of attention, psychomotor tasks and memory were still detectable 12–24 hours after drug use. However, evidence for longer-term impairment was not found. Finally, female marijuana-users should note studies showing that use of the drug during pregnancy can affect the memory performance of children (Fried and Watkinson, 1990).

The **benzodiazepines** are an important class of psychoactive drugs, the best-known of which are probably lorazepam (ativan) and diazepam (valium). They can be used either as a hypnotic (to promote sleep) or an anxiolytic (to reduce anxiety). Under normal conditions of use, benzodiazepines can impair mental function, including memory. Ativan taken as an overnight hypnotic, for example, produces a small memory impairment when subjects are tested the following morning (File and Bond, 1979). However, if given under appropriate conditions, some benzodiazepines can induce a temporary amnesic state. Brown and colleagues (1983) gave doses of intravenous diazepam or lorazepam to a group of medical students. The drugs had no appreciable effect on memory span, but produced a marked anterograde amnesia. Neither drug had any effect on the recall of information presented shortly before drug administration, indicating that the drugs impair some aspect of acquisition. File and co-workers (1992) examined the effects of lorazepam on performance of a range of tasks, and found that they were restricted to tests involving episodic memory, with those entailing semantic memory and implicit memory unaffected – findings which, with some exceptions, are characteristic of benzodiazepine effects more generally (see Polster, 1993; Danion et al., 1993, for reviews).

Benzodiazepine-induced amnesia for events recently made news when several Parisian prostitutes were prosecuted for extortion. Their method was to 'lace' their clients' drinks with valium – a cocktail which resulted in temporary amnesia. In this condition the clients wrote cheques for large amounts of money, but when 'sobered up' could remember nothing about the experience. Fortunately there are more constructive uses for this induced amnesia. Dentists now routinely use benzodiazepines as a means of sedating patients with dental phobia. One procedure involves giving the drug midazolam to promote relaxation, and, once the procedure is over, using the drug flumazenil to counteract the sedation. This procedure is very effective in that it both sedates the patient and renders them amnesic for the events of the surgery, thereby preventing the retention of negative experiences that might enhance the phobia (e.g. Bigl et al., 1992; see also File et al., 1991).

Memory and Anaesthesia

For a number of reasons one would expect – indeed hope – that general anaesthesia would render us incapable of remembering anything during the time we were unconscious. However, there are a number of grounds to suspect that this reasonable assumption is wrong. Suspicions about learning during anaesthesia were first aroused in a study that would be unlikely to gain ethical approval nowadays. Levinson (1965) arranged for ten dental patients to be exposed to a mock crisis while undergoing general anaesthesia. This involved the anaesthetist suddenly announcing 'Stop the operation. I don't like the patients' colour. His lips are much too blue. I'm going to give a little oxygen.' Thankfully, patients had little explicit recall of these events, but four of them were able to repeat what the anaesthetist said when tested under hypnosis.

There are a number of problems with this study. First, as we saw in chapter 3, hypnosis is a highly questionable means of facilitating accurate retrieval from memory, and it is possible that some of the recall arose from suggestion rather than genuine recollection. There is also the question of whether the patients were all properly anaesthetized. The possibility that people could learn during anaesthesia has been extensively reviewed by Andrade (1995), and a number of important points come out of her study. Most important, perhaps, is that there is no good evidence that patients can have explicit recall for events during an operation provided that they have been properly anaesthetized. However, when implicit tests of memory are considered, there appears to be good evidence that some learning can take place.

Jelicic and colleagues (1992b) used a conceptual priming task in which subjects were presented with category exemplars while under an anaesthetic and were then, after the operation, required to generate exemplars to category cues. They found that subjects were more likely to give exemplars presented during the operation, thus suggesting that some memory had been acquired despite the anaesthesia. Kihlstrom and co-workers (1990) presented anaesthetized subjects with 'cue–target' paired associates, and then, about an hour after awakening, asked subjects to free-associate to the first member of each pair. Subjects had no explicit memory for the word pairs, but produced the response words with an above chance probability when asked to free-associate to the cue words. Other studies have reported similar types of result (e.g. Humphreys et al., 1990), but some have not (e.g. Eich et al., 1985).

Jelicic and colleagues (1992a) claimed that subjects could learn the answers to obscure general knowledge questions during an operation, but in a subsequent study failed to get the same finding (Jelicic et al., 1993). Preference judgement tasks also yield conflicting results. Block and co-workers (1991) presented patients with unfamiliar nonsense words, and post-operatively found that patients preferred those words to novel non-words even though they could not remember hearing them. However, a comparable study involving unfamiliar melodies failed to show any implicit preference (Winograd et al., 1990).

Inconsistencies in the influence of anaesthetics on memory are difficult to resolve, because there appear to be so many methodological differences between the studies. However, a study by Schwender and colleagues (1993) does suggest one interesting possibility. Patients undergoing surgery were played the story of Robinson Crusoe while attached to an electro-encephalogram (EEG) monitor which enabled the pattern of brain activity associated with different anaesthetic administrations to be examined. EEG monitoring showed that cortical activity during story presentation with one type of anaesthetic was similar to that in the awake brain, whereas in two other groups the anaesthetics did not allow this activity. Implicit memory was assessed by asking subjects to free-associate to the word 'Friday'. Half the patients who had an 'awake' pattern of brain activity showed priming in that they produced 'Robinson Crusoe' as a response to 'Friday', but none of the other patients, including a group of non-exposed subjects, did. This finding suggests that implicit memory in anaesthesia may depend on using anaesthetics which do not block aspects of brain activity associated with the conscious processing of information (see also Schwender et al., 1994).

Memory during Pregnancy and the Menopause

Studies of cognitive performance during and after pregnancy are scarce, which is surprising given the physical, hormonal and emotional changes that occur at this point in a woman's life. Hormonal changes, in particular, are known to influence memory, so there is good reason to expect that a pregnant woman's memory may be different in some way. Poser and co-workers (1986), using data from questionnaires detailing 67 pregnancies, revealed that 28 women had difficulties in reading, confusion, disorienta-tion and forgetfulness, and that all these women regarded these symptoms as normal features of pregnancy, even though the number of women in this group was less than that in the group which did not exhibit these symptoms. They defined this group of cognitive disturbances as 'benign encephalopathy of pregnancy', and claim that it is transient, is not due to either sleepiness, lack of concentration or irritability, that its aetiology is unknown, and that, being mild, it can easily be overcome or compensated for by simply becoming aware of its existence.

A few researchers have recently undertaken experimental studies of pregnancy and memory impairment. In a Swedish project, Silber and co-workers (1990) examined the performance of pregnant women on several cognitive tests of both memory and attention. Tests were administered in five stages spanning more than a year, beginning with the end of pregnancy and finishing at 12 months post-partum. They found that the pregnant women's performance on some of the tests improved significantly more than controls after the 6- and 12-months testing. They attempted to correlate this improvement with falling levels of plasma oxytocin, but were unsuccessful. However, the pregnant subjects did have significantly higher levels of plasma oxytocin up to 3 months post-partum.

Brindle and colleagues (1991) attempted to discover any differences between the performance of primagravidae and multigravidae pregnant women on tests of both explicit and implicit memory (see chapter 3). They found that primagravidae in their second trimester of pregnancy showed an impairment in implicit memory, as measured by word stem completion, compared to multigravidae and controls. They also discovered that this impairment in implicit memory correlated with lower subjective ratings of memory ability in the primagravidae group. A later study by Sharp and colleagues (1993) has provided more information concerning memory loss during pregnancy. Eight separate tests plus a self-assessment of memory were administered in total. Recall, recognition and priming memory were tested, and both primagravidae and multigravidae pregnant women were compared to control subjects. Both pregnant groups revealed a deficit in a recall test involving the incidental learning of word lists, and also in two measures of priming memory (word stem completion and pronunciation priming). This corresponded with results from the subjective rating, in which 81 per cent of the pregnant women considered their memory to be worse at the time of the experiment compared to before becoming pregnant.

As well as providing objective evidence concerning the relation between pregnancy and memory, the study of Brindle and co-workers (1991) is of particular interest, because it gives evidence for a variable that affects implicit memory while leaving explicit memory intact. The study of Sharp and colleagues (1993) also indicates an effect of pregnancy on implicit memory, but here it is noticeable that on tests of recall the pregnant women also show an impairment, even though there is no equivalent deficit on a test of recognition. There is a possibility, therefore, that the apparent deficit in implicit memory might be mediated by a pregnancy-induced impairment in explicit memory, the argument being that, despite overt task demands, subjects confronted with a word stem completion task may well attempt to recall the learning episode as an aid to responding.

Before leaving this topic, we must also consider the effects of the **menopause** on memory. A number of studies employing subjective report methods have suggested that the menopause causes increased forgetfulness. Polit and LaRocco (1980) found that 25 per cent of their sample reported forgetfulness, but that this was linked to lower levels of health and education and in mothers who had children at a relatively early age. More recently, Mathews and co-workers (1994) found that forgetfulness characterized 35 per cent of menopausal women, and that the symptom was most noticeable at the onset of the menopause. Two studies (Phillips and Sherwin, 1992; Kampen and Sherwin, 1994) have examined memory in women who have had the menopause induced surgically and then been treated with oestrogen to alleviate effects. By measuring memory before and after treatment it has been possible to examine whether any memory impairment stems specifically from hormonal deficiencies caused by the menopause. Both studies have shown memory improvement in oestrogen-treated women in comparison with untreated women. Most recently Kimura (1995) has suggested that there may be a direct link between lowered oestrogen in the post-menopausal period and intellectual ability.

Transient disorders of organic origin arise from a number of causes, including transient cerebral ischemia, toxins, head injury, ECT and drugs. All these disorders are characterized by anterograde amnesia, but RA varies between conditions. At a general level these disorders have the same characteristics as the amnesic syndrome. TGA and drug-induced amnesia appear to be completely reversible phenomena, whereas PTA may leave its victims with some residual impairment. ECT does not appear to damage memory permanently, although the possibility that some individuals might be peculiarly susceptible needs to be considered. Memory also appears to be temporarily impaired during pregnancy, and forgetfulness is also associated with the menopause.

10 Psychogenic Disorders of Memory

On 8 November 1987 the people of Enniskillen, Northern Ireland, gathered for their annual Remembrance Day service. In the crowd was 60-year-old Gordon Wilson and his daughter Marie. Suddenly there was a terrible explosion: IRA terrorists had planted a bomb in the nearby community centre. Within moments Gordon Wilson and his daughter were buried in rubble. Gordon survived, but Marie died in hospital. Despite his own terrible sadness, Gordon bore no ill will to the terrorists, but he hoped that the awful events would be a turning-point in the affairs of the province. Gordon's message caught the imagination of the people, and it was repeated all over the world. More publicity followed: he was voted 'man of the year' by a national radio station, and the Queen mentioned him personally in her Christmas message. Pressure mounted for Gordon to lead a peace movement and make a lecture tour of the United States. All Gordon wanted was privacy, and one day his mind 'snapped' and he lost his memory. Sitting at the kitchen table, he asked his wife, 'Where's Marie? Surely she should be home by now' (Moller, 1988, p. 54).

Loss of memory in the absence of any detectable brain pathology is known as **psychogenic amnesia**, a name that reflects its psychological rather than organic cause. To avoid confusion, the reader should note that the term **functional amnesia** is often used as an alternative name for these disorders. Psychogenic amnesia, as exemplified in Gordon Wilson's case, almost always follows some unpleasant and emotionally disturbing set of events, and the degree of impairment can be extremely variable.

Psychogenic amnesias are known to be one sign of a class of mental illnesses known as **dissociative disorders**. These disorders all involve some breakdown in identity, but the extent is variable (note that in some of the older literature these disorders are referred to as **hysterias**). In **dissociative amnesia** there is an inability to remember specific sets of events. **Dissociative fugue** involves loss of personal identity and in some cases the adoption of a new identity. The third form is dissociative identity disorder, which is perhaps better known as **multiple personality**.

Dissociative Amnesia

The classic studies of dissociative amnesia were carried out by Janet (1904). One case concerned Irene, a 20-year-old girl who nursed her mother through a slow and painful terminal illness under squalid conditions. After her mother's death, Irene's behaviour changed radically. She accepted that her mother was dead, but could not remember how it had occurred. During dissociative amnesia, lost memories can often be recollected under special conditions. Thus Irene was able to recount their traumatic experiences when in a trance-like state which Janet described as 'somnambulism'. Similarly, Freud's 'Elizabeth von R.', through psychoanalysis, came to recall her wish that her sister might die so that she could marry her brother-in-law. However, as Erdeyli and Goldberg (1979) point out, there are difficulties in accepting such recall as the unequivocal return of lost memory. Many cases of hysterical amnesia involve matters of personal embarrassment, so the initial failure to remember might reflect a response bias in that the individual cannot face telling the examiner certain things that they have always been fully aware of. In addition, much of what is supposedly recalled in such situations may not be true, but unless the examiner has knowledge of what actually happened, this cannot be verified.

Amnesia for combat experience provides a more convincing demonstration of memory recovery. The amnesia has a straightforward origin, and the circumstances can often be verified independently. Grinker and Spiegel (1945) studied a large number of men who had developed amnesia following traumatic wartime episodes. They made use of the **sodium pentothal interview**, in which the patient is sedated by slow intravenous injection of the drug. Its first effect is to relieve any anxiety that the patient might be experiencing, followed by the development of drowsiness. At this point the injection is halted, and the interview begins. Because the interviewer knows the circumstances, he can cue the patient about the traumatic incident. As recall becomes more detailed, the subject may become more and more agitated, as this extract shows:

> The terror exhibited in moments of extreme danger, such as the imminent explosion of shells, the death of a friend before the patient's eyes . . . is electrifying to watch. The body becomes increasingly tense and rigid; the eyes widen and the pupils dilate, while the skin becomes covered in fine perspiration. The hands move about convulsively, seeking a weapon, or a friend to share the danger. The breathing becomes incredibly rapid and shallow. The intensity of the emotion sometimes becomes unbearable; and frequently, at the height of the reaction, there is collapse and the patient falls back in bed and remains

quiet . . . usually to resume the story at a more neutral point. (p. 80)

More recently, the effects of combat experience on memory have been studied within the broader context of **post-traumatic stress disorder** (PTSD). PTSD is a complex of symptoms induced by the experience of a traumatic event. These symptoms include anxiety and poor sleep along with vivid recollection and rumination about the precipitating trauma. At present, however, it is unclear whether vivid recollection of trauma is an essential element of PTSD. Layton and Wardi-Zonna (1995), for example, described two cases of PTSD where there was a clear dissociative amnesia for the trauma. McNally and colleagues (1995) studied groups of Vietnam War veterans who either did or did not have PTSD. The veterans were given an autobiographical cueing test (see chapter 8) in which they were asked to retrieve memories in response to either positive (e.g. 'loyal') or negative (e.g. 'guilty') cue words. PTSD subjects had difficulty with the task, particularly when it involved positive cues. Interestingly, this deficit was especially pronounced in veterans suffering from PTSD who were still wearing their army regalia (e.g. medals, uniform). Most subjects tended to concentrate their recall on more recent events, thus suggesting avoidance of war memories. However, PTSD veterans who still wore their regalia disproportionately retrieved memories from the war period, leading to the view that 'wearing regalia in everyday life may be emblematic of psychological fixation to a war fought more than two decades ago' (p. 619).

Dissociative Fugue

Dissociative fugue can be defined as the 'sudden onset of wandering with clouding of consciousness and a more or less complete amnesia for the event' (Berrington et al., 1956). During a fugue the patient is unaware that anything is wrong, and will often adopt a new identity. Fugues are identified only when the patient 'comes to', days, months or even years after the precipitating event, usually some distance from where they were originally living.

Most patients emerging from a fugue regain their normal identity and past history, the only amnesia being for events of the fugue period itself. Less commonly, patients may become aware that they have lost their identity, but progress no further. In these circumstances the patient has to adopt a new permanent identity and relearn skills. Akhtar and co-workers (1981) describe the case of a middle-aged woman found unconscious in a bookshop. On admission to hospital, the only sign of abnormality was a small bump on her head, presumably caused when she passed out. She showed no signs of mental impairment other than a total inability to remember her identity and past history. The investigators went to extreme lengths to find out who she was: the FBI were contacted, her fingerprints were taken, and the police circulated her picture to local hotels. Under hypnosis the patient never mentioned relatives, but frequently gave the names of friends and acquaintances. However, when these were traced, none of them could identify her. After two months she was discharged, at which time she 'guessed that she was 58 . . . unmarried, childless, Christian, and a legal secretary from somewhere in Illinois'. Being a competent secretary, she contacted various employment agencies, and, somewhat amusingly, turned up at the hospital where she had been studied to work for a day. As the authors note, 'She still did not know who she was or where she came from, but she was not a bad typist!' (p. 48).

A more typical fugue is illustrated in a report by Schacter and colleagues (1982) involving a 21-year-old man (PN) found wandering in Toronto. When stopped by the police, he had no identification, and could provide little useful information about himself. His picture was published in the local newspaper and identified by his cousin. PN did not recognize his cousin when she went to visit him, but she was able to tell the hospital that the patient's grandfather, to whom he had been very close, had died the previous week. When questioned, PN could not remember anything about his grandfather or the recent funeral. The next evening PN was watching a funeral sequence in the serial *Shogun*. This prompted him to remember his grandfather's death and the funeral. Over the new few days his amnesia cleared, and the only residual deficit was an inability to recall events occurring during the fugue state itself.

The investigators were able to test various aspects of PN's memory both during and after the clearance of his fugue. On standard memory and intelligence tests PN's ability changed little after he emerged from fugue. However, his responses to the autobiographical cueing procedure were markedly different on the two occasions. Whilst amnesic, almost all the memories he recalled referred to events during his four-day fugue state. Of those that referred to earlier experiences, most related to one specific time, suggesting that some 'islands' of past memory survived the fugue. When the fugue had cleared, the cueing procedure elicited very few memories from the fugue period, with the vast majority relating to the patient's life prior to this.

Dissociative Identity Disorder (Multiple Personality)

No discussion of psychogenic memory disorders would be complete without some discussion of **multiple personality disorder** (MPD). Because of their dramatic nature, multiple personalities have been the subject of intense media interest, and a number of popular books describing individual cases have appeared (e.g. The *Three Faces of Eve*, Thigpen and

Cleckley, 1957). This has given rise to concerns that many apparent cases of MPD are a product of cultural suggestion – a proposal which would explain why MPD has been transformed from a rare condition to an 'epidemic' during the last few years. There are also arguments that MPD may be 'iatrogenic', in that the diagnosis is manufactured by psychiatrists with a commitment to believing in the existence of the disorder (e.g. Merskey, 1992; Seltzer, 1994).

The problem of accepting multiple personality is illustrated by the case of the 'Hillside Strangler'. Kenneth Bianchi was charged with the rape and murder of several women, but despite strong evidence against him, he persistently denied his guilt, and claimed that he could remember nothing about the crimes. Under hypnosis, however, another personality called 'Steve' emerged. He was very different from Ken, and claimed responsibility for the murders. When removed from the hypnotic trance, Ken Bianchi could apparently remember nothing of the conversations Steve had engaged in with the hypnotist.

If two or more personalities can co-exist within the same individual, it creates difficult legal problems. In Bianchi's case, prosecution of Ken could be seen as unjust, because it was Steve who had committed the crimes. However, the ruling went against Bianchi, because the court refused to accept that he genuinely possessed two personalities. A number of psychologists pointed out that Bianchi's other personality emerged only in hypnotic sessions, in which the examiner informed him that he would reveal another part of himself. In the discussion of hypnosis in chapter 3, we saw that a major problem with interpreting hypnotic effects on memory is compliance. In Bianchi's case, hypnosis allowed the suggestion that another personality could exist, and Bianchi may have seized the opportunity to confess by complying in this manner. Furthermore, his general knowledge about psychiatric diagnosis and the features of multiple personality may have provided Bianchi with a basis for responding more convincingly.

In MPD the individual appears to have two or more very distinct identities with correspondingly different memories and personalities. The various *alter egos* of the patient are often separated by an 'amnesic barrier', so one personality may not know of the existence of some or all of the other personalities. However, it is notable that clinical diagnosis of MPD does not require 'inter-personality amnesia' to be present, and this may in part explain the apparently high incidence of the disorder.

A typical MPD case is described by Schacter and colleagues (1989). This 24-year-old woman, known as IC, had four *alter egos*: Heather, Joan, Gloria and Alpha. All the *alter egos* were aware of each other, but IC herself knew nothing of any of them. IC was given an autobiographical cueing task, and, like typical young subjects (see p. 138), she tended to recall very recent events. However, her bias towards recent events was somewhat exaggerated, and a further test showed that she was unable to remember any event from before the age of ten.

The absence of childhood memories in IC suggests that the genesis of MPD may involve a history of sexual abuse, and indeed, there was other evidence indicating this. The use of multiple personality to cope with childhood abuse is neatly demonstrated by the case of 'Lucy' (Coons et al., 1982). Hospitalized following a drug overdose, Lucy had been suffering from amnesia and hallucinations for two years as a result of being raped. Psychological examination revealed that she had four 'personalities'. Aside from her normal friendly personality there was 'Linda', an aggressive person whom she used when recounting the physical and sexual abuse she endured as a young child; 'Sally', a distrustful secluded person whom she used to give accounts of the rape incident; and 'Sam', an imaginary male character who served to rescue her when she was feeling suicidal. More recently, Bryant (1995) described a patient, HS, who was only willing to talk about traumatic events when in an alternative child personality.

As we have seen, MPD patients may have a degree of inter-personality amnesia. Nissen and co-workers (1988) investigated this in a woman who had manifest 22 different personalities. These included 'Alice', who was studying to be a ministerial counsellor; 'Charles', a profane and aggressive heavy drinker; 'Ellen', who enjoyed bird-watching; and 'Gloria', an artist and one of three left-handed personalities. Gloria was also the only one to adopt a different surname so that she could get her own social security number. The patient was able to change personalities at the request of her psychiatrist, and Nissen and her colleagues used this to examine what one personality might be able to remember about information presented to another. On tests of explicit learning there appeared to be little transfer across personalities, in that successive presentations of, for example, a short story, to several of the personalities did not result in an upward trend in the amount retained. But implicit memory testing yielded a different picture. Both perceptual identification (see figure 10.1) and fragment completion were facilitated when the priming stimulus was presented to a different personality. However, on implicit tests involving more conceptual information (e.g. interpreting an ambiguous paragraph), there was little evidence of transfer. Nissen and co-workers concluded that inter-personality transfer occurred only for information that could not be differentially interpreted by the different personalities.

Explanations of Dissociative Memory Disorders

Since dissociative amnesias involve the disruption of episodic memory, there is a temptation to make comparisons with temporary organic amnesias (see chapter 9). However, there are important differences which rule out a common explanation. First, organic disorders almost always produce anterograde amnesia (although see the discussion of focal retro-grade amnesia in chapter 6). Psychogenic disorders, by contrast, show the reverse, being, with just one or two exceptions, exclusively retrograde in nature. Second, loss of personal identity – the defining feature of fugue – rarely occurs in even the most severe organic disorders. Similarly, multiple personality has never been reported as a symptom of organic brain injury. Finally, the observation that psychogenic amnesia can often be alleviated by procedures such as the pentothal interview has no parallel in organic disorders.

Janet (1904) was probably the first to offer a comprehensive account of dissociative amnesia and fugue. Under normal conditions, psychological functions, including memory, were assumed to be integrated within a unified personality. However, under adverse conditions, such as an emo-tionally disturbing experience, it was possible for memories to become detached from personal identity and therefore impossible to recall. Janet believed that the appearance of hysterical amnesia was genetically deter-mined. Each individual possessed a certain amount of 'energy' which bound together different elements of the personality; psychogenic amnesia

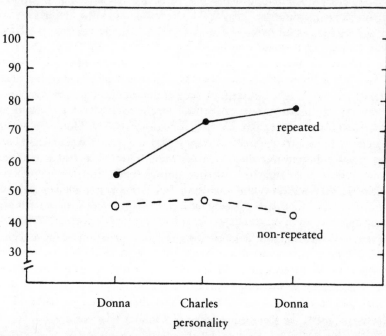

Figure 10.1 Data from Nissen et al., 1988, showing results of a perceptual identification experiment involving two personalities contained within the same person. Words shown initially to 'Donna' were subsequently identified more easily by 'Charles', and this effect remained when the words were shown a third time to 'Donna'.

was most likely to occur, therefore, in individuals whose level of energy was low. Janet's theory was physiological, in that the prime determinant of hysterical amnesia was the individual's innate level of 'mental energy'.

Modern accounts of dissociative disorders attribute them to the operation of **repression**. According to this idea, memory is a dynamic system in which memories containing information injurious to the ego can be suppressed. In this way the memory system could produce a 'defence reaction' that suppresses unpleasant experiences. The concept of repression is mainly associated with Freud, although its origins as an explanation of forgetting stem from the philosopher Nietzsche. Freud's concept of repression is linked specifically with his theory of personality; thus the key factor determining forgetting is the relevance of memories to the individual's psycho-sexual status. Few memory researchers would endorse this view, but the more general claim, that memory has a self-defence capability, is considered by many to be a useful framework for understanding psychogenic memory disorders. It explains why dissociative disorders occur only following adverse events; moreover, it is consistent with the high incidence of depression and other psychiatric disorders in patients subsequently developing psychogenic disorders. This correlation has led some to suppose that psychogenic disorders may be a means of avoiding depression or suicide – an idea expressed in the term 'fugue' which derives from the Latin *fugere*, meaning to run away or flee.

A recent example of how a repressive mechanism might allow a better mental life is described by Kaminer and Lavie (1991). They examined sleep patterns and dream recall in well-adjusted and less-adjusted survivors of the Holocaust. The less-adjusted group took longer to get to sleep, and their sleep pattern was poorer – both symptomatic of PTSD. However, when subjects in both groups were woken up at the point where their eye movements indicated that they were dreaming, the well-adjusted survivors were significantly less able to recall their dreams. The authors argue that the decreased dream recall may be one factor facilitating better adjustment, and this ability may be attributable to some form of repressive mechanism operating.

Even if we accept the 'defence reaction' interpretation of dissociative amnesia and fugue, it is still necessary to explain how memory can be organized to produce sudden and selective forgetting of past events and, in more extreme cases, loss of personal identity. In chapter 2 we saw that a crucial property of episodic memories was their self-referential quality; episodic memories have meaning only because they relate to the individual. Similarly, the fact that an individual can reflect on a set of personal experiences provides an essential component of identity. In an argument that has some similarities with Janet's proposed 80 years earlier, Schacter and colleagues (1982) have proposed that personal identity serves as a 'control element' under which episodic memories are organized. The process of repression might exert its effect by forcing a dissociation between episodic memory and personal identity. Where this dissociation is partial, a limited dissociative amnesia will arise; but when total dissociation occurs, a fugue develops, episodic memories can no longer be utilized, because their frame of reference is unavailable, and personal identity is lost because it cannot be anchored to any set of personal memories. This is a plausible theory, but we have yet to explain how memory is organized so as to allow these degrees of dissociation.

Morton (1994) has provided an account of dissociative amnesia in terms of his **headed records** account of memory. This model likens memory to a filing system in which, for each event, there is a folder which records the details of that event. To enable efficient search, it is suggested, each record is indexed with a heading that contains information about the record. At retrieval a description is formed, and only records matching that description are accessed. To explain dissociative states, Morton argues that the concept of 'self' may be lacking in the description used to search memory, thus rendering the vast majority of memories inaccessible. Turning to MPD, Morton argues that 'multiple self markers' are set up, with given events being associated with different markers, thus accounting for the frequent observation of inter-personality amnesia.

The type of account offered by Morton may perhaps explain a case that I studied with psychiatrist Hans Stampfer (Parkin and Stampfer, 1995). It entailed a woman known as Elizabeth, who, following a psychotic episode, found herself unable to remember much about her past. It was easy to see some value in this for her. Her childhood had been traumatic, she had been seriously assaulted, and her first child had died; but when we interviewed her, she felt that her only problem was that she could not remember her past. We decided to investigate her neuropsychological status, and, to our surprise, found that she had evidence of frontal lobe dysfunction. Her condition remained stable for several months, but then her amnesia began to lift, and, at the same time, evidence of frontal lobe impairment also disappeared.

While these events are purely circumstantial, they suggest that her amnesia may have been linked to an impairment of the frontal lobe processes involved in memory. This is perfectly feasible, as we saw in chapter 7 that damage to the frontal lobes can cause a disruption of retrieval. Thus to account for Elizabeth's amnesia, we need only suggest that a temporary disruption of these processes took place so as to prevent the recollection of episodes. Thus, in Morton's terms, her past memories were inaccessible because 'self' was not part of the description being used to specify memories of the past.

Any explanation of psychogenic disorders must also consider the possibility that organic factors may play some role. Kopelman and colleagues (1994) describe a London man, KG, who had been a credit controller and had embezzled a sum of £35,000. Immediately after being found out he experienced two episodes of fugue, one of which resulted in him turning up in Glasgow without any recollection of how he got there. Although these fugues lifted, thus supporting a psychogenic interpretation, KG has never been able to remember the offence he committed. As we shall see, psychogenic amnesia for crime is a well-known phenomenon, so its association with the experience of fugue should come as no great surprise. However, further investigation of KG showed that he had damage in both the frontal and temporal lobe region, and that his amnesia for the offence could have been genuine.

Amnesia and Crime

Amnesia for crime, especially homicide, has been widely documented. Surveys have shown that between 23 and 65 per cent of murderers have, or claim to have, amnesia for their crime. Other crimes appear to elicit amnesia with far less frequency, but where this occurs, the crimes are usually violent. Taylor and Kopelman (1984) examined 203 men on remand for violent and non-violent offences. Of these, 19 reported amnesia for their crimes of which nine were homicides, six entailed personal violence and arson, and four criminal damage. Amnesia was not observed in any one charged with a non-violent crime. Hopwood and Snell (1933) conducted a retrospective interview of 100 prisoners in Broadmoor who, at the time of their trials, had claimed amnesia for their crime. They concluded that 78 per cent of these amnesias were genuine, whereas the rest were either doubtful or fake. By contrast, a review by Schacter (1986a) claimed that 'many claims of amnesia after crimes are simulated'.

We will consider the issue of faking memory loss in more detail later, but for now note that there may not be a strict line between genuine and simulated psychogenic memory loss. O'Connell (1960) considered that many prisoners had a 'passive disregard' for their crimes; they knew that the memories were there, but somehow managed to keep them at bay. A good example of this is Ian Brady, one of the 'Moors murderers'. He was contacted by parents of children he was convicted of killing and asked where he had buried the bodies. At the time he refused to reply, noting that 'I have to keep the mental blocks up and keep control'. However, some years later, he showed the police where the bodies were.

Not all amnesia for crime has a psychogenic origin. First, there is a high incidence of schizophrenia and depression amongst criminals who cannot remember their crimes, both of which are disorders that can be associated with marked impairments of memory. Indeed, some have suggested that schizophrenia can produce a memory impairment as severe as that in the amnesic syndrome (McKenna et al., 1990, 1995).

Another line of explanation stems from the fact that many murders are committed during 'alcoholic black-outs'. According to a recent survey by Kopelman (1995a), about 35 per cent of amnesias associated with crime involve intoxication at the time of crime, and about 46 per cent of amnesic offenders are known to be alcohol abusers. Black-outs are a common phenomenon, occurring in both alcoholics and normal drinkers who overindulge. During a black-out the individual is not incapacitated, and is usually in possession of most mental faculties; the person is therefore drunk but not stuporous or unconscious. Two forms of black-out can be identified: an 'en bloc' form in which the black-out has a clear start and finish, with amnesia for the intervening events, with the individual knowing he has a 'lost period', and a form in which the individual is not aware that amnesia has occurred. In the latter case the individual may have exhibited memory lapses during the drinking bout (e.g. asking the same question repeatedly) but have no recollection of it.

In chapter 3 we considered the phenomenon of state-dependent learning, in which memories formed in one particular state were more easily remembered when subjects were in the same state at testing. Furthermore, a number of studies showed that alcoholic intoxication was an effective means of inducing these effects. This being so, alcoholic black-outs could be a form of state-dependent forgetting. A number of studies have explored this possibility, including a unique experiment carried out by Wolf (1980). If amnesia for crime committed during a state of drunkenness is due to state-dependent learning, then it should be possible, under appropriate conditions, to reinstate memory for the events. Wolf studied five Eskimos with a history of alcoholism who had been convicted of murder. All five were known to have been drunk when they committed the crime, and all of them claimed amnesia for that period. One subject, he wrote,

> drank 22 cans of beer over about 5 hr. He remembered leaving the bar with friends and later being held on the floor and choked. . . . He remembered nothing more until the next morning. In the first interval he went home, got his gun, came back the half mile to the bar, walked in, and without saying anything, raised his gun and shot the man next to him. He was then thrown to the floor and choked. Subsequently he was arraigned, booked and transported to the nearest jail, but remembered nothing of this. (p. 459)

As they became more intoxicated the convicts became increasingly angry, and their conversation was often accompanied by intense emotion, but at no time did any of the convicts recall the circumstances of their crime. When they sobered up, the convicts had varying degrees of amnesia for the events of the experiment.

On the assumption that Wolf's subjects were intoxicated at similar levels to those experienced during their crime, the above findings argue against a state-dependent explanation of amnesia for crime. This conclusion agrees with those of other studies (e.g. Goodwin, 1974; Lisman, 1974) which have also failed to confirm a state-dependent explanation of alcoholic black-outs.

These findings leave us with two possible explanations for alcohol-induced amnesia. It could, as some have argued, be of psychogenic origin, in that the individual represses knowledge of shameful acts committed during a black-out. There seem to be a number of arguments against this. Black-outs do not appear to be related to the nature of events occurring during the amnesic period. If the amnesia were of psychogenic origin, one would expect black-outs to be more frequent for unpleasant and embarrassing events. The behaviour of individuals observed during black-outs also argues against a psychogenic cause. Ryback (1971) observed a number of alcoholics during black-outs and noted a profound anterograde amnesia. As we saw earlier, psychogenic disorders almost always involve a selective RA (see also Hashtroudi et al., 1984). Finally, if black-outs were psychogenic in origin, it should be possible to reinstate memory for the lost period under conditions that have been effective with other disorders, but this is not the case. The generally accepted explanation is that black-outs arise because the original level of alcohol intoxication was sufficient to disrupt the physiological basis underlying memory formation.

Studies of alcoholic murderers therefore provide no support for a state-dependent learning interpretation of amnesia for crime. However, this conclusion does not lead us to entirely reject state-dependent learning as an explanation of amnesia for crime. In most circumstances crimes of violence are associated with states of extreme emotion that are unlikely to be experienced at any other time. There is some evidence that emotion itself, like alcohol and other psychoactive agents, can cause state-dependent learning. Briefly, it has been suggested that memories congruent with a subject's mood state are more easily recalled than those associated with a different mood (see chapter 3). Given this relationship, is it possible that some instances of amnesia for crime might be explicable in the same way?

At present there is little evidence to support this possibility. One problem lies in re-creating the emotional state presumed to have existed at the time the crime was committed, a much more difficult task than achieving a comparable level of intoxication! Bower (1981) has reported observations of Robert Kennedy's assassin, Sirhan Sirhan. Throughout his trial and subsequent imprisonment, Sirhan denied any memory of the assassination. Under hypnosis, however, a psychiatrist was able to induce in him a highly agitated state, at which point he began to 'scream out the death curses, "fire" the shots, and then choke as he re-experienced the Secret Service bodyguard nearly throttling him after he was caught'.

Bower suggests that Sirhan's amnesia may be of state-dependent origin; he is unable to remember because, without hypnotic assistance, he cannot re-create the highly emotional state associated with his memory of the crime. However, it must be said that not everyone accepts Bower's interpretation of Sirhan's case. Centor (1982) notes 'amnesia is easily feigned and difficult to disprove in criminal cases; in the 11-yr experience of the author . . . no case of psychological [psychogenic] amnesia in the absence of a psychotic episode, brain tumour, or brain syndrome was ever confirmed' (p. 240). While this is a strong claim, it alerts us to the topic of the next section. How can we be sure that someone with a psychogenic memory disorder is not just faking?

Malingering

Identifying **malingering**, the deliberate faking of impairments, can often be a difficult business. In 1930 a journal reported 'the first pure case of . . . complete and isolated loss of memory retention'. The patient, known as B, had been found unconscious at work overcome by carbon monoxide (CO) fumes. He quickly regained consciousness, and on initial assessment did not show evidence of memory impairment. He was discharged from hospital after a week, but reappeared about five weeks later, disoriented and complaining that his memory for recent events was 'nil'. His memory span was so poor that it was necessary to ask questions in very short forms and repeat them many times. He forgot instructions immediately, and seemed totally unable to remember anything new. By contrast, he was able to remember most of his life up until the accident, including events on the day itself.

The discovery of such a 'pure' memory deficit attracted considerable attention, but also aroused suspicion. It was noted that B was atypical with respect to other CO poisoning cases, and showed no signs of neurological impairment. Furthermore, the fact that compensation had still to be agreed shed further doubt on the authenticity of his amnesia. Initially B was co-operative with investigators, but, after some years, he refused to be examined further. This led two psychiatrists to adopt a rather devious means of observing him. Posing as tourists, they visited B's home town and made contact with him. At first B behaved normally, but when the 'tourists' revealed their true identity, he began to exhibit his amnesic symptoms and adopt an evasive manner (Zangwill, 1967).

The procedures used to investigate the true nature of B's amnesia were at times underhand and subject to ethical criticism. Fortunately there have been some important developments since then, in that specific procedures have been devised to 'catch out' people who are faking a memory disorder. The basis of these procedures is that people attempting to simulate a memory impairment are not conversant with the true nature of amnesia, and will therefore make mistakes.

The case of B probably provides us with a good example of malingered amnesia. First, there was an issue of compensation hanging over his case. It is well known that many victims of brain injury exaggerate their memory loss in an effort to increase the size of their damages payment (see e.g. Guthkelch, 1980). In many instances this is a blatant attempt at fraud, but not every patient is deliberately faking. Instead, the attempt to simulate memory loss may be linked to other aspects of the person's mental health. Pseudo-dementia, which we considered in chapter 8, resembles real dementia in many ways, but is entirely linked to other factors such as depression. In those seeking compensation, there may also be depression and anxiety, which, in turn, may lead the person to simulate a memory disorder – perhaps as a means of reducing responsibility for their predicament. This type of response may also occur in the absence of any financial inducement. The British comedian Tony Hancock, for example, was involved in a car accident in which he suffered a mild concussion. Following the accident, he claimed that his memory was defective, and insisted on performing 'The Blood Donor' almost entirely from mug boards. It is unlikely that he was performing in a state of post-traumatic amnesia; more likely, his brief experience of memory loss caused him a disproportionate, neurotic loss of confidence.

Returning to the case of B, we could, with reasonable certainty, predict that he would have had a reduced memory span. As we saw in chapter 6, memory span (usually measured by digit span) is almost always normal in amnesic patients, so B's apparent deficit should immediately have given cause for concern. In current clinical practice, reduced forward memory span is regarded as prime evidence for a malingered amnesia: the task appears to be quite hard, so the 'amnesic' person believes that they should perform badly, when in fact they should do well. We also saw in chapter 6 that skills tend to be preserved in amnesia, so impairment on tasks such as riding a bicycle also give rise to suspicion.

There are also a number of specific memory tests that have been devised by psychologists to identify patients who are pretending to be memory-impaired. One of the simplest was recently reported by Kapur (1995). Called the 'coin in hand' test, it involves placing a coin in one hand and then clenching the hands in a fist. Then, after a brief period of distraction, the subject is asked which hand the coin is in. Kapur found that patients who were densely amnesic had no trouble with this task, but a man suspected of malingering performed *below chance* on the test. More elaborate procedures for identifying malingered memory disorders are described by Leng and Parkin (1995).

The methods we have considered so far are mainly addressed to people pretending to have organic amnesia, but how might we detect simulated dissociative states? Brandt and colleagues (1985) investigated LG, a man on trial for murdering his wife who claimed total amnesia for the event. He was shown a list of 20 words, and then given a forced-choice recognition test in which a word from the list was paired with a new word, and he had to indicate which one he had seen before. On this task pure guessing would produce 50 per cent correct, but LG's score was significantly below this, indicating that he really remembered the words and was trying to simulate amnesia. However, being unaware of the level of chance performance, he rather overdid the amnesia, thus revealing his malingering.

This study indicates that some people simulating dissociative states may be caught out by special malingering tests, but this is not always the case. Kopelman and colleagues (1994) studied a woman, AT, who had suffered a fugue episode lasting 7 days. When admitted to hospital, she claimed to have no idea who she was or how she had come to be in London. Five months later she was identified as a woman from the United States, but expressed surprise that this was her true identity. Her amnesia persisted, but evidence was uncovered showing that her inability to remember her identity was fake. She had, for example, written to her 11-year-old daughter telling her that she had cancer and had decided to spare the family her suffering, and, subsequently she had forged a letter to her family saying that she had died and had been buried in Devon.

Kopelman and co-workers gave AT a number of tests used to detect simulated amnesia, but on most of these she appeared entirely normal – these included recognition tests rather like those used by Brandt and his colleagues (1985). However, on other tests she did show some abnormalities. When given an autobiographical memory test, she showed an extreme recency effect, whereas normal people and also those with amnesia will almost always recall some childhood memories. She was also given a recognition test in which she had to identify which of four names were familiar. The names were either from her own 'forgotten past' or those of unknown people. In addition, she was asked whether more cues might help her to remember the correct name. Schacter (1986b) has shown that people who have genuinely forgotten something tend to believe that more cues will help, whereas subjects told to pretend they are amnesic do not. AT did not believe that more cues would help her, and this was the same whether the names she was looking at came from her own past or from someone else's.

Amnesia and the Legal System

If a defendant is amnesic for a crime with which he or she is charged, it can have important implications for the trial. First, it may be argued that the defendant is unfit to plead. However, following the precedent set by the famous trial of Gunther Padola, this is unlikely. Padola claimed no memory for the murder he was alleged to have committed. During the trial there was much discussion about the origin of Padola's fugue state. He had sustained a minor head injury at the time of arrest, but the jury felt that his amnesia was not genuine – interestingly, part of the reason given was that he still possessed all his skills, something we would not regard as unusual with our modern knowledge of memory disorder. On appeal, the original court decision was upheld, with the additional point that even if Padola's amnesia had been genuine, he would still have been fit to plead.

A second issue is that amnesia for a crime can provide the basis for a plea of **automatism**. The term refers to behaviour that is carried out involuntarily, without conscious intent. Two forms of automatism can be identified. The first, **sane automatism**, involves conscious involuntary movements, such as reflex actions carried out under duress. An example of crime arising from this form of automatism might be a driver attacked by a hornet who, by taking reflexive evasive action, unintentionally steers his car on to the pavement. In this case the charge of reckless driving could be defended against by arguing that the driver was out of control through no fault of his own.

In a well-known case Hill and Sargent (1943) described a man on trial for murdering his mother. He offered the defence that he committed the murder whilst in an epileptic state (see chapter 9) brought on by consuming four pints of beer on an empty stomach. To confirm this possibility, the defendant was given the same amount of 'mild ale' under controlled conditions which produced an abnormal EEG and other symptoms of an epileptic attack. This demonstration was sufficient to bring in a verdict of **insane automatism**, which can be defined as a crime committed in an automatic state but not involving any external agency. Recently, crimes committed while sleep-walking (**somnambulism**) have also come into this category. There are now many reported instances of a sleep-walker carrying out a violent attack, most commonly on their sleeping partner. Usually the person awakes after the act of violence, but appears confused, with no recollection of the event (Fenwick, 1990).

Acquittal due to a temporary organic amnesic state is rare. However, a British case does provide an example. On 11 October 1984 a slow-moving goods train was hit from behind by a passenger train. The driver of the passenger train had passed through a number of red signals, each time cancelling the automatic warning signal. On questioning by the police, it became clear that the driver had no memory for events in the two or three minutes preceding the accident. There were no abnormal signs, and the driver had appeared normal at the start of the journey. Neurological examination subsequently revealed that the driver suffered migraine-like symptoms, had lost his sense of smell, and had received a blow on the head three months prior to the accident. The investigators concluded that the accident occurred because a sudden attack of transient global amnesia had led him to forget that he was going through stop signals (HMSO, 1986). The train driver was thus acquitted because of circumstantial neurological evidence.

Infantile Amnesia

Few people can remember events in their lives before the age of about three and a half (see figure 10.2). This phenomenon is known as **infantile amnesia**, and its inclusion in this chapter reflects early attempts to explain it in terms of repression rather than any general belief that it has a psychogenic origin. According to Freudian theory, certain crucial stages in personality development take place during early childhood, and repression of these early experiences is thought to be a consequence of normal development. Freudian accounts of infantile amnesia are generally not accepted any more, and the phenomenon is now thought to involve crucial changes in the way memory comes to be organized (e.g. Neisser, 1967). The first point to note is that children under the age of 4 do have memories for events, as this excerpt of a 3-year-old's memory shows.

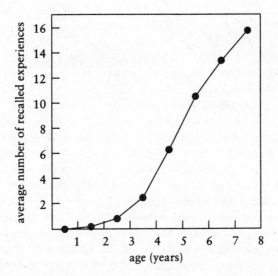

Figure 10.2 Average number of experiences recalled by adults as a function of age at the time of experience.
(*Data from Waldfogel, 1948, adapted by Kail, 1990.*)

Child.	Once on Hallowe'en the kids was over and I had a princess dress on me.
Adult.	You had a princess dress on? Did you get any candy? Did you go door to door? What happened?
Child.	We went treating.
Adult.	You went treating! and who took you?
Child.	Andrea's mother took us. And my mom . . . and we brought a pumpkin too.
Adult.	What did you do with the pumpkin?
Child.	We lighted it.
Adult.	What did it look like? Was it scary?
Child.	Uh-huh. Dad made cuts in it with a razor. He made a face too. That was funny.

(Fivush and Hamond, 1990, p. 223)

When we recollect an experience, we are usually fairly certain that it is correct. This indicates that autobiographical memories must have some component that confirms their authenticity (although, as we have seen repeatedly in this chapter, this mechanism is by no means infallible!). Perner and Ruffman (1995) argue that children under the age of 4 do not have this capability, and that their recollections, as illustrated above, are highly dependent on prompting. As a result, these early memories are not amenable to spontaneous recall in later life. Howe and Courage (1993) argue that the development of autobiographical memory is dependent on the parallel emergence of a sense of self. They reviewed various studies showing that infants learn to recognize themselves in a mirror by the age of 18 months, and equated this with the development of a self concept. They then suggest that 'the fact that this period corresponds with the onset of autobiographical memory is, we believe, more than mere coincidence' (p. 319). If Howe and Courage are right, we would expect the infantile amnesia barrier to be around 18 months to 2 years, but this is somewhat earlier than the infantile amnesia barrier. Children as young as 2 years can talk about their experiences (Hamond and Fivush, 1991), but, as we saw above, this is not the spontaneous recall of events we associate with later memory.

An alternative explanation has been put forward by Nelson and colleagues (e.g. Hudson, 1990; Nelson, 1993). Their **social interaction theory** proposes that the development of autobiographical memory depends crucially on acquiring the ability to describe experiences in a narrative form. Tessler and Nelson (1994) noted that mothers interacting with children could be divided into two basic types: **elaborative** mothers, who talk about events in narrative terms (e.g. when something happened) and **pragmatic** mothers, who talked mainly in instrumental terms (e.g.

where you put your shoes). This distinction was found to have implications for what children remembered about a visit to a museum. Children of elaborative mothers recalled more than those with pragmatic mothers, suggesting that the way parents talk about memory has important implications for how memory develops.

The social interaction theory proposes that autobiographical memory development depends on an increasing use of the narrative form. Infantile amnesia may therefore occur because memories formed prior to the age of 4 may not have a good narrative structure, and thus may be inaccessible to the narrative form used in the post-infantile amnesia period. Further support for this theory comes from a study by Fivush and co-workers (1995) which found a marked change in the narrative structure of memories between the ages of 4 and 5.

At present, there are thus some interesting ideas around as to why infantile amnesia occurs, but as yet no firm conclusions (for a more extensive review, see Parkin, in press).

Recovered versus False Memory

On 22 September 1969 Susan Nason disappeared while running an errand for her mother, and two months later her body was found in a ravine outside her home town in California. Despite the presence of many clues, Susan's murderer was not found, and the crime remained unsolved until a curious sequence of events 20 years later.

Eileen Franklin-Lipsker, a childhood friend of Susan, was feeding her young son when her older daughter Jessica looked up at her and asked her a question. For some reason the look on her daughter's face suddenly brought back images of Susan's final moments of life, and for the next few months Eileen began to reassemble detailed recollections of the events leading up to Susan's death. She recalled her father taking both of them for a car ride, stopping in the countryside, her father's attempts to rape Susan, and, finally, Susan's brutal murder. Almost a year after recalling these awful events, Eileen contacted the police and told them everything. Her father was arrested and tried, and started serving a life sentence. Recently, following doubts about the evidence, the guilty verdict was overturned.

This case led to a surge of other people claiming to have recovered repressed memories of unpleasant childhood experiences. Among them was the American actress Roseanne Barr Arnold, who, following therapy, recollected her mother abusing her when she was an infant until about 7 years of age. Her story, like many others, was featured heavily in magazines and newspapers. Following this, a number of other prosecutions were made successfully on the basis of recovered memories, but, notably, others were not. The phenomenon of **recovered memory** is now extremely wide-spread – so much so, in fact, that those accused by people apparently recovering memories have formed a society known as the False Memory Society.

What, then, is the truth about recovered memory? In this chapter we have reviewed a range of dissociated amnesic states, and have used the concept of repression to explain at least part of what is happening in these disorders. If we accept this, then surely the phenomenon of recovered memory is entirely plausible. In principle, this is true; the problem is the sheer scale on which people with apparently recovered memories are coming forward. Can repressed memory really be that common? Or is there some other reason for this phenomenon?

A high proportion of repressed memories are uncovered in psychotherapy sessions, and there is a strong belief among experimental psychologists that the emergence of recovered memories has much to do with the way this therapy is carried out (Loftus, 1993, 1994; Schacter et al., 1996a). A first, and very important, point is that therapists tend to believe that repression does occur, and that through therapy these memories can be unlocked. In addition, surveys have shown that therapists are highly inclined to believe recovered memories, even when they involve improbable events such as satanic abuse (e.g. Bottoms et al., 1994). In addition, therapists can be willing to accept very early memories as genuine recollections, despite our widespread knowledge about infantile amnesia (see above).

The next important point is that therapists often appear to encourage the emergence of these memories during therapy. Addressing this aspect, Loftus (1993, p. 526) provides a sample of quotes from therapists, all indicating that therapists encourage the production of memories of abuse: for example, 'You know in my experience, a lot of people who are struggling with many of the same problems you are, have often had some really painful things happen to them as kids – maybe they were beaten or molested. And I wonder if anything like that ever happened to you?' And, 'It is crucial . . . that clinicians ask about sexual abuse during therapy.'

It should also be remembered that therapy involving this kind of 'memory work' is often conducted under hypnosis, which, as we saw in chapter 3, may well be a situation in which an individual is highly compliant with their interrogator. Furthermore, it is well established that hypnosis can implant memories for events that never happened. Laurence and Perry (1983) asked 27 highly hypnotizable subjects to choose a night from the previous week and to think about what they were doing just before they went to bed. A suggestion was then made that a loud noise had woken them up that night. After hypnosis, about half the subjects believed that the event had actually occurred, and even when told that the noise memory had been implanted, still insisted it was true. However, hypnosis is not crucial for the implantation of false memories in adults. There is, for example, an extensive literature on the 'misinformation effect' whereby adults can be made to believe that false events actually occurred. Initially these studies showed that it was possible to distort an adult's memory for details of an event (e.g. the colour of a car), but it has been extended to show that entire episodes can be implanted (Garry et al., 1994; Loftus and Coan, 1995).

Another factor is that the sheer detail and vividness of recovered memories often appear to convince people that the memories are true. However, psychologists should overcome these impressions, and look more closely at the evidence. In the Franklin case, Eileen's memory appeared to be authentic because of the details it contained. In fact, many of these details were reported widely at the time of the crime, and other details of her recollection could not be verified. Moreover, parts of her testimony changed across tellings, thus casting doubt on the truth of some of her memories.

Glover (1929) noted that 'When the memory image is of a sufficiently traumatic nature, it is possible that it may be too easily accepted at its face value'. This is wise advice, yet it seems to have been ignored. It is probably the case that the apparent satanic abuse memories of the Orkney children owed part of their acceptance to their bizarre nature. Good (1993) provides an interesting detailed case-study also exemplifying this point. Mrs E. was suffering from anxiety, and reported difficulties with her sex life. During the course of therapy it emerged that her mother had been extremely angry with her for masturbating, and, in order to prevent this, had made her wear plaster-of-Paris panties. Later she claimed that her mother had taken her to a doctor, and that her clitoris had been removed. Describing this account, Good notes: 'Her affectively charged description sounded credible, albeit astonishing. At no time did she express doubt about her memories' (p. 86). After 4 months of therapy she was asked whether she had ever talked to her gynaecologist about her childhood operation. Six months later she made an appointment and discovered that she was anatomically normal. This case provides a good example of how a childhood memory can become distorted by other factors. It seems likely that this patient was prevented from masturbating, and she may well have had a gynaecological examination involving surgical instruments. However, in her subsequent life these events had been transformed into an entirely new and frightening memory which appeared central to the generation of her anxiety.

An alternative approach is to examine populations of adults who are known, via medical or other evidence, to have been sexually abused and see whether any of these people have repressed memory for their abuse. Pope and Hudson (1996) set out to do this by examining several studies that claimed to have found evidence for repressed memory of abuse. Some of the studies appeared to find some such individuals, but the authors concluded that methodological shortcomings ruled out any firm conclusions. One problem was that not all studies made use of a 'clarification interview'. Sexual abuse is a very difficult thing to talk about, so it remains possible that repression of these memories is really just reluctance to admit them. To get around this, it is necessary to confront the patient with your knowledge of their sexual abuse. This can change everything. Della Femina and colleagues (1990) describe a woman whose mother attempted to drown her and whose stepfather sexually abused her. When interviewed initially, she did not recall any of this, but at clarification she said: I didn't say it cuz I wanted to forget. I wanted it to be private. I only cry when I think about it.' Linked with this, a recent study by Kuyken and Brewin (1995) found that patients who had experienced childhood sexual abuse did not deny those memories, but tended to avoid recalling them on an autobiographical memory test.

From the foregoing it is clear that we must be extremely cautious in accepting recovered memories of sexual abuse as accurate recollections on the basis of which to prosecute others. This does not mean that genuine repression of memory of abuse could not occur (see e.g. Harvey and Herman, 1994; Nash, 1994 – see also Schacter et al., 1996a for an overview). What seems clear, however, is that the true incidence of the phenomenon has been dramatically overestimated, and that many apparently recovered memories may be products of other things. What is needed is greater education about how memory works. In particular, therapists need to become more aware that memory for events is not robust, and can easily be tampered with (Lindsay, 1994).

Psychogenic memory disorders are a fascinating but poorly understood set of phenomena. They are instances of a dissociative state in which the individual becomes partly or wholly separated from their memories. Dissociative amnesia is the least severe of these disorders, affecting only part of an individual's life. In fugue the disorder results in a complete loss of personal identity, whereas in MPD a number of personalities are set up to handle different aspects of an individual's past life. Although theoretical explanations are still vague, it seems clear that psychogenic states serve to protect an individual from harmful memories. Dissociative amnesia is frequently associated with crime; this may be due to attendant problems with alcoholism or schizophrenia, but there is also evidence for dissociative amnesia. Dissociative states are often malingered, and detection of this remains a clinical challenge. Amnesia for crime is no excuse in law except under certain unusual circumstances. Infantile amnesia describes the finding that early memories cannot be recalled later in life. Recently there has been a spate of people claiming to have recovered memories of abuse during childhood. It is likely that many of these claims have been manufactured during therapy.

11 Remediation

Loss of memory following brain damage is a common occurrence, and its effects on a victim's life can be devastating. Normal employment is usually impossible, because the patient is a hazard both to themselves and to others. The home also becomes a dangerous environment for amnesic patients, and they need constant supervision to ensure that accidents do not occur. Amnesic patients can also become bored and frustrated, in that reading a book, watching a film or following a conversation all require an intact memory; so the patient is often reduced to low-level activities to pass the time. Amnesia can also affect the patient's social life, extreme forgetfulness and the tendency to repeat the same question over and over again creating tension in even the most sympathetic relative or friend. Problems in remembering new information present the major difficulty to an amnesic, but retrograde amnesia can also have disturbing consequences. Some patients, such as those with Korsakoff's Syndrome, seem to accept their impairment; but for others, loss of memory is a source of distress which can lead to psychiatric illness. A person with impaired memory is therefore likely to be unemployed, at risk, bored, frustrated and even anxious or depressed.

The debilitating effects of amnesia have been commented on since the study of amnesia began, but serious consideration of remediation has taken place only during the last 15 years. The development of memory therapy may have been held back by the mistaken belief that nothing can be done about organic memory impairments. We will see later that the achievements of memory therapy are modest, but their importance within the therapeutic setting should not be underestimated. Patients and relatives can often gain considerable satisfaction from even minor improvements in memory; and memory therapy can also reduce depressive symptoms (Wilson, 1995).

One problem is knowing where to start helping someone with memory difficulties. In aphasia (loss of language), for example, there is often some residual function that can be identified immediately and serve as the foundation for improvement. Amnesics do, of course, have residual memory functions, such as the ability to acquire new procedural memory. However, only those with a specialized knowledge of amnesia are aware of this. Thus a relative or therapist faced with an amnesic person may be surprised to hear that learning to program a computer is a possible therapeutic option for such a patient (see below). One of the goals of neuropsychology, therefore, is dissemination of knowledge about amnesia and potential therapeutic options.

Confronted with an amnesic person, it is useful to have some idea of the various treatment possibilities. First, there are a number of things that can be done just by using common sense:

- Use labels to indicate where things go (e.g. which cupboards are for crockery, food, etc.).
- Place signs in places where the patient may well forget to do something (e.g. a sign by the door reminding them to remember their key). Placing things on the floor by the door – e.g. keys, library books, etc. – helps people to remember.
- Use a prominent wall chart to indicate the date and any events that are taking place that day. Effective use of this can reduce the amount of repetitive questioning that sometimes occurs when people have a memory impairment and also increase self-reliance.
- Encourage the person to use a diary and write notes. This will also reduce repetitive questioning and increases self-reliance.
- If the person has problems finding certain places, then try to make them distinctive. The toilet, for example, can be made easier to find by painting the door a different colour from the rest. Alternatively, the path to it can be marked with distinctive masking tape.
- If there are certain items that the person habitually misplaces (e.g. glasses), put a flow chart on the wall giving instructions about which places to look for them.
- Try to stick to a regular routine. There is plenty of evidence that memory-impaired people can pick up routines and that they can become quite unsettled if these routines are interrupted and they are not told – don't take it for granted that they 'know' what's going on.
- Do not make regular changes to the environment; keep things in the same places as much as possible. This will enhance the possibility of the person learning where things are.
- Keep a notepad by each telephone so that the person can take messages. Try to ensure that the caller's number is always recorded. A specially designed memo pad is useful here, with specific spaces for time of call, name of caller, telephone number and message.
- Using the memory function for more commonly dialled numbers on the telephone can help greatly, avoiding the need to recall a number.

Telephone diallers are also becoming more common, consisting of a pocket-sized device which stores names and telephone numbers, enabling a number to be found easily, and will activate automatic dialling if used with a multi-frequency telephone exchange.

● Display photographs of family and friends prominently, and label them with their names.

External Aids

Above we listed a number of external memory aids which can help amnesic people live more independently. However, having a diary or a timetable, for example, is no use if you do not remember to consult it regularly. Harris (1984) lists three criteria which external cueing devices must meet to be maximally effective.

● The cue must be given as close as possible to the time when a desired act is required.
● It must be active rather than passive; that is, it must alert the individual to the fact that something needs to be done. It is no good reminding an amnesic in the morning that they must do something at lunchtime.
● It should specify as clearly as possible what needs to be done. Cues such as a knotted handkerchief are inadequate because they provide no information about what should be done.

The ideal cueing mechanism is a timer which can be programmed to display specific messages at set times. Recently a system that does just this has been developed and evaluated on a number of patients. Known as 'NeuroPage' (Lynch, 1995; Hersh and Treadgold, 1994), this system involves a cueing device attached to the patient which can be remotely activated to display messages at particular times. In one evaluation of this system a severely amnesic man was prompted daily to carry out a range of tasks (e.g. take medication, make lunch, feed the dog) all of which he failed to do when left to his own devices (Aldrich, 1995b). In another study it was used to prompt a severely amnesic woman who would otherwise spend inordinate amounts of time in the bath. NeuroPage has considerable potential, in that it relies on a minimal degree of learning (all the patient must learn is that the cue means a message is being displayed), is highly adaptable, and can deal with many clients simultaneously.

NeuroPage is not yet commercially available, but there are alternatives that can work as effectively (for reviews see Harris, 1992, and Kapur, 1995). Kurlychek (1983) taught a man with early Alzheimer's Disease to consult his diary every time his watch alarm sounded, and Naugle and co-workers (1988) used an 'alarm display' as an effective means of delivering memory prompts to an amnesic patient. The potential of personal organizers (POs) has also been explored. Kapur (1995) has evaluated their potential by examining how POs could help four memory-impaired subjects. For two of them, POs were every effective, but for the other two, POs did not help, because the patients could not grasp how to use the machine.

Memory as a Muscle?

It is often assumed that an analogy can be drawn between the workings of memory and those of a muscle. The latter, as we all know, will improve in strength with repeated exercise, and a similar view has also been held about memory. The experimental evidence, however, provides little indication that repetitive practice leads to any general improvement in memory performance. Ericsson and Chase (1980) recruited an undergraduate (SF) and asked him to spend 1 hour a day, 3–5 days a week, practising the digit span task. At the outset his digit span was 7, but by the end of the training it had increased to almost 80 digits. Although this involved 230 hours of training, the gains here were enormous. But what exactly had been achieved? Digit span is assumed to reflect the operation of STS, so one conclusion might be that training had increased his STS capacity. If this were so, then SF should have shown superior performance on any memory span task; but when digits were replaced by consonants, his performance was only 7 items. Analysis of SF's performance indicated that his enhanced memory span for digits stemmed from a complex strategy that he had developed which allowed him to group numbers into 'chunks', making them easier to remember. There was no suggestion that his STS had undergone any general increase in capacity.

Godfrey and Knight (1985) gave Korsakoff patients 32 hours of practice on paired-associate learning, but found no improvement in performance. In a more extensive study, Prigatano and colleagues (1984) put a group of head-injured patients through a rehabilitation programme which included repetitive practice on a number of memory tasks. To evaluate its effectiveness, after six months the patients' performance on three subcomponents of the WMS – logical memory, hard paired associates and visual reproduction – plus other tests were compared with their ability on the same tests before treatment. The programme produced modest but statistically significant improvements in memory performance of approximately one item on each component of the WMS. Discussing this study, Schacter (1986) notes that the 625 hours of training involved in the programme indicated an improvement rate of 1/625th of an item per patient per hour – hardly a cost-effective exercise! Other studies, using computer-based drills, have come to similar conclusions. Middleton and co-workers (1991), for example, found no evidence of improved memory following 32 hours of computer-based training, and Skilbeck and Robertson (1992), following a review of the literature, concluded that there was no firm evidence for memory improvement using any computer-based memory drill.

Memory Strategies

An alternative to repetitive practice is to equip the amnesic patient with more efficient memory strategies, the aim being to make more effective any residual memory capacity the patient has. In chapter 4 we reviewed a number of **mnemonics** – artificial strategies for remembering information more efficiently – and therapists have seized upon some of these as a means of improving defective memory. Gardner (1977) taught an amnesic the following song to help him learn his personal details:

> *Henry's my name;*
> *Memory's the game;*
> *I'm in the VA in Jamaica Plain;*
> *My bed's on 7D;*
> *The year is '73;*
> *Every day I make a little gain.*

Rhymes are easier to learn than prose, because they constrain the possible responses that a patient can make. However, the range of situations in which they could be used would seem to be rather restricted.

First-letter mnemonics, especially acronyms, are a more general way of teaching amnesics information they would otherwise find difficult to remember. Thus a shopping list might be remembered by arranging it so that the first letters of each item form a word (e.g. carrots, yoghurt, cucumber, lentils, eggs, spinach). Glasgow and colleagues (1977) used a first-letter mnemonic to help a head injury victim remember a strategy for studying prose more effectively. Known as PQRST, it instructed the patient to

P – Preview (preview material quickly)
Q – Question (ask key question)
R – Read (read thoroughly)
S – State (state answers)
T – Test (test yourself on answers)

Taking selected passages, it was found that the patient remembered them much better using PQRST. Furthermore, the patient was able to generalize the method to newspaper articles. Wilson (1982) used PQRST with Mr B., a man rendered amnesic following a stroke. The man remembered what each letter meant and was able to retain 80–100 per cent of the information derived from the strategy for half an hour. Wilson (1987) describes a number of studies showing PQRST to be superior to rote learning, but in a follow-up study (Wilson, 1991), none of the subjects taught the method previously was using it spontaneously.

Of all the techniques used by memory therapists, those based on mental imagery are the most popular. In the discussion of mental imagery (chapter 4) it was noted that imagery is an effective means of promoting paired-associate learning provided the image is interactive. Lewinsohn and colleagues (1977) found that similar instructions given to amnesic patients improved their performance (see also Cermak, 1975). Robertson-Tchabo and co-workers (1976) taught elderly people with memory problems the method of loci. The patients used the mnemonic to learn three different word lists presented on different days, and no evidence of interference between lists was found. However, as with PQRST, the authors note that the subjects never employed the technique unless specifically instructed to do so.

There seems little doubt that amnesic patients remember more when instructed to use mental imagery mnemonics. But whether these strategies can be of any value to the patient in everyday life is unclear. The method of loci is often considered a good way of remembering a shopping list, but wouldn't a written list be easier? However, in one sphere it is possible that imagery mnemonics do have a practical value. Learning new names is something that amnesic patients find particularly difficult, and writing a person's name down is not much help if you are trying to recognize a number of different people.

Wilson's (1982) patient Mr B. was successfully taught new names using an imagery technique similar to that of Lorayne and Lucas (1975; see page 59). To remember Barbara, for example, the patient was told to imagine a barber holding a large letter A and associate this image with her face. Within 12 days the patient could name 12 people with 100 per cent accuracy. The technique was also used to provide him with correct orientation information. At the outset of therapy he invariably gave 'Harold Wilson' as the name of the Prime Minister, but successful learning of an image depicting a woman thatching the roof of 10 Downing St resulted in him learning the correct response – Mrs Thatcher. Grunberg and colleagues (1991) used the simple procedure of turning a name into a picture to promote face–name learning (e.g. Neil Kinnock becomes an image of a kneeling king knocking), and found it to be effective in learning-disabled children.

The association of distinctive images with faces in order to learn names seems an effective strategy for some amnesic patients. However, it has limitations. Deriving a suitable image can sometimes require a considerable degree of ingenuity (proponents of the imagery method have an uncanny knack of picking suitable names to illustrate their method), and this may be beyond the scope of many brain-damaged people. Even when a name suggests a suitable image, there may be difficulties in making it precise enough for the patient to decode it unambiguously. Wilson (1995) gives the following example:

> [I] once tried to teach a memory-impaired man the name of his social worker, which was Mary Thorne, by drawing a picture of a merry thorn. The man looked at the picture carefully, understanding what was required of him. However, when next asked the name of the social worker, he closed his eyes, thought about the drawing and replied confidently, 'Gay Holly'. (p. 468)

A major problem with training patients to use strategies is, as we have seen, that they do not appear to use them spontaneously (e.g. Wilson, 1987). Berg and colleagues (1991) compared a 'strategy rehabilitation' programme with a 'pseudo-rehabilitation' (memory drill) condition and the effects of no treatment. The strategies were devised for individual patients, and were given to them in a notebook, which they were to consult when attempting to remember something. The main strategies were:

1 Use external aids wherever possible.
2 Pay more attention.
3 Spend more time.
4 Repeat information you wish to remember.
5 Make associations to the things you are trying to remember.
6 Organize what you are trying to remember.
7 Try to make learning and retrieval contexts as similar as possible.

Four months after training ceased the subjects were given three memory tests: learning a word list, learning face–name pairs, and remembering a shopping list. The group taught the strategies performed much better, but this does not mean that the strategies were being used spontaneously. The authors chose the three tests precisely because they were amenable to the strategies that had been taught; thus the tasks themselves may have prompted retrieval of the strategies.

The above review is not exhaustive, but illustrates the range of mnemonics that can promote learning in brain-damaged patients. Within the therapeutic setting any success in remembering must be regarded as valuable; but if we are interested in the broader issue of rehabilitation, we must consider whether these strategies generalize to the patients' normal life. We have already noted that amnesics fail to implement strategies they have found successful in the laboratory, and this would generally seem to be the case. Returning to Wilson's Mr B., he learnt a number of useful strategies in the laboratory, but implemented them only occasionally when he returned home.

Spacing and Impaired Memory

In chapter 4 we discussed evidence that expanding spaced retrieval could improve memory. Schacter and co-workers (1985) investigated how this technique might help memory-impaired people. The subjects were four 29–68-year-olds with mild or severe memory problems who were presented with 192 pictures of human faces on slides and asked to learn various characteristics of those faces. Expanding spaced retrieval was found to be very effective, and there was also evidence of learning in that two subjects came to use the technique in the absence of explicit cues from the experimenter. The spaced retrieval technique has also recently been applied to memory impairments in Alzheimer's Disease (McKintrick and Camp, 1993).

Domain-specific Knowledge: The Method of Vanishing Cues

Schacter and Glisky (1986) have argued that teaching amnesics mnemonic strategies in the hope that they will lead to general improvements in memory is unrealistic. Instead, he argues that therapy should be aimed at teaching **domain-specific knowledge** – that is, information relating to a particular setting in which the amnesic patient currently experiences difficulty.

One method to emerge from this approach is that of **vanishing cues** (VC; Glisky and Schacter, 1987, 1989). VC is a computer-based training method which elicits target information from prompts, which gradually fade as learning progresses. The method was originally devised by behaviourists as a learning method which taught the learner 'to respond to reduced cues' (Hollingworth, 1932). However, Glisky and Schacter have argued that learning in amnesics using VC procedure arises because VC taps into preserved implicit memory ability. More specifically, it involves the same learning processes that underlie preserved fragment and stem completion priming (see chapter 3).

Glisky and Schacter (1986) compared the VC method with a traditional rote learning approach. Their aim was to teach four amnesic patients a small vocabulary of computer-related words, with half the words being taught using VC, the other half by rote. In VC subjects were shown a definition (e.g. 'to store a program') together with the stem of the target word. On the first presentation the stem was increased letter by letter until the subject identified the word, or the whole answer had been revealed (e.g. _____, S___, SA__, SAV_, SAVE). On subsequent presentations the stem was one letter shorter than required for successful identification on the previous trial, with this procedure continuing until the response could be produced without any cues at all. In rote learning, the definition was always presented without cues, and the answer given in full when the subject did not know the answer.

Learning by the memory-impaired group was slow, with many repetitions being needed. However, the VC method proved by far the more effective of the two, with more items being learned and retained over a 6-week retention interval. Glisky and her colleagues carried out further investigations which showed that VC could be used to teach patients computer procedures such as how to write, edit and execute simple programs, and how to store and retrieve data. Recently the VC procedure has been extended to teach word processing, computer data entry, microfilming and database management (Butters and Glisky, 1993; Glisky, 1993; Glisky, 1995; Glisky and Schacter, 1987; Glisky and Schacter, 1988). Other researchers have also reported success with VC. Leng and colleagues (1991) and Prevey and colleagues (1991) have also used VC to teach computer knowledge. Heinrichs and co-workers (1992) used the technique to teach basic orientation information to a severely amnesic man, and Breuning and co-workers (1989) showed that VC could be used to teach a patient the names of hospital staff.

Recently a number of studies have investigated whether VC is the best method for teaching memory-impaired people novel information. Thoene and Glisky (1995) compared VC with two alternative ways of learning face–name associations. In the 'video' condition, people appeared on the screen, introduced themselves, and gave other personal details. In the mnemonic condition, the experimenter provided a verbal elaboration of the name, and suggested a visual image to associate with the face (e.g. 'Her first name "Carol" sounds like Christmas carol, and her last name "Oliphant" sounds like elephant with an O at the beginning. Try to imagine her riding an elephant singing Christmas carols'). The mnemonic method was the most effective, with VC no more effective than the video condition.

The apparent advantage of VC has been called into question as a result of an investigation of VC carried out by Nikki Hunkin and myself (Hunkin and Parkin, 1995). We too concentrated on computer vocabulary, but used twice as many subjects. We found no difference between VC and rote learning even though learning was good, with each subject attaining at least 75 per cent accuracy on one method. We also reported a second experiment in which the VC method was modified to reduce any influence of explicit memory. This experiment involved 16 subjects, and, if anything, showed an advantage for rote learning over VC. Aldrich (1995a) also carried out an extensive investigation of VC in both amnesics and older adults.

Again, there was no evidence for any advantage of VC over rote learning.

On balance, it would seem that VC does not confer any advantage over rote learning methods when attempting to teach new information to memory-impaired people. However, it should be borne in mind that VC is an effective learning method in so far as it makes fewer demands on a therapist's time. Thus, a mnemonic strategy may be a better way of learning names, but far more costly in terms of instructional demands than an automated VC procedure. This point is emphasized by Aldrich, who, despite finding no advantage for VC over rote learning, noted that all her patients preferred the VC procedure. Further, Hunkin and I found that VC is a more attractive learning method for subjects with lower verbal IQ or impaired frontal lobe functioning.

Errorless Learning

Baddeley and Wilson (1994) have pointed out that a frequent problem in trying to teach amnesic subjects new information is that they tend to remember errors, and that these get in the way of their acquiring correct responses. They go on to argue that implicit memory methods are particularly sensitive to interference from errors, and that amnesic subjects are particularly prone to this problem because they cannot explicitly recollect having made them before. By contrast, someone with intact explicit memory can eliminate an error, because they remember making it previously.

In support of their view, Baddeley and Wilson compared the effectiveness of an **errorless** learning procedure with one in which errors could be generated during learning. In the errorless condition subjects heard an instruction such as 'I am thinking of a five-letter word beginning with QU and the word is QUOTE. Please write that down.' By contrast, the errorful condition involved subjects trying to guess what the word might be. After allowing a number of incorrect guesses, subjects were then told the correct answer. Following this, a cued recall test was given, using each letter stem as a cue, and this showed a reliable advantage for the errorless procedure. These findings have since been extended through a series of single case-studies, all of which show an advantage for errorless learning in teaching the names of people and objects, general knowledge, orientation, and how to program an electronic aid (Wilson et al., 1994). Hunkin and colleagues (submitted) have also shown that errorless learning is an effective means of teaching basic word processing skills.

Squires, Hunkin and I (1996) compared errorless and errorful training methods as means of teaching novel picture–picture associations to a severely amnesic man, Mr S. In the errorless condition Mr S. was shown a picture and told to look up which picture went with this in a notebook. In the errorful condition he was allowed to have three guesses before looking up the answer. The errorless method produced significantly better learning, which was still apparent after a 10-week delay. This study also had an ulterior motive. Mr S., like many amnesic patients, had a tendency to ask the same questions over and over again. Usually these questions were about his daily routine, and it was thought that things could be much improved, particularly for his wife, if he could learn to look up the answers to these questions in a notebook. Accordingly, the errorless learning procedure was adapted to train Mr S. to look up facts about daily events. In the training 10 daily events were selected (e.g. 'Where are you going at 2 o'clock this afternoon?'), and Mr S. was required to look them up in his notebook, thus mimicking the errorless learning procedure he had previously undergone. This training continued for 4 weeks, after which Mr S.'s tendency to ask repetitive questions was assessed relative to his performance before the training. The results showed a marked reduction in repetitive questioning, and indicates that an artificial learning procedure can be adapted to teach an amnesic patient a useful skill.

To assess the generality of the errorless learning advantage in the acquisition of novel associations, we have recently carried out two group studies of verbal association learning (Squires et al., submitted). Each study involved 16 memory-impaired subjects, and in both studies, half the associations were taught by an errorless method, and half by an errorful method. In the first study, we compared the effectiveness of the two methods when subjects were required to learn associations that were remotely linked (e.g. MENU – 'pepper'), and in the second study, we compared the effectiveness of the two methods in the acquisition of totally novel associations. In both studies subjects showed an advantage for items learned by the errorless method, and this was most pronounced for the learning of novel associations. On these grounds it would seem that errorless learning is an effective means of helping memory-impaired patients acquire novel associations, and we are hopeful that this method can be effectively transferred to the rehabilitation setting.

Memory Groups

A number of psychologists now run memory 'clinics'. This is a rather misleading term, because it tends to imply that attendance will somehow make memory better. These clinics usually operate by assigning the memory-impaired patient to a 'memory group'. The outstanding benefit obtained in these groups has been twofold. First, they provide an environment in which people can discuss problems with others who understand from first-hand experience the specific difficulties encountered. In many cases this has led to relief when participants discover that their problems are shared by the majority of people, when previously they had thought themselves to be alone and abnormal (particularly with problems in dealing with anger and frustration). Secondly, they gave rise to 'self-help' discussions, with participants passing on tips for coping with problems, which were typically better received coming from other 'sufferers' than from carers or other experts. In these groups patients often practise using strategies to help them remember things. Because these are often effective, temporarily at least, the patients receive a boost to their self-esteem. For reasons that we have already discussed, the benefits of learning about these strategies do not readily generalize to everyday life. However, there is evidence that, despite this, patients attending these groups become less depressed (Evans and Wilson, 1992), and one study has produced some evidence of improved memory (Steinglass et al., 1994).

Loss of memory is extremely debilitating for the patient, and can place great strain on carers. Along with the application of common sense, there are other means of helping. External aids, particularly those that can prompt at relevant times, are particularly effective. Memory is not like a muscle, and thus cannot be improved just by repetitive practice. Only the acquisition of more effective memory strategies will enhance memory. Some strategies have been found to be effective, but the problem is that patients do not use them spontaneously. An alternative is to teach knowledge restricted to particular domains. The VC technique appears to be an effective means of doing this, although its superiority to normal rote learning has been questioned. An alternative approach using errorless learning seems to show promise.

Suggestions for Further Reading

Chapters 1-4

These chapters are based on my recent book *Memory: Phenomena, Experiment and Theory* (Parkin, 1993) which, along with a more detailed account of experimental research, provides an account of memory development and ageing. Baddeley (1996) provides an update of his comprehensive book on human memory, and Eysenck and Keane (1995) provide an account of memory within the broader context of cognitive psychology. Anderson (1995) also provides an account of memory, including a detailed discussion of mental imagery.

Chapter 5

There are a number of summaries of memory assessment, including mine with Leng (Parkin and Leng, 1993) and that by Baddeley et al. (1995). More generally, neuropsychological testing is covered by Lezak (1995), Spreen and Strauss (1991) and Crawford et al. (1992). Kolb and Whishaw (1996) provide an excellent introduction to human neuropsychology which includes a section on neuropsychological assessment.

Chapters 6 and 7

Parkin and Leng (1993) provide an overview of the amnesic syndrome, and Squire and Butters (1992) contains a number of useful chapters on amnesia. Campbell and Conway (1995) contains chapters on many different types of amnesia. I also provide a theoretical account of amnesia in my recent book *Explorations in Cognitive Neuropsychology* (1996a), which includes discussion of the frontal lobes and memory. Kapur (1994) provides a thorough review of amnesia and other memory disorders from a clinical perspective. Bradshaw and Mattingley (1995) also provide an account of memory disorders. A good introduction to neuro-imaging is provided by Posner and Raichle (1994).

Chapter 8

Kausler (1994) provides a clear and authoritative account of ageing and memory. Pathological aspects of ageing and dementia are covered by Backman (1992) and Huppert et al. (1994).

Chapter 9

Kapur (1994) provides a clinical account of most of the transient disorders covered in this chapter, and Cahill and Frith (1995) provide a recent overview of ECT and memory.

Chapter 10

Schacter (1996) provides a recent, very interesting account of psychogenic memory loss, which includes discussion of the recovered memory debate.

Chapter 11

Baddeley et al.'s *Handbook of Memory Disorders* (1995) contains several useful chapters on memory remediation, and Wilson and Moffat (1992) is an entire edited volume concerned with this topic. The use of computer-based remediation is discussed extensively in Bradley et al. (1993).

References

Abel, E. L. (1971) Marijuana and memory: acquisition or retrieval? *Science*, 173, 1038–40.

Abernathy, E. M. (1940) The effect of changed environmental conditions upon the results of college examinations. *Journal of Psychology*, 10, 293–301.

Akhtar, S., Lindsey, B., and Kahn, F. L. (1981) Sudden amnesia for personal identity. *Pennsylvania Medicine*, 84, 46–8.

Albert, M. S., and Moss, M. (1984) The assessment of memory disorders in patients with Alzheimer's Disease. In L. R. Squire and N. Butters (eds), *Neuropsychology of Memory*, 236–46. New York: Guildford.

Albert, M. S., Butters, N., and Levin, J. (1979) Temporal gradients in the retrograde amnesia of patients with alcoholic Korsakoff's disease. *Archives of Neurology*, 36, 211–16.

Aldrich, F. K. (1995a) Can implicit memory be exploited to facilitate the learning of novel associations? Unpublished D.Phil. thesis, University of Sussex.

Aldrich, F. K. (1995b) Support for prospective memory: use of a paging device by a young, amnesic man. Unpublished research report.

Alzheimer, A. (1907) Uber eine eigenartige Erkrankung der Hirnrinde. *Allgemeine Zeitschrift für Psychiatrie Psychoisch-Gerichtliche Medicin*, 64, 146–8.

Anderson, J. R. (1995) *Cognitive Psychology and its Implications*, 4th edn. New York: Freeman.

Anderson, J. R., and Bower, G. H. (1972) *Human Associative Memory*. Washington, DC: Winston.

Andrade, J. (1995) Learning during anaesthesia: a review. *British Journal of Psychology*, 86, 479–506.

Andrews, E., Poser, C. M., and Kessler, M. (1982) Retrograde amnesia for forty years. *Cortex*, 18, 441–58.

Anonymous (1996) Desert brainstorm. *British Medical Journal*, 312, 1485–6.

Anooshian, L. J., Mammarella, S. L., and Hertel, P. T. (1989) Adult age differences in knowledge of retrieval processes. *International Journal of Aging and Human Development*, 29, 39–52.

Atkinson, R. C. (1975) Mnemotechnics in second-language learning. *American Psychologist*, 30, 821–8.

Atkinson, R. C. and Shiffrin, R. M. (1968) Human memory: A proposed system and its control processes. In K. W. Spence and J. T. Spence (eds), *Psychology of Learning and Motivation*, vol. 2. New York: Academic Press.

Backman, L. (1992) *Memory Functioning in Dementia: Advances in Psychology.* Amsterdam: North-Holland.

Baddeley, A. D. (1976) *The Psychology of Memory.* New York: Basic Books.

Baddeley, A. D. (1984) Memory theory and memory therapy. In B. A. Wilson and N. Moffat (eds), *The Clinical Management of Memory Problems*, 5–27. London: Croom Helm.

Baddeley, A. D. (1986) *Working Memory.* Oxford: Churchill Livingstone.

Baddeley, A. D. (1990) *Human Memory: Theory and Practice.* Boston: Allyn and Bacon.

Baddeley, A. D. (1996) *Human Memory: Theory and Practice*, 2nd edn. Hove: Erlbaum.

Baddeley, A. D., and Hitch, G. J. (1974) Working memory. In G. A. Bower (ed.), *The Psychology of Learning and Motivation*, vol. 8, 47–90. New York: Academic Press.

Baddeley, A. D., and Lewis, V. J. (1981) Inner active processes in reading: the inner voice, the inner ear and the inner eye. In A. M. Lesgold and C. A. Perfetti (eds), *Interactive Processes in Reading*, 107–30. Hillsdale, NJ: Erlbaum.

Baddeley, A. D., Thomson, N., and Buchanan, M. (1975) Word length and the structure of short-term memory. *Journal of Verbal Learning and Verbal Behaviour*, 14, 575–89.

Baddeley, A. D., and Wilson, B. A. (1994) When implicit learning fails: amnesia and the problem of error elimination. *Neurospychologia*, 32, 53–68.

Baddeley, A. D., Bressi, S., Della Sala, S., Logie, R., and Spinnler, H. (1991) The decline of working memory in Alzheimer's disease. *Journal of Clinical and Experimental Neuropsychology*, 13, 372–80.

Baddeley, A. D., Wilson, B. A. and Watts, F. N. (1995) *Handbook of Memory Disorders.* Chichester: Wiley.

Bancaud, J., Brunet-Bourgin, F., Chauvel, P., and Halgren, E. (1994) Anatomical origin of déjà vu and vivid 'memories' in human temporal lobe epilepsy. *Brain*, 117, 71–90.

Baron, J. C., Petit-Taboue, M. C., Le Doze, F., Desgranges, B., Ravenel, N., and Marchal, G. (1994) Right frontal cortex hypometabolism in transient global amnesia. *Brain*, 117, 545–52.

Bassili, J., Smith, M., and MacLeod, C. (1989) Auditory and visual word stem completion: separating data-driven and conceptually driven processes. *Quarterly Journal of Experimental Psychology*, 41, 439–53.

Beatty, W. W., Goodkin, D. E., Monson, N., Beatty, P. A., and Herstgaard, D. (1988) Anterograde and retrograde amnesia in patients with chronic progressive multiple sclerosis. *Archives of Neurology*, 45, 611–19.

Beaumont, J. G., and Davidoff, J. (1992) Assessment of visual-perceptual dysfunction. In J. R. Crawford et al., *Handbook of Neuropsychological Assessment*, 115–40. Hove: Erlbaum.

Becker, J. T. (1988) Working memory and secondary memory deficits in Alzheimer's disease. *Journal of Clinical and Experimental Neuropsychology*, 10, 739–53.

Benson, D. F., and Geschwind, N. (1967) Shrinking retrograde amnesia. *Journal of Neurology, Neurosurgery and Psychiatry*, 30, 539–44.

Berg, I. J., Koning-Haanstra, M., and Deelman, B. G. (1991) Long-term effects of memory rehabilitation: a controlled study. *Neuropsychological Rehabilitation*, 1, 87–111.

Berkowitz, B. (1953) The Wechsler–Bellvue performance of white males past 50. *Journal of Gerontology*, 8, 76–80.

Berrington, W. P., Liddell, D. W., and Foulds, G. A. (1956) A re-evaluation of the fugue. *Journal of Mental Science*, 102, 280–6.

Berry, D. C., and Broadbent, D. E. (1984) On the relationship between task performance and associated verbalisable knowledge. *Quarterly Journal of Experimental Psychology*, 36A, 209–31.

Berry, D. C., and Dienes, Z. (1992) *Implicit and Explicit Learning in Human Performance*. Hillsdale, NJ: Erlbaum.

Bigl, P., Hess, L., and Pavek, V. (1992) Our experience with midazolam and flumazenil in dentistry. *Current Therapeutic Research*, 51, 92–6.

Blakemore, C. (1977) *Mechanics of the Mind*, Cambridge: Cambridge University Press.

Blaney, P. H. (1986) Affect and memory: a review. *Psychological Bulletin*, 99, 229–46.

Block, R. I., and Wittenborn, J. R. (1985) Marijuana effects on associative processes. *Psychopharmacology*, 85, 426–30.

Block, R. I., Ghonheim, M. M., Sum-Ping, S. T., and Ali, M. A. (1991) Human learning during general anaesthesia and surgery. *British Journal of Anaesthesia*, 66, 170–8.

Bolles, R. C. (1975) *Learning Theory*. New York: Holt, Rinehart and Winston.

Bondi, M. W., and Kaszniak, A. W. (1991) Implicit and explicit memory in Alzheimer's disease and Parkinson's disease. *Journal of Clinical and Experimental Neuropsychology*, 13, 339–58.

Bottoms, B. L., and Goodman, G. S. (1994) Perceptions of children's credibility in sexual assault cases. *Journal of Applied Social Psychology*, 24, 702–32.

Botwinick, J., and Storandt, M. (1974) *Memory, Related Functions, and Age*. Springfield, Ill.: C. C. Thomas.

Bower, G. H. (1970) Imagery as a relational organizer in associative learning. *Journal of Verbal Learning and Verbal Behavior*, 9, 529–33.

Bower, G. H. (1981) Mood and memory. *American Psychologist*, 36, 129–48.

Bower, G. H., Gilligan, S. G., and Monteiro, K. P. (1981) Selectivity of learning caused by affective states. *Journal of Experimental Psychology: General*, 110, 451–73.

Bowles, N. L., and Poon, L. W. (1985) Aging and retrieval of words in semantic memory. *Journal of Gerontology*, 40, 71–7.

Bradley, V. A., Welch, J. L., and Skilbeck, C. (1993) *Cognitive Retraining Using Computers*. Hove: Erlbaum.

Bradshaw, J. L., and Mattingley, J. B. (1995) *Clinical Neuropsychology. Behavioural and Brain Science*. London: Academic Press.

Brandt, J., and Rich, J. B. (1995) Memory disorders in the dementias. In A. D. Baddeley, B. A. Wilson and F. N. Watts (eds), *Handbook of Memory Disorders*, Chichester: Wiley.

Brandt, J., Rubinsky, E., and Lassen, G. (1985) Uncovering malingered amnesia. *Annals of the New York Academy of Sciences*, 444, 502–3.

Breuning, E., Van Loon Vervoorn, W. A., and Van Dieren, M. P. (1989) Geheugentraining bij Korsakov-patienten met behulp van de methode der 'vanishing cues': een effect-meting (Memory training with Korsakoff patients using the 'vanishing cues' method: measurement of the effect). *Tijdschrift voor Alcohol, Drugs en Andere Psychotrope Stoffen*, 15, 213–21.

Brindle, P. M., Brown, M. W., Brown, J. Griffith, H. B., and Turner, G. M. (1991) Objective and subjective memory impairment in pregnancy. *Psychological Medicine*, 21, 647–53.

Broadbent, D. E., Cooper, P. E., Fitzgerald, P., and Parkes, K. R. (1982) Cognitive Failures Questionnaire (CFQ). *British Journal of Clinical Psychology*, 21, 1–16.

Brooks, L. R. (1968) The suppression of visualization by reading. *Quarterly Journal of Experimental Psychology*, 19, 289–99.

Brown, J., Brown, M. W., and Bowes, J. B. (1983) Effects of lorazepam on rate of forgetting, on retrieval from semantic memory and on manual dexterity. *Neuropsychologia*, 21, 501–12.

Bruce, P. R., Coyne, A. C., and Botwinick, J. (1982) Adult age differences in metamemory. *Journal of Gerontology*, 37, 354–7.

Bryant, R. A. (1995) Autobiographical memory across personalities in dissociative identity disorder: a case report. *Journal of Abnormal Psychology*, 104, 625–31.

Burke, M., and Mathews, A. (1992) Autobiographical memory and clinical anxiety. *Cognition and Emotion*, 6, 23–36.

Butterfield, E. C., Nelson, T. O., and Peck, V. (1988) Developmental aspects of feeling of knowing. *Developmental Psychology*, 24, 654–63.

Butters, M. A., and Glisky, E. L. (1993) Transfer of new learning in memory-impaired patients. *Journal of Clinical and Experimental Neuropsychology*, 15, 219–30.

Butters, N. (1984) Alcoholic Korsakoff's Syndrome: An update. *Seminars in Neurology*, 4, 226–44.

Butters, N., and Cermak, L. S. (1980) *Alcoholic Korsakoff's Syndrome. An Information Processing Approach to Amnesia*. New York: Academic Press.

Buzan, T. (1972) *Use Your Head*. London: BBC Publications.

Cahill, C., and Frith, C. (1995) Memory following electroconvulsive therapy. In A. D. Baddeley et al. (eds), *Handbook of Memory Disorders*, 319–36. Chichester: Wiley.

Calev, A., Ben-Tzvi, E., Shapira, B., Drexler, H., et al. (1989) Distinct memory impairments following electroconvulsive therapy and imipramine. *Psychological Medicine*, 19, 111–19.

Cameron, D. G. (1994) ECT: sham statistics, the myth of convulsive therapy, and the case for consumer misinformation. *Journal of Mind and Behavior*, 15, 177–98.

Campell, R., and Conway, M. A. (1995) *Broken Memories*. Oxford: Blackwell.

Centor, A. (1982) Criminals and amnesia: comment on Bower. *American Psychologist*, 37, 240.

Cermak, L. S. (1975) Imagery as an aid to retrieval in Korsakoff patients. *Cortex*, 11, 163–9.

Cermak, L. S., Talbot, N., Chandler, K., and Woolbarst, L. R. (1985) The perceptual priming phenomenon in amnesia. *Neuropsychologia*, 23, 615–22.

Chan, A. S., Butters, N., Paulsen, J. S., Salmon, D. P., Swenson, M. R., and Maloney, L. (1993a) An assessment of the semantic network in patients with Alzheimer's disease. *Journal of Cognitive Neuroscience*, 5, 254–61.

Chan, A. S., Butters, N., Salmon, D. P., and McGuire, K. A. (1993b) Dimensionality and clustering in the semantic networks of patients with Alzheimer's disease. *Psychology and Aging*, 8, 411–19.

Chan, A. S., Butters, N., Johnson, S. A., Paulsen, J. S., Salmon, D. P., and Swenson, M. R. (1995) Comparison of the semantic networks in patients with dementia and amnesia. *Neuropsychology*, 9, 177–86.

Chiarello, C., and Hoyer, W. J. (1988) Adult age differences in implicit and explicit memory: time course and encoding effects. *Psychology and Aging*, 3, 359–66.

Clark, D. M., and Teasdale, J. D. (1981) Diurnal variation in clinical depression and accessibility of positive and negative experiences. *Journal of Abnormal Psychology*, 91, 87–95.

Cockburn, J., and Smith, P. T. (1993) Correlates of everyday memory among residents of part III homes. *British Journal of Clinical Psychology*, 32, 75–7.

Cohen, G. D. (1990) Psychopathology and mental health in the mature and elderly adult. In J. E. Birren and K. W. Schaie (eds), *Handbook of the Psychology of Aging*, 359–71. New York: Academic Press.

Comfort, A. (1976) *A Good Age*. New York: Simon & Schuster.

Coons, P. M., Milstein, V., and Marley, C. (1982) EEG studies of two multiple personalities. *Archives of General Psychiatry*, 39, 823–5.

Corkin, S. (1968) Acquisition of motor skill after bilateral medial temporal lobe-excision. *Neuropsychologia*, 6, 255–65.

Corkin, S. (1982) Some relationships between global amnesias and the memory impairments in Alzheimer's Disease. In S. Corkin et al. (eds), *Alzheimer's Disease: A Report of Progress*, 149–64. New York: Raven Press.

Craik, F. I. M. (1977) Depth of processing in recall and recognition. In S. Dornic (ed.), *Attention and Performance*, vol. 6, 679–98. New York: Academic Press.

Craik, F. I. M., and Jacoby, L. L. (1976) A process view of short-term retention. In F. Restle (ed.), *Cognitive Theory*, vol. 1, 173–92. Hillsdale, NJ: Erlbaum.

Craik, F. I. M., and Lockhart, R. S. (1972) Levels of processing: a framework for memory research. *Journal of Verbal Learning and Verbal Behavior*, 11, 671–84.

Craik, F. I. M., and McDowd, J. M. (1987) Age differences in recall and recognition. *Journal of Experimental Psychology: Learning, Memory and Cognition*, 13, 474–9.

Craik, F. I. M., and Tulving, E. (1975) Depth of processing and retention of words in episodic memory. *Journal of Experimental Psychology: General*, 104, 268–94.

Crawford, J. R., Parker, D. M., and McKinlay, W. W. (eds), (1992) *A Handbook of Neuropsychological Assessment*. Hove: Erlbaum.

Cremer, R. and Zeef, E. J. (1987) What kind of noise increases with age? *Gerontology*, 42, 515–18.

Crovitz, H. F., Harvey, M. T., and McClanahan, S. (1981) Hidden memory: a rapid method for the study of amnesia using perceptual learning. *Cortex*, 17, 273–8.

204 References

Curran, H. V., Gardiner, J. M., Java, R. I., and Allen, D. (1993) Effects of lorazepam upon recollective experience in recognition memory. *Psychopharmacology*, 110, 374–8.

Damasio, H., Grabowski, T., Frank, R., Galaburda, A. M., and Damasio, A. R. (1994) The return of Phineas Gage: clues about the brain from the skull of a famous patient. *Science*, 264, 1102–5.

Danion, J. M., Weingartner, H. J., File, S. E., Jaffard, R., et al. (1993) Pharmacology of human memory and cognition: illustrations from the effects of benzodiazepines and cholinergic drugs. *Journal of Psychopharmacology*, 7, 371–7.

Darley, C. F., Tinklenberg, J. R., Roth, W. T., Hollister, L. E., and Atkinson, R. C. (1974) Influence of marijuana on storage and retrieval processes in memory. *Memory and Cognition*, 1, 196–200

Davison, G. C., and Neale, J. M. (1994) *Abnormal Psychology*, 6th edn. New York: Wiley.

Delbecq-Derousne, J., Beauvois, M. F., and Shallice, T. (1990) Preserved recall versus impaired recognition. *Brain*, 113, 1045–74.

della Femina, D., Yeager, C. A., and Lewis, D. O. (1990) Child abuse: adolescent records vs. adult recall. *Child Abuse and Neglect*, 14, 227–31.

De Renzi, E., Lucchelli, F., Muggia, S., and Spinnler, H. (1995) Persistent retrograde amnesia following a minor trauma. *Cortex*, 31, 531–42.

Devanand, D. P., Verma, A. K., Tirumalasetti, F., and Sackeim, H. A. (1991) Absence of cognitive impairment after more than 100 lifetime ECT treatments. *American Journal of Psychiatry*, 148, 929–32.

De Wardener, H. E., and Lennox, B. (1947) Cerebral beri-beri. *Lancet*, 1, 11.

Digman, J. M. (1959) Growth of a motor skill as a function of distribution of practice. *Journal of Experimental Psychology*, 57, 310–16.

Dikmen, S., Temkin, N., Mclean, A., Wyler, A., and Machamer, J. (1987) Memory and head injury severity. *Journal of Neurology, Neurosurgery and Psychiatry*, 50, 1613–18.

Dillard, A. (1982) *Teaching a Stone to Talk*. London: Picador.

Dinges, D. F., Whitehouse, W. G., Orne, E. C., and Powell, J. W. (1992) Evaluating hypnotic memory enhancement (hypermnesia and reminiscence) using multi-trial forced recall. *Journal of Experimental Psychology: Learning, Memory and Cognition*, 18, 1139–47.

Dixon, R. A., and Hultsch, D. F. (1983) Structure and development of meta-memory in adulthood. *Journal of Gerontology*, 38, 682–8.

Downes, J. J., Davis, E. J., De Mornay Davies, P., Perfect, T. J., Wilson, K., Mayes, A. R., and Sagar, H. J. (1996) Stem completion priming in Alzheimer's disease: the importance of target word articulation. *Neuropsychologia*, 34, 63–75.

Drachman, D. A., and Sahakian, B. J. (1979) Effects of cholinergic agents on human learning and memory. In R. Barbeau et al. (eds), *Nutrition and the Brain*, Vol. 5, 351–66. New York: Raven Press.

Druckman, D., and Swets, R. (eds) (1994) *Enhancing Human Performance. Issues, Theories and Techniques*. Washington, DC: National Academy Press.

Dusoir, H., Kapur, N., Byrnes, D. P., et al. (1990) The role of diencephalic pathology in human memory disorder. *Brain*, 113, 1695–1706.

Ebbinghaus, H. (1885) *Über das Gedachtnis*. Leipzig: Dunker.

Eich, J. E. (1980) The cue-dependent nature of state-dependent retrieval. *Memory and Cognition*, 8, 157–73.

Eich, J. E. (1984) Memory for unattended events: remembering with and without awareness. *Memory and Cognition*, 12, 105–11.

Eich, J. E., and Metcalfe, J. (1989) Mood-dependent memory for internal versus external events. *Journal of Experimental Psychology: Learning, Memory, and Cognition*, 15, 443–55.

Eich, E., Reeves, J. L., and Katz, R. L. (1985) Anaesthesia, amnesia and the memory/awareness distinction. *Anaesthesia & Analgesia*, 64, 1143–8.

Erdeyli, M. H., and Goldberg, B. (1979) Let's not sweep repression under the rug: toward a cognitive psychology of repression. In J. F. Kihlstrom and F. J. Evans (eds), *Functional Disorders of Memory*, 355–402. Hillsdale, NJ: Erlbaum.

Ericsson, K. A., and Chase, W. G. (1980) Acquisition of a memory skill. *Science*, 208, 1181–2.

Eslinger, P. J., and Grattan, L. M. (1993) Frontal lobe and frontal-striatal substrates for different forms of human cognitive flexibility. *Neuropsychologia*, 31(1), 17–28.

Evans, J. J., and Wilson, B. A. (1992) A memory group for individuals with brain injury. *Clinical Rehabilitation*, 6, 75–81.

Eysenck, M. W., and Keane, M. (1995) *Handbook of Cognitive Psychology*, 3rd edn. Hove: Erlbaum.

Fenwick, P. (1990) *Automatism, Medicine and the Law*. Psychological Medicine Monographs, suppl. 17. Cambridge: Cambridge University Press.

File, S. E., and Bond, A. J. (1979) Impaired performance and sedation after a single dose of lorazepam. *Psychopharmacology*, 66, 309–13.

File, S. E., Easton, P., and Skelly, A. M. (1991) Amnesia for dental procedures and mood change following treatment with nitrous oxide or midazolam. *International Clinical Psychopharmacology*, 6, 169–78.

File, S. E., Sharma, R., and Shaffer, J. (1992) Is lorazepam-induced amnesia specific to the type of memory or to the task used to assess it? *Journal of Psychopharmacology*, 6, 76–80.

Fink, M. (1984) ECT-verdict. Not guilty. *Behavioral and Brain Sciences*, 7, 26–7.

Fitzgerald, J. M. (1992) Autobiographical memory and conceptualisations of the self. In M. A. Conway, D. C. Rubin, H. Spinnler and W. A. Wagenaar (eds), *Theoretical Perspectives on Autobiographical Memory*, 99–114. Dordrecht: Kluwer Academic Press.

Fivush, R., and Hamond, N. (1990) Autobiographical memory across the pre-school years: toward reconceptualizing childhood amnesia. In R. Fivush and J. A. Hudson (eds), *Knowing and Remembering in Young Children*, 223–48. Cambridge: Cambridge University Press.

Fivush, R., Haden, C., and Adam, S. (1995) Structure and coherence of pre-schooler's personal narratives over time: implications for childhood amnesia. *Journal of Experimental Child Psychology*, 60, 32–56.

Fletcher, P. C., Frith, C. D., Grasby, P. M., Shallice, T., et al. (1995) Brain systems for encoding and retrieval of auditory-verbal memory: an in vivo study in humans. *Brain*, 118, 401–16.

Folstein, M. F., Folstein, S. E., and McHugh, P. R. (1975) 'Mini Mental State'. *Journal of Psychiatric Research*, 12, 189–98.

Freeman, C. P. L., Weeks, D., and Kendell, R. E. (1980) ECT: patients who complain. *British Journal of Psychiatry*, 137, 17–25.

Fried, P. A., and Watkinson, B. (1990) 36- and 48-month neurobehavioural follow up of children prenatally exposed to marijuana, cigarettes, and alcohol. *Journal of Developmental and Behavioural Paediatrics*, 11, 49–58.

Fuld, P. A., Katzman, R., Davies, P., and Terry, R. D. (1982) Intrusions as a sign of Alzheimer's dementia: chemical and pathological verification. *Annals of Neurology*, 11, 155–9.

Gabrieli, J. D. E., Cohen, N. J., and Corkin, S. (1983) The acquisition of lexical and semantic knowledge in amnesia. *Society for Neuroscience Abstracts*, 9, 238.

Gainotti, G., and Marra, C. (1994) Some aspects of memory disorders clearly distinguish dementia of the Alzheimer type from depressive pseudo-dementia. *Journal of Clinical and Experimental Neuropsychology*, 16, 65–78.

Gardiner, J. M. (1988) Functional aspects of recollective experience. *Memory and Cognition*, 16, 309–13.

Gardiner, J. M., and Java, R. I. (1993) Recognizing and remembering. In A. Collins, M. A. Conway, S. E. Gathercole and P. E. Morris (eds), *Theories of Memory*, 163–88. Hillsdale, NJ: Erlbaum.

Gardiner, J. M., and Parkin, A. J. (1990) Attention and recollective experience in recognition memory. *Memory and Cognition*, 18, 579–83.

Gardner, H. (1977) *The Shattered Mind: The Person after Brain Damage*. London: Routledge and Kegan Paul.

Garry, M., Loftus, E. F., and Brown, S. W. (1994) Memory: a river runs through it. *Consciousness and Cognition*, 3, 438–51.

Gasquoine, P. G. (1991) Learning in post-traumatic amnesia following extremely severe closed head injury. *Brain Injury*, 5, 169–75.

Geiselman, R., and Machlovitz, H. (1987) Hypnosis memory recall: implications for forensic use. *American Journal of Forensic Psychology*, 5, 37–47.

Gick, M., Craik, F. I. M., and Morris, R. G. (1988) Task complexity and age differences in working memory. *Memory and Cognition*, 16, 353–61.

Glanzer, M., and Cunitz, A. R. (1966) Two storage mechanisms in free recall. *Journal of Verbal Learning and Verbal Behaviour*, 5, 351–60.

Glanzer, M., and Razel, M. (1974) The size of the unit in short-term storage. *Journal of Verbal Learning and Verbal Behavior*, 13, 114–31.

Glasgow, R. E., Zeiss, R. A., Barrera, M., and Lewinsohn, P. M. (1977) Case studies on remediating memory deficits in brain-damaged individuals. *Journal of Clinical Psychology*, 33, 1049–54.

Glenberg, A. M., Bradley, M. M., Stevenson, J. A., et al. (1980) A two-process account of long-term serial position effects. *Journal of Experimental Psychology: Human Learning and Memory*, 6, 692–704.

Glisky, E. L. (1993) Training persons with traumatic brain injury for complex computer jobs: the domain-specific learning approach. In D. F. Thomas, F. E. Menz and D. C. McAlees (eds), *Community-Based Employment Following Traumatic Brain Injury*, 3–27. Menomonie, Wis.: University of Wisconsin Press.

Glisky, E. L. (1995) Acquisition and transfer of word processing skill. *Neuropsychological Rehabilitation*, 5, 299–318.

Glisky, E. L., and Schacter, D. L. (1986) Remediation of organic memory disorders: current status and future prospects. *Journal of Head Trauma Rehabilitation*, 1(3), 54–63.

Glisky, E. L., and Schacter, D. L. (1987) Acquisition of domain-specific knowledge in organic amnesia: training for computer-related work. *Neuropsychologia*, 25, 893–906.

Glisky, E. L., and Schacter, D. L. (1988) Long-term memory retention of computer learning by patients with memory disorders. *Neuropsychologia*, 26, 173–8.

Glisky, E. L., and Schacter, D. L. (1989) Extending the limits of complex learning in organic amnesia: computer training in a vocational domain. *Neuropsychologia*, 27, 107–20.

Glisky, E. L., Polster, M. R., and Routhieaux, B. C. (1995) Double dissociation between item and source memory. *Neuropsychology*, 9, 229–35.

Gloor, P. (1990) Experiential phenomena of temporal lobe epilepsy. *Brain*, 113, 1673–94.

Glover, E. (1929) The 'screening' function of traumatic memories. *International Journal of Psychoanalysis*, 10, 90–3.

Godden, D., and Baddeley, A. D. (1975) Context-dependent memory in two natural environments. *British Journal of Psychology*, 66, 325–31.

Godden, D., and Baddeley, A. D. (1980) When does context influence recognition memory? *British Journal of Psychology*, 71, 99–104.

Godfrey, H. P. D., and Knight, R. G. (1985) Cognitive rehabilitation of memory functioning in amnesic alcoholics. *Journal of Clinical and Consulting Psychology*, 53, 555–7.

Goldenberg, G. (1995) Transient global amnesia. In A. D. Baddeley, B. A. Wilson and F. N. Watts (eds), *Handbook of Memory Disorders*, 109–34. Chichester: Wiley.

Goldstein, F. C., and Levin, H. S. (1995) Post-traumatic and anterograde amnesia in head injury. In A. D. Baddeley, B. A. Wilson and F. N. Watts (eds), *Handbook of Memory Disorders*, 187–210. Chichester: Wiley.

Good, M. I. (1993) The reconstruction of early childhood trauma: fantasy reality, and verification. *Journal of the American Psychoanalytical Association*, 42, 79–101.

Goodglass, H., and Kaplan, E. (1983) *The Boston Diagnostic Aphasia Examination*, Philadelphia: Lea & Febiger.

Goodwin, D. W. (1974) Alcoholic blackout and state-dependent learning. *Federation Proceedings*, 33, 1833–5.

Graf, P., and Schacter, D. L. (1985) Implicit and explicit memory for novel associations in normal and amnesic subjects. *Journal of Experimental Psychology: Learning, Memory and Cognition*, 11, 501–18.

Graf, P., Squire, L. R., and Mandler, G. (1984) The information that amnesic patients do not forget. *Journal of Experimental Psychology: Learning, Memory and Cognition*, 9, 164–78.

Grinker, R. R., and Spiegel, J. P. (1945) *Men Under Stress*. New York: McGraw-Hill.

Grosse, D. A., Wilson, R. S., and Fox, H. J. (1990) Preserved word-stem-completion priming of semantically encoded information in Alzheimer's Disease. *Psychology & Aging*, 5, 304–6.

Grossman, M. (1987) Lexical acquisition in alcoholic Korsakoff psychosis. *Cortex*, 23, 631–44.

Grunberg, M. M. (1987) *Linkword Language System*. London: Corgi.

Grunberg, M. M., Sykes, R. N., and Hammond, V. (1991) Face–name association in learning-disabled adults: the use of a visual associative strategy. *Neuropsychological Rehabilitation*, 1, 113–16.

Guthkelch, A. N. (1980) Post-traumatic amnesia, post-concussional symptoms and accident neurosis. *European Neurology*, 19, 91–102.

Halligan, P. W., Hunt, M., Marshall, J. C., and Wade, D. T. (1996) When seeing is feeling: acquired synaesthesia or phantom touch? *Neurocase*, 2, 21–9.

Hamann, S. B., and L. R. Squire (1994) New semantic learning in amnesia. 35th Annual Meeting of the Psychonomic Society.

Hamilton, E. (1961) *Plato: The Collected Dialogues*. Princeton: Princeton University Press.

Hamond, N. R., and Fivush, R. (1991) Memories of Mickey Mouse: young children recount their trip to Disneyworld. *Cognitive Development*, 6, 433–48.

Hanley, J. R., and Davies, A. D. M. (1997) Impaired recall and preserved recognition. In A. J. Parkin (ed.), *Case Studies in the Neuropsychology of Memory*. Hove: Psychology Press.

Hanley, J. R., Davies, A. D. M., Downes, J. J., and Mayes, A. R. (1994) Impaired recall of verbal material following rupture and repair of an anterior communicating artery aneurysm. *Cognitive Neuropsychology*, 11, 543–78.

Harlow, J. M. (1993) Recovery from the passage of an iron bar through the head. *History of Psychiatry*, 4, 271–81.

Harris, J. (1984) Methods of improving memory. In B. Wilson and N. Moffat (eds), *The Clinical Management of Memory Problems*, 44–62. London: Croom Helm.

Harris, J. (1992) Ways to help memory. In B. Wilson and N. Moffat (eds), *The Clinical Management of Memory Problems*, 2nd edn, 59–85. London: Croom Helm.

Harrison, J., Baron-Cohen, S., Pavlescu, E., et al. (1995) The physiology of coloured hearing: a PET activation study of colour-word synaesthesia. *Brain*, 118, 661–76.

Hart, R. P., Kwentus, J. A., Harkins, S. W., and Taylor, J. R. (1988) Rate of forgetting in mild Alzheimer's-type dementia. *Brain and Cognition*, 7, 31–8.

Hartley, A. A. (1993) Evidence for the selective preservation of spatial selective attention in old age. *Psychology and Aging*, 8, 371–9.

Harvey, M. R., and Herman, J. L. (1994) Amnesia, partial amnesia, and delayed recall among adult survivors of childhood trauma. *Consciousness and Cognition*, 3, 295–306.

Hasher, L., and Zacks, R. T. (1988) Working memory comprehension, and aging: a review and a new view. In G. H. Bower (ed.), *The Psychology of Learning and Motivation*, vol. 22, pp. 193–225. San Diego, Calif.: Academic Press.

Hayslip, B., and Kenelly, K. J. (1982) Short-term memory and crystalized-fluid intelligence in adulthood. *Research on Aging*, 4, 314–22.

Hebb, D., A. (1949) *The Organization of Behavior.* New York: Wiley.

Heinrichs, R. W., Levitt, H., Arthurs, A., Gallardo, C., Hirscheimer, K., MacNeil, M., Olshansky, E., and Richards, K. (1992) Learning and retention of a daily activity schedule in a patient with alcoholic Korsakoff's syndrome. *Neuropsychological Rehabilitation*, 2, 43–58.

Hersh, N., and Treadgold, L. (1994) NeuroPage: the rehabilitation of memory dysfunction by prosthetic memory and cueing. *NeuroRehabilitation*, 4, 186–97.

Hertzog, C., Dixon, R. A., and Hultsch, D. F. (1990) Relationships between metamemory, memory predictions, and memory task performance in adults. *Psychology and Aging*, 5, 215–27.

Hewitt, K. (1973) Context effects in memory: a review. Unpublished manuscript, Cambridge University Psychological Laboratory.

Higbee, K. (1977) *Your Memory: How it Works and How to Improve it.* Englewood Cliffs, NJ: Prentice-Hall.

Higbee, K. L., and Kunihira, S. (1985) Cross-cultural applications of Yodai mnemonics in education. *Educational Psychology*, 20, 57–64.

Hill, D., and Sargent, W. (1943) A case of matricide. *Lancet*, 1, 526–7.

Hill, L. B. (1957) A second quarter century of delayed recall or relearning at 80. *Journal of Educational Psychology*, 48, 65–8.

Hirshman, E., Snodgrass, J. G., Mindes, J., and Feenan, K. (1990) Conceptual priming in fragment completion. *Journal of Experimental Psychology: Learning, Memory, and Cognition*, 16, 634–47.

Hirst, W., and Volpe, B. T. (1988) Memory strategies with brain damage. *Brain and Cognition*, 8, 1–33.

HMSO (1986) *Railway Accident Report on the Collision that Occurred on 11th October 1984 near Wembley Central Station.* London: HMSO.

Hodges, J. R. (1991) *Transient Amnesia: Clinical and Neuropsychological Aspects*, London: W. B. Saunders.

Hodges, J. R. (1994) Semantic memory for frontal executive function during TGA. *Journal Neurology, Neurosurgery and Psychiatry*, 57, 605–8.

Hodges, J. R. (1995) Retrograde amnesia, In *Handbook of Memory Disorders*, A. D. Baddeley, B. A. Wilson and F. N. Watts (eds), 81–108. Chichester: Wiley.

Hodges, J. R., and Warlow, C. P. (1990) Syndromes of transient amnesia: towards a classification. A study of 153 cases. *Journal of Neurology, Neurosurgery and Psychiatry*, 53, 834–43.

Holding, D. H. *Principles of Training.* Oxford: Pergamon.

Holland, C. A., and Rabbitt, P. M. A. (1991) Ageing memory: use versus impairment. *British Journal of Psychology*, 82, 29–38.

Hollingworth, H. L. (1932) What is learning? *Scientific Monthly*, 35, 63–5.

Hopwood, J. S., and Snell, H. K. (1933) Amnesia in relation to crime. *Journal of Mental Science*, 79, 27–41.

Houx, P. J., Vreeling, F. W., and Jolles, J. (1991) Rigorous health screening reduces age effect on memory scanning task. *Brain and Cognition*, 15, 246–60.

Howard, D., and Howard, J. H. (1992) Adult age differences in the rate of learning serial patterns: evidence from direct and indirect tests. *Psychology and Aging*, 7, 232–41.

Howard, D., and Orchard-Lisle, V. M. (1984) On the origin of semantic errors in naming: evidence from the case of a global dysphasic. *Cognitive Neuropsychology,* 1, 163–90.

Howard, D. V., Shaw, R. J., and Heisey, J. G. (1986) Aging and the time course of semantic activation. *Journal of Gerontology,* 41, 195–203.

Howe, M. L., and Courage, M. L. (1993) On resolving the enigma of infantile amnesia. *Psychological Bulletin,* 113, 305–26.

Hudson, J. A. (1990) The emergence of autobiographic memory in mother–child interactions. In R. Fivush and J. A. Hudson (eds), *Knowing and Remembering in Young Children,* 166–96. New York: Cambridge University Press.

Hughes, C. P., Berg, L., Dabziger, W. L., Coben, L. A., and Martin, R. L. (1982) A new clinical scale for the staging of dementia. *British Journal of Psychiatry,* 140, 566–72.

Hughlings-Jackson, H. J. (1889) On a particular variety of epilepsy ('intellectual aura'), one case with symptoms of organic brain disease. *Brain,* 11, 189–207.

Humphreys, K. J., Asbury, A. J., and Millar, K. (1990) Investigation of awareness by homophone priming during computer controlled anaesthesia. In B. Bonke, W. Fitch, and K. Millar (eds), *Memory and Awareness in Anaesthesia,* 101–9. Lisse/ Amsterdam: Swets & Zeitlinger.

Hunkin, N. M., and Parkin, A. J. (1993) Recency judgements in Wernicke–Korsakoff and post-encephalitic amnesia: influences of proactive interference and retention interval. *Cortex,* 29, 485–500.

Hunkin, N. M., and Parkin, A. J. (1995) The method of vanishing cues: an evaluation of its effectiveness in teaching memory-impaired individuals. *Neuropsychologia,* 33, 1255–79.

Hunkin, N. M., Parkin, A. J., and Longmore, B. E. (1994) Aetiological variation in the amnesic syndrome: comparisons using the temporal list discrimination task. *Neuropsychologia,* 32, 819–26.

Hunkin, N. M., Parkin, A. J., Bradley, V. A., Aldrich, F. K., and Jansari, A. (1995) Focal retrograde amnesia following closed head injury: A caseStudy and theoretical account. *Neuropsychologia,* 33, 509–23.

Hunkin, N. M., Squires, E. J., Aldrich, F. K., and Parkin, A. J. (submitted), The use of errorless learning in the acquisition of word processing skills: preliminary findings.

Hunter, I. M. L. (1977) Imagery, comprehension and mnemonics. *Journal of Mental Imagery,* 1, 65–72.

Huppert, F. A., and Piercy, M. (1978a) Recognition memory in amnesic patients: a defect of acquisition? *Neuropsychologia,* 15, 643–52.

Huppert, F. A., and Piercy, M. (1978b) The role of trace strength in recency and frequency judgements by amnesic and control subjects. *Quarterly Journal of Experimental Psychology,* 30, 346–54.

Huppert, F. A., Brayne, C., and O'Connor, D. W. (1994) *Dementia and Normal Ageing.* Cambridge: Cambridge University Press.

Incisa della Rocchetta, A., and Milner, B. (1993) Strategic search and retrieval inhibition: the role of the frontal lobes. *Neuropsychologia,* 31, 503–24.

Jacobs, D., Salmon, D. P., Troster, A. I., and Butters, N. (1990) Intrusion errors in the figural memory of patients with Alzheimer's and Huntington's disease. *Archives of Clinical Neuropsychology,* 5, 49–57.

Jacoby, L. L. (1991) A process dissociation framework: separating automatic from intentional uses of memory. *Journal of Memory and Language*, 30, 513–41.

Jacoby, L. L., and Dallas, M. (1981) On the relationship between autobiographical memory and perceptual learning. *Journal of Experimental Psychology: General*, 110, 306–40.

James, W. (1890) *Principles of Psychology*, vol. 1. New York: Henry Holt.

James, W. (1899) *Talks to Teachers on Psychology: And to Students on Some of Life's Ideals*. New York: Henry Holt.

Janet, P. (1904) *Neuroses et Idées Fixes*, 2nd edn. Paris: Felix Alcan.

Janis, I. (1950) Psychological effects of electro-convulsive treatments. *Journal of Nervous and Mental Disease*, 111, 359–82.

Janowsky, J. S., Shimamura, A. P., and Squire, L. R. (1989a) Memory and metamemory: comparisons between patients with frontal lobe lesions and amnesic patients. *Psychobiology*, 7, 3–11.

Janowsky, J. S., Shimamura, A. P., and Squire, L. R. (1989b) Source memory impairment in patients with frontal lobe lesions. *Neuropsychologia*, 27, 1043–56.

Jansari, A. S. (1995) *The Reminiscence Bump in Autobiographical Memory*. Unpublished D. Phil. thesis, University of Sussex.

Jansari, A., and Parkin, A. J. (1996) Things that go bump in your life: explaining reminiscence effects in autobiographical memory. *Psychology and Aging*, 11, 85–91.

Java, R. I., and Parkin, A. J. (submitted) Measures of perceptual speed as determinants of age-related deficits in recall and recognition.

Jelicic, M., De Roode, A., Bovill, J. G., and Bonke, B. (1992a) Unconscious learning during anaesthesia. *Anaesthesia*, 47, 835–7.

Jelicic, M., Bonke, B., Wolters, G., and Phaf, R. H. (1992b) Implicit memory for words presented during anaesthesia. *European Journal of Cognitive Psychology*, 4, 71–80.

Jelicic, M., Asbury, A. J., Millar, K., and Bonke, B. (1993) Implicit learning during enflurane anaesthesia in spontaneously breathing patients. *Anaesthesia*, 48, 766–8.

Jenkins, J. J., Mink, W. D., and Russell, W. A. (1952) Associative clustering as a function of verbal association strength. *Psychological Reports*, 4, 127–36.

Jenkins, V. A., and Parkin, A. J. (submitted) Novel association priming in amnesia does not depend on residual explicit memory.

Jones, M. (1974) Imagery as a mnemonic aid after left temporal lobectomy: contrast between material-specific and generalized memory disorders. *Neuropsychologia*, 12, 21–30.

Judge, E., and Parkin, A. J. (submitted) Recognition performance distinguishes multi-infarct dementia from Alzheimer's Disease.

Kail, F. (1990) *The Development of Memory in Children*, 3rd edn. New York: Freeman

Kaminer, H., and Lavie, P. (1991) Sleep and dreaming in Holocaust survivors. Dramatic decrease in dream recall in well-adjusted survivors. *Journal of Nervous and Mental Disease*, 179, 664–9.

Kampen, D. L., and Sherwin, B. B. (1994) Estrogen use and verbal memory in healthy post-menopausal women. *Obstetrics and Gynaecology*, 83, 979–83.

Kaplan, E. F., Goodglass, H., and Weintraub, S. (1983) *The Boston Naming Test*, 2nd edn. Philadelphia: Lea & Febiger.

Kapur, N. (1992) Focal retrograde amnesia in neurological disease: a critical review. *Cortex*, 29, 217–34.

Kapur, N. (1993) Transient epileptic amnesia – a clinical update and a reformulation. *Journal of Neurology, Neurosurgery and Psychiatry*, 56, 1184–90.

Kapur, N. (1994) *Memory Disorders in Clinical Practice*, 2nd edn. Hove: Erlbaum.

Kapur, N. (1995) Memory aids in rehabilitation. In A. D. Baddeley, B. A. Wilson and F. N. Watts (eds), *Handbook of Memory Disorders*, 533–56. Chichester: Wiley.

Kapur, N., Young, A. W., Bateman, D., and Kennedy, P. (1989) A long-term clinical and neuropsychological follow-up of focal retrograde amnesia. *Cortex*, 25, 387–402.

Kapur, N., Ellison, D., Smith, M. P., McLellan, D. L., and Burrows, E. H. (1992) Focal retrograde amnesia following bilateral temporal lobe pathology. *Brain*, 115, 73–85.

Kapur, N., Ellison, D., Parkin, A. J., Hunkin, N. M., et al. (1994) Bilateral temporal lobe pathology with sparing of medial temporal lobe structures: lesion profile and pattern of a memory disorder. *Neuropsychologia*, 32, 23–38.

Kausler, D. H. (1991) *Experimental Psychology, Cognition and Human Aging*, 2nd edn. New York: Springer.

Kausler, D. H. (1994) *Learning and Memory in Normal Aging*. San Diego, Calif.: Academic Press.

Kausler, D. H., and Kleim, D. M. (1978) Age differences in processing-relevant versus irrelevant stimuli in multiple item recognition memory. *Journal of Gerontology*, 33, 87–93.

Kihlstrom, J. F. (1980) Attempting to breach hypnotic amnesia. *Journal of Abnormal Psychology*, 89, 603–26.

Kihlstrom, J. F., Schacter, D. L., Cork, R. C., et al. (1990) Implicit and explicit memory following surgical anaesthesia. *Psychological Science*, 1, 303–6.

Kimura, D. (1995) Estrogen replacement therapy may protect against intellectual decline in post-menopausal women. *Hormones and Behavior*, 29, 312–21.

Kintsch, W. (1970) Models for free recall and recognition. In D. A. Norman (ed.), *Models of Human Memory*, 333–74. New York: Academic Press.

Knopman, D. S., and Ryberg, R. (1989) A verbal memory test with high predictive accuracy for dementia of the Alzheimer type. *Archives of Neurology*, 46, 141–5.

Knowlton, B. J., Ramus, S. J., and Squire, L. S. (1992) Intact artificial grammar learning in amnesia: dissociation of classification learning and explicit memory for specific instances. *Psychological Science*, 3, 172–9.

Knowlton, B. J., Squire, L. R., and Gluck, M. A. (1994) Probabilistic classification learning in amnesia. *Learning & Memory*, 1, 106–20.

Kolb, B., and Whishaw, I. Q. (1996) *Fundamentals of Human Neuropsychology*, 4th edn. New York: Freeman.

Kopelman M. D. (1989) Remote and autobiographical memory, temporal context memory and frontal atrophy in Korsakoff and Alzheimer patients. *Neuropsychologia*, 27, 437–60.

Kopelman, M. D. (1995a) The assessment of psychogenic amnesia. In A. D. Baddeley, B. A. Wilson and F. N. Watts (eds), *Handbook of Memory Disorders*, 427–50. Chichester: Wiley.

Kopelman, M. D. (1995b) The Korsakoff Syndrome. *British Journal of Psychiatry*, 166, 154–73.

Kopelman, M., Wilson, B. A., and Baddeley, A. D. (1990) *The Autobiographical Memory Interview*, Bury St Edmunds: Thames Valley Test Company.

Kopelman, M. D., Green, R. E. A., Guinan, E. M., Lewis, P. D. R., and Stanhope, N. (1994) The case of the amnesic intelligence officer. *Psychological Medicine*, 24, 1037–45.

Kosslyn, S. M. (1983) *Ghosts in the Mind's Machine: Creating and Using Images in the Brain*. New York: Norton.

Kosslyn, S. M. (1994) *Image and Brain: The Resolution of the Imagery Debate*. Cambridge, Mass.: MIT Press.

Kurlychek, R. T. (1983) Use of a digital alarm chronograph as a memory aid in early dementia. *Clinical Gerontologist*, 1, 93–4.

Kuyken, W., and Brewin, C. R. (1995) Autobiographical memory functioning in depression and reports of early abuse. *Journal of Abnormal Psychology*, 104, 585–91.

Landauer, T. K., and Bjork, R. A. (1978) Optimum rehearsal patterns and name learning. In M. M. Gruneberg et al. (eds), *Practical Aspects of Memory*, 625–32. New York: Academic Press.

Laurence, J., and Perry, C. (1983) Hypnotically created memory among highly hypnotizable subjects. *Science*, 222, 523–4.

Layton, B. S., and Wardi-Zonna, K. (1995) Post-traumatic stress disorder with neurogenic amnesia for the traumatic event. *Clinical Neuropsychologist*, 9, 2–10.

Leininger, B. E., Gramling, S. E., Farrell, A. S., Kreutzer, J. S. and Peck, E. A. (1990) Neuropsychological deficits in symptomatic minor head injury patients after concussion and mild concussion. *Journal of Neurology, Neurosurgery and Psychiatry*, 53, 293–6.

Leng, N. R. C., and Parkin, A. J. (1988) Amnesic patients can benefit from instructions to use imagery: evidence against the cognitive mediation hypothesis. *Cortex*, 24, 33–9.

Leng, N. R. C., and Parkin, A. J. (1995) The detection of exaggerated or simulated memory disorder by neuropsychological methods. *Journal of Psychosomatic Research*, 39, 767–76.

Leng, N. R., Copello, A. G., and Sayegh, A. (1991) Learning after brain injury by the method of vanishing cues: a case study. *Behavioural Psychotherapy*, 19, 173–81.

Levin, H. S., and Goldstein, F. C. (1986) Organization of verbal memory after severe closed-head injury. *Journal of Clinical and Experimental Neuropsychology*, 8, 643–56.

Levin, H. S., High, W. M., Meyers, C. A., von Laufen, A., Hayden, M. E., and Eisenberg, H. (1985) Impairment of remote memory after closed head injury. *Journal of Neurology, Neurosurgery and Psychiatry*, 48, 55–63.

Levinson, B. W. (1965) States of awareness during general anaesthesia. *British Journal of Anaesthesia*, 37, 544–6.

Lewinsohn, P. M., Danaher, B. G., and Kikel, S. (1977) Visual imagery as a mnemonic aid for brain-injured persons. *Journal of Clinical and Consulting Psychology*, 45, 717–23.

Lezak, M. D. (1995) *Neuropsychological Assessment*, 3rd edn. New York: Oxford University Press.

L'Hermitte, F., and Signoret, J. L. (1972) Analyse neuropsychologique et differenciation des syndromes amnesiques. *Revue Neurologique*, 126, 86–94.

Light, L. L., and Carter-Sobell, L. (1970) Effects of changed semantic context on recognition memory. *Journal of Verbal Learning and Verbal Behavior*, 9, 1–11.

Light, L. L., and Singh, A. (1987) Implicit and explicit memory in young and older adults. *Journal of Experimental Psychology: Learning, Memory and Cognition*, 13, 531–41.

Light, L. L., Singh, A., and Capps, J. L. (1986) The dissociation of memory and awareness in young and older adults. *Journal of Clinical and Experimental Neuropsychology*, 8, 62–74.

Lindsay, D. S. (1994) Contextualizing and clarifying criticisms of memory work in psychotherapy. *Consciousness and Cognition*, 3, 426–37.

Lisman, S. A. (1974) Alcoholic blackout: state-dependent learning? *Archives of General Psychiatry*, 30, 46–53.

Lloyd, G. G., and Lishman, W. A. (1975) Effect of depression on the speed of recall of pleasant and unpleasant experiences. *Psychological Medicine*, 5, 173–80.

Loewen, E. R., Shaw, R. J., and Craik, F. I. M. (1990) Age differences in components of metamemory. *Experimental Aging Research*, 16, 43–8.

Loftus, E. F. (1993) The reality of repressed memories. *American Psychologist*, 48, 518–37.

Loftus, E. F. (1994) The repressed memory controversy. *American Psychologist*, 49, 443–5.

Loftus, E. F., and Coan, D. (1995) The construction of childhood memories. In D. Peters (ed.), *The Child Witness in Context: Cognitive, Social and Legal Perspective*. Dordrecht: Kluwer.

Loftus, E. F., and Loftus, G. R. (1980) On the permanence of stored information in the human brain. *American Psychologist*, 35, 409–20.

Loftus, E. F., Maryanne, G., Brown, S. W., et al. (1994) Near natal memories, past life memories, and other memory myths. *American Journal of Clinical Hypnosis*, 36, 176–9.

Lorayne, H., and Lucas, J. (1975) *The Memory Book*. London: W. H. Allen.

Lovelace, E. A., and Marsh, G. R. (1985) Prediction and evaluation of memory performance by young and old adults. *Journal of Gerontology*, 37, 432–7.

Lucchelli, F., Muggia, S., and Spinnler, H. (1995) The 'Petites Madeleines' phenomenon in two amnesic patients. *Brain*, 118, 167–83.

Luria, A. R. (1968) *The Mind of a Mnemonist*. Harmondsworth: Penguin.

Lynch, W. J. (1995) You must remember this: assistive devices for memory impairment. *Journal of Head Trauma Rehabilitation*, 10, 94–7.

Lynn, S. J., and Nash, M. R. (1994) Truth in memory: ramifications for psychotherapy and hypnotherapy. *American Journal of Clinical Hypnosis*, 36, 194–208.

MacMillan, M. B. (1986) A wonderful journey through the skull and brains: the travels of Mr Gage's tamping iron. *Brain and Cognition*, 5, 67–107.

Madigan, S. A. (1969) Intraserial repetition and coding processes in free recall. *Journal of Verbal Learning and Verbal Behavior*, 8, 828–35.

Malhotra, N. K. (1991) Mnemonics in marketing: a pedagogical tool. *Journal of the Academy of Marketing Science*, 19, 141–9.

Malpass, R. S., and Devine, P. G. (1981) Guided memory in eyewitness identification responses. *Journal of Applied Psychology*, 66, 343–50.

Mandler, G. (1980) Recognising: the judgement of a previous occurrence. *Psychological Review*, 27, 252–71.

Mathews, K. A., Wing, R. R., Kuller, L. H., et al. (1994) Influence of perimenopause cardiovascular risk factors and symptoms of middle-aged healthy women. *Archives of Internal Medicine*, 154, 2349–55.

Mayes, A. R. (1988) *Human Organic Memory Disorders*. Cambridge: Cambridge University Press.

Mayes, A. R., and Gooding, P. (1989) Enhancement of word completion priming in amnesics by cueing with previously novel associates. *Neuropsychologia*, 27, 1057–72.

Mayes, A. R., Baddeley, A. D., Cockburn, J., et al. (1988) Why are amnesic judgements of recency and frequency made in a qualitatively different way from those of normal people? *Cortex*, 25, 479–88.

McAndrews, M. P., Glisky, E. L., and Schacter, D. L. (1987) When priming persists: long-lasting implicit memory for a single episode in amnesic patients. *Neuropsychologia*, 25, 497–506.

McCarty, D. (1980) Investigation of a visual imagery mnemonic device for acquiring face–name associations. *Journal of Experimental Psychology: Human Learning and Memory*, 6, 145–55.

McGeoch, J. A. (1932) Forgetting and the law of disuse. *Psychological Review*, 39, 352–70.

McKenna, P., and Warrington, E. K. (1983) *Graded Naming Test*. London: NFER-Nelson.

McKenna, P. J., Tamlyn, D., Lund, C. E., et al. (1990) Amnesic syndrome in schizophrenia. *Psychological Medicine*, 20, 967–72.

McKenna, P. J., Clare, L., and Baddeley, A. D. (1995) Schizophrenia. In A. D. Baddeley, B. A. Wilson and F. N. Watts (eds), *Handbook of Memory Disorders*, 271–92. Chichester: Wiley.

McKintrick, L. A., and Camp, C. J. (1993) Relearning the names of things: the spaced-retrieval intervention implemented by a caregiver. *Clinical Gerontologist*, 14, 60–2.

McNally, R. J., Lasko, N. B., Macklin, M. L., Pitman, R. (1995) Autobiographical memory disturbance in combat-related posttraumatic stress disorder. *Behaviour Research and Therapy*, 33, 619–30.

McNeil, M. R., and Prescott, T. E. (1978) *Revised Token Test*. Austin, Tex.: Pro-Ed.

Melton, A. W. (1967) Repetition and retrieval from memory. *Science*, 158, 532.

Merskey, H. (1992) The manufacture of personalities. *British Journal of Psychiatry*, 160, 327–40.

Meudell, P. R., and Mayes, A. R. (1981) The Claparède phenomenon: a further example in amnesics, a demonstration of a similar effect in normal people with attenuated memory, and a reinterpretation. *Current Psychological Research*, 1, 75–88.

Meudell, P. R., Mayes, A. R., Ostergaard, A., and Pickering, A. (1985) Recency and frequency judgments in alcoholic amnesias and normal people with poor memory. *Cortex*, 21, 487–511.

Micco, A., and Masson, M. E. J. (1992) Age-related differences in the specificity of verbal encoding. *Memory & Cognition*, 20, 244–53.

Middleton, D. K., Lambert, M. J., and Seggar, L. B. (1991) Neuropsychological rehabilitation: microcomputer-assisted treatment of brain-injured adults. *Perceptual and Motor Skills*, 72, 527–30.

Milner, B. (1966) Amnesia following operation on the temporal lobes. In C. W. M. Whitty and O. L. Zangwill (eds), *Amnesia*, 109–33. London: Butterworths.

Milner, B. (1971) Interhemispheric differences in the location of psychological processes in man. *British Medical Bulletin*, 27, 272–7.

Milner, B., Corsi, P., and Leonard, G. (1991) Frontal-lobe contribution to recency judgements. *Neuropsychologia*, 29(6), 601–18.

Moller, D. (1988) Enniskillen's prayer for peace. *Reader's Digest*, 133, 51–6.

Monti, L. A., Gabrieli, J. D. E., Reminger, S. L., et al. (1996) Differential effects of aging and Alzheimer's Disease on conceptual implicit and explicit memory. *Neuropsychology*, 10, 101–12.

Moonen, C. T. W. (1995) Imaging of human brain activation with functional MRI. *Biological Psychiatry*, 37, 141–3.

Morris, R. G., Gick, M. L., and Craik, F. I. M. (1988) Processing resources and age differences in working memory. *Memory & Cognition*, 16, 362–6.

Morton, J. (1994) Cognitive perspectives on memory recovery. *Applied Cognitive Psychology*, 8, 389–98.

Moscovitch, M. (1989) Confabulation and the frontal system: strategic versus associative retrieval in neuropsychological theories of memory. In H. L. Roediger and F. I. M. Craik (eds), *Varieties of Memory and Consciousness: Essays in Honour of Endel Tulving*, 133–60. Hillsdale, NJ: Lawrence Erlbaum Associates.

Mumenthaler, M., Kaeser, H. E., Meyer, A., and Hess, T. (1979) Transient global amnesia after clioquinol. *Journal of Neurology, Neurosurgery and Psychiatry*, 42, 1084–90.

Musen, G., and Squire, L. R. (1991) Normal acquisition of novel verbal information in amnesia. *Journal of Experimental Psychology: Learning, Memory & Cognition*, 17, 1095–1104.

Musen, G., and Squire, L. R. (1993) On the implicit learning of novel associations by amnesic patients and normal subjects. *Neuropsychology*, 7, 119–35.

Nash, M. (1994) Memory distortion and sexual trauma: the problem of false negatives and false positives. *International Journal of Clinical and Experimental Hypnosis*, 42, 346–62.

Naugle, R., Naugle, C., Prevey, M., et al. (1988) New digital watch as a compensatory device for memory dysfunction. *Cognitive Rehabilitation*, 6, 22–3.

Nebes, R. D. (1989) Semantic memory in Alzheimer's disease. *Psychological Bulletin*, 106, 377–94.

Nebes, R. D., Boller, F., and Holland, A. (1986) Use of semantic context by patients with Alzheimer's disease. *Psychology and Aging*, 1, 261–9.

Neisser, U. (1967) *Cognitive Psychology*. Englewood Cliffs, NJ: Prentice-Hall.

Nelson, H. E. (1976) A modified card sorting test sensitive to frontal lobe defects. *Cortex*, 12, 313–24.

Nelson, H. E. (1991) *National Adult Reading Test (NART): Test Manual*, rev. edn. Windsor: NFER-Nelson.

Nelson, H. E., and O'Connell, A. (1978) Dementia: the estimation of premorbid intelligence levels using the New Adult Reading Test. *Cortex*, 14, 234–44.

Nelson, K. (1993) The psychological and social origins of autobiographical memory. *Psychological Science*, 4, 7–14.

Nichols, B. (1926) *Twenty-five: Being a Young Man's Candid Recollections of his Elders and Betters*. London: Cape.

Nigro, G., and Neisser, U. (1983) Point of view in personal memories. *Cognitive Psychology*, 15, 467–82.

Nissen, M. J., Ross, J. L., Willingham, D. B., Mackenzie, T. B., and Schacter, D. L. (1988) Memory and awareness in a patient with multiple personality disorder. *Brain and Cognition*, 8, 117–34.

Norman, D. A., and Shallice, T. (1986) Attention to action: willed and automatic control of behaviour. In R. J. Davidson, G. E. Schwartz and D. E. Shapiro (eds), *Consciousness and Self-regulation*, vol. 4, 1–18. New York: Plenum Press.

Norman, K. A., and Schacter, D. L. (in press) Implicit memory, explicit memory and false recollection: a cognitive neuroscience perspective. To appear in L. M. Reder (ed.), *Implicit Memory and Metacognition*. Hillsdale, NJ: Erlbaum.

O'Connell, B. A. (1960) Amnesia and homicide. *British Journal of Delinquency*, 10, 262–76.

O'Connor, M., Butters, N., Miliotis, P., Eslinger, P., and Cermak, L. S. (1992) The dissociation of anterograde and retrograde amnesia in a patient with Herpes encephalitis. *Journal of Clinical and Experimental Neuropsychology*, 14, 159–78.

Owen, A. M., Downes, J. J., Sahakian, B. J., Polkey, C. E., and Robbins, T. W. (1990) Planning and spatial working memory following frontal lobe lesions in man. *Neuropsychologia*, 28, 1021–34.

Owens, W. A. (1959) Is age kinder to the initially more able? *Journal of Gerontology*, 14, 334–7.

Owens, W. A. (1966) Age and mental ability: a second follow up. *Journal of Educational Psychology*, 57, 311–25.

Paivio, A. (1971) *Imagery and Verbal Processes*. New York: Holt, Rinehart and Winston.

Paivio, A. (1986) *Mental Representations: A Dual Coding Approach*. Oxford: Oxford University Press.

Palmini, A. L., Gloor, P., and Jones-Gotman, M. (1992) Pure amnesic seizures in temporal lobe epilepsy. *Brain*, 115, 749–69.

Parker, D. M., and Crawford, J. R. (1992) Assessment of frontal lobe function. In J. R. Crawford, D. M. Parker, and W. W. McKinlay (eds), *Handbook of Neuropsychological Assessment*, 267–94. Hove: Erlbaum.

Parkin, A. J. (1979) Specifying levels of processing. *Quarterly Journal of Experimental Psychology*, 31, 175–95.

Parkin, A. J. (1992) Functional significance of etiological factors in human amnesia. In L. R. Squire and N. Butters (eds), *Neuropsychology of Memory*, 2nd edn, 122–9. New York: Guildford.

Parkin, A. J. (1993) *Memory: Phenomena, Experiment and Theory.* Oxford: Blackwell.

Parkin, A. J. (1996a) *Explorations in Cognitive Neuropsychology.* Oxford: Blackwell.

Parkin, A. J. (1996b) Focal retrograde amnesia: a multi-faceted disorder? *Acta Neurologica Belgica*, 96, 43–50.

Parkin, A. J. (1997) The long and winding road: twelve years of frontal amnesia. In A. J. Parkin (ed.), *Case Studies in the Neuropsychology of Memory*. Hove: Psychology Press.

Parkin, A. J. (in press) The development of declarative and procedural memory. In N. Cowan (ed.), *Memory Development*. London: UCL Press.

Parkin, A. J., and Hunkin, N. M. (1991) Memory loss following radiotherapy for naso-pharyngeal cancer. *British Journal of Clinical Psychology*, 30, 349–57.

Parkin, A. J., and Hunkin, N. M. (1993) Impaired temporal context memory on anterograde but not retrograde tests in the absence of frontal pathology. *Cortex*, 29, 267–80.

Parkin, A. J., and Lawrence, A. (1994) A dissociation between memory performance and frontal lobe functions in the normal elderly. *Neuropsychologia*, 32, 1523–33.

Parkin, A. J., and Leng, N. R. C. (1993) *Neuropsychology of the Amnesic Syndrome.* Hove: Erlbaum.

Parkin, A. J., and Russo, R. (1990) Implicit and explicit memory and the automatic/effortful distinction. *European Journal of Cognitive Psychology*, 2, 71–80.

Parkin, A. J., and Stampfer, H. G. (1995) Keeping out the past. In R. Campbell and M. Conway (eds), *Broken Memories*, 81–92. Oxford: Blackwell.

Parkin, A. J., and Streete, S. (1988) Implicit and explicit memory in young children and adults. *British Journal of Psychology*, 79, 361–9.

Parkin, A. J., and Walter, B. (1992) Ageing, conscious recollection, and frontal lobe dysfunction. *Psychology and Aging*, 7, 290–8.

Parkin, A. J., Bell, W. P., and Leng, N. R. C. (1988) Metamemory in amnesic and normal subjects. *Cortex*, 24, 141–7.

Parkin, A. J., Montaldi, D., Leng, N. R. C., and Hunkin, N. (1990a) Contextual cueing effects in the remote memory of alcoholic Korsakoff patients. *Quarterly Journal of Experimental Psychology*, 42A, 585–96.

Parkin, A. J., Reid, T., and Russo, R. (1990b) On the differential nature of implicit and explicit memory. *Memory & Cognition*, 18, 507–14.

Parkin, A. J., Blunden, J., Rees, J. E., and Hunkin, N. M. (1991) Wernicke–Korsakoff Syndrome of non-alcoholic origin. *Brain and Cognition*, 15, 69–82.

Parkin, A. J., Dunn, J. C., Lee, C. W., O'Hara, P. F., and Nussbaum, L. (1993) Neuropsychological sequelae of Wernicke's encephalopathy in a 20-year-old woman: selective impairment of a 'frontal memory system'. *Brain and Cognition*, 21, 1–19.

Parkin, A. J., Rees, J. E., Hunkin, N. M., and Rose, P. E. (1994) Impairment of memory following discrete thalamic infarction. *Neuropsychologia*, 32, 39–51.

Parkin, A. J., Yeomans, J., and Binschaedler, C. (1994) Further characterization of the executive memory impairment following frontal lobe lesions. *Brain and Cognition*, 26, 23–42.

Parkin, A. J., Walter, B. M., and Hunkin, N. M. (1995) Relationships between normal aging, frontal lobe function, and memory for temporal and spatial information. *Neuropsychology*, 9, 304–12.

Parkin, A. J., Bindschaedler, C., Harsent, L., and Metzler, C. (1996) Pathological false alarm rates following damage to the left frontal cortex. *Brain and Cognition*, 32, 14–27.

Parkin, A. J., Bindschaedler, C., and Squires, E. (in preparation) Encoding factors in the generation of high false alarm rates in left frontal lobe disease.

Paulescu, E., Harrison, J., Baron-Cohen, S., et al. (1995) The physiology of coloured hearing: a PET activation study of colour-word synaesthesia. *Brain*, 118, 661–76.

Penfield, W. (1958) Some mechanisms of consciousness discovered during electrical stimulation of the brain. *Proceedings of the National Academy of Sciences*, 44, 51–66.

Penfield, W., and Roberts, L. (1959) *Speech and Brain Mechanisms*. Princeton, NJ: Princeton University Press.

Perner, J., and Ruffman, T. (1995) Episodic memory and autonoetic consciousness: developmental evidence and a theory of infantile amnesia. *Journal of Experimental Child Psychology*, 59, 516–48.

Phillips, S. M., and Sherwin, B. B. (1992) Effects of estrogen on memory function in menopausal women. *Psychoneuroendocrinology*, 17, 497–506.

Polit, D. F., and LaRocco, S. A. (1980) Social and psychological correlates of menopausal symptoms. *Psychosomatic Medicine*, 42 334–45.

Pollock, V. E., Earleywine, M., and Gabrielli, W. F. (1995) Personality and EEG in older adults with alcoholic relatives. *Alcoholism: Clinical and Experimental Research*, 19, 37–43.

Polster, M. R. (1993) Drug-induced amnesia: implications for cognitive neuropsychological investigations. *Psychological Bulletin*, 114, 477–93.

Pope, H. G., and Hudson, J. I. (1995) Can memories of childhood sexual abuse be repressed? *Psychological Medicine*, 25, 121–6.

Pope, H. G., Gruber, A. J., and Yurgelun-Todd, D. (1995) The residual neuropsychological effects of cannabis: the current status of research. *Drug and Alcohol Dependence*, 38, 25–34.

Poser, C. M., Kassirer, M. R., and Peyser, J. M. (1986) Benign encephalopathy of pregnancy: preliminary clinical observations. *Acta Neurologica Scandinavica*, 73, 39–43.

Posner, M. I. (1973) *Cognition: An Introduction*. Glenview, Ill: Scott, Foresman.

Posner, M. I., and Raichle, M. E. (1994) *Images of Mind*. New York: Freeman.

Prevey, M., Delaney, R. C., De l'Aune, W., and Mattson, R. H. (1991) A method of assessing the efficacy of memory rehabilitation techniques using a 'real-world' memory task: learning a computer language. *Journal of Rehabilitation Research and Development*, 28(4), 53–60.

Prigatano, G. P., Fordyce, D. J., Zeiner, H. K., Roueche, J. R., Pepping, M., and Wood, B. C. (1984) Neuropsychological rehabilitation after closed head injury in young adults. *Journal of Neurology, Neurosurgery and Psychiatry*, 47, 505–13.

Pylyshyn, Z. W. (1979) Imagery theory: not mysterious – just wrong. *Behavioral and Brain Sciences*, 2, 561–3.

Rabbitt, P. M. A., and Abson, V. (1991) Do older people know how good they are? *British Journal of Psychology*, 82, 137–51.

Reber, A. S. (1989) Implicit learning and tacit knowledge. *Journal of Experimental Psychology: General*, 118, 219–35.

Reder, L. M., Anderson, J. R., and Bjork, R. A. (1974) A semantic interpretation of encoding specificity. *Journal of Experimental Psychology*, 102, 648–56.

Regard, M., and Landis, T. (1984) Transient global amnesia: neuropsychological dysfunction during attack and recovery of two 'pure' cases. *Journal of Neurology, Neurosurgery and Psychiatry*, 47, 668–72.

Remple-Clower, N. L., Zola, S. M., Squire, L. R., and Amaral, D. G. (1996) Three cases of enduring memory impairment after bilateral damage limited to the hippocampal formation. *Journal of Neuroscience*, 16, 5233–55.

Rey, A. (1964) *L'Examen clinique en psychologie*. Paris: Presses Universitaires de France.

Ribot, T. (1882) *Diseases of Memory*. New York: Appleton.

Riddoch, M. J., and Humphreys, G. W. (1995) *Birmingham Object Recognition Battery*. Hove: Erlbaum.

Robertson-Tchabo, E. A., Hausman, C. P., and Arenberg, D. (1976) A classical mnemonic for older learners: a trip that works. *Educational Gerontologist*, 1, 215–26.

Robinson, J. A. (1976) Sampling autobiographical memory. *Cognitive Psychology*, 8, 578–95.

Roediger, H. L., and Blaxton, T. (1987) Effects of varying modality, surface features and retention interval on priming in word fragment completion. *Memory & Cognition*, 15, 379–88.

Romaniuk, M. (1981) Reminiscence and the second half of life. *Experimental Aging Research*, 7, 315–36.

Rundus, D. (1971) Analysis of rehearsal processes in free recall. *Journal of Experimental Psychology*, 89, 63–77.

Russell, E. W. (1975) A multiple scoring method for the assessment of complex memory functions. *Journal of Consulting and Clinical Psychology*, 43, 800–9.

Russell, W. R. (1971) *The Traumatic Amnesias*. London: Oxford University Press.

Russell, W. R., and Smith, A. (1961) Post-traumatic amnesia in closed head injury. *Archives of Neurology*, 5, 16–29.

Russo, R., and Parkin, A. J. (1993) Age differences in implicit memory: more apparent than real. *Memory & Cognition*, 21, 73–80.

Ryback, R. (1971) The continuum and specificity of the effects of alcohol on memory. *Quarterly Journal of Studies in Alcoholism*, 32, 995–1016.

Salthouse, T. A. (1980) Age and memory: strategies for localizing the loss. In L. W. Poon et al. (eds), *New Directions in Aging*. Hove: Erlbaum.

Salthouse, T. A. (1982) *Adult Cognition*. New York: Springer-Verlag.

Salthouse, T. A. (1984) Effects of age and skill in typing. *Journal of Experimental Psychology: General*, 113, 345–71.

Salthouse, T. A. (1985) *A Theory of Cognitive Ageing*. Amsterdam: North-Holland.

Salthouse, T. A. (1991) *Theoretical Perspectives on Cognitive Ageing*. Hove: Erlbaum.

Salthouse, T. A. (1994) Aging associations: influence of speed on adult age differences in associative learning. *Journal of Experimental Psychology: Learning, Memory and Cognition*, 20, 1486–1503.

Salthouse, T. A., and Fristoe, N. M. (1995) Process analysis of adult age effects on a computer administered trail making test. *Neuropsychology*, 9, 518–28.

Salthouse, T. A., and Kersten, A. W. (1993) Decomposing adult age differences in symbol arithmetic, *Memory & Cognition*, 21, 699–710.

Schacter, D. L. (1986a) Amnesia and crime: how much do we really know? *American Psychologist*, 41, 286–95.

Schacter, D. L. (1986b) Feeling-of-knowing ratings distinguish between genuine and simulated forgetting. *Journal of Experimental Psychology*, 12, 30–41.

Schacter, D. L. (1990) Perceptual representation systems and implicit memory: toward a resolution of the multiple memory systems debate. In A. Diamond (ed.), *The Development and Neural Bases of Higher Cognitive Functions*, 543–71. New York: New York Academy of Sciences.

Schacter, D. L. (1992) Understanding implicit memory. *American Psychologist*, 47, 559–69.

Schacter, D. L. (1996) *Searching for Memory: The Brain, the Mind, and the Past*. New York: Basic Books.

Schacter, D. L., and Glisky, E. L. (1986) Memory remediation: restoration, alleviation and the acquisition of domain-specific knowledge. In B. P. Uzzell and Y. Gross (eds), *Clinical Neuropsychology of Intervention*, 257–82. Nijhoff: Martinus.

Schacter, D. L., Wang, P. L., Tulving, E., and Freedman, M. (1982) Functional retrograde amnesia: a quantitative case study. *Neuropsychologia*, 20, 523–32.

Schacter, D. L., Harbluk, J. L., and McLachlan, D. R. (1984) Retrieval without recollection: an experimental analysis of source amnesia. *Journal of Verbal Learning and Verbal Behavior*, 23, 593–611.

Schacter, D. L., Rich, S. A., and Stampp, M. S. (1985) Remediation of memory disorders: experimental evaluation of the spaced-retrieval technique. *Journal of Clinical and Experimental Neuropsychology*, 7, 79–96.

Schacter, D. L., Kihlstrom, J. F., and Kihlstrom, L. C. (1989) Autobiographical memory in a case of multiple personality disorder. *Journal of Abnormal Psychology*, 98, 508–14.

Schacter, D. L., Cooper, L. A., and Delaney, S. M. (1990) Implicit memory for unfamiliar objects depends on access to structural descriptions. *Journal of Experimental Psychology: General*, 119, 5–24.

Schacter, D. L., Curran, T., and Galluccio, L. (1996a) False recognition and the right frontal lobe. *Neuropsychologia*, 34, 793–808.

Schacter, D. L., Reiman, E., Curran, T., et al. (1996b) Neuroanatomical correlates of veridical and illusory recognition memory: evidence from positron emission tomography, *Neuron*, 17, 267–74.

Schwender, D., Kaiser, A., Klasing, S., et al. (1993) Explicit and implicit memory and mid-latency auditory evoked potentials during cardiac surgery. In P. S. Sebel, B. Bonke, and E. Winograd (eds), *Memory and Awareness in Anaesthesia*, 85–98. Englewood Cliffs, NJ: Prentice-Hall.

Schwender, D., Madler, C.,Klasing, S., et al. (1994) Anaesthetic control of 40-Hz brain activity and implicit memory. *Consciousness and Cognition*, 3, 129–47.

Scoville, W. B., and Milner, B. (1957) Loss of recent memory after bilateral hippocampal lesions. *Journal of Neurology, Neurosurgery and Psychiatry*, 20, 11–21.

Seltzer, A. (1994) Multiple personality: a psychiatric misadventure. *Canadian Journal of Psychiatry*, 39, 442–5.

Shallice, T. (1988) *From Neuropsychology to Mental Structure*. Cambridge: Cambridge University Press.

Shallice, T., Fletcher, P., Grasby, P., Frackowiak, R. S., and Dolan, R. J. (1994) Brain regions associated with acquisition and retrieval of verbal episodic memory. *Nature*, 368, 633–5.

Sharp, K., Brindle, P. M., Brown, M. W., and Turner, G. M. (1993) Memory loss during pregnancy. *British Journal of Obstetrics and Gynaecology*, 100, 209–15.

Shields, I. W., and Knox, V. J. (1986) Level of processing as a determinant of hypnotic hypermnesia. *Journal of Abnormal Psychology*, 95, 358–64.

Shimamura, A. P. (1994) Memory and frontal lobe function. In M. S. Gazzaniga (ed.), *The Cognitive Neurosciences*, 803–14. Cambridge, Mass.: MIT Press.

Shimamura, A., and Squire, L. R. (1987) A neuropsychological study of fact memory and source amnesia. *Journal of Experimental Psychology: Learning, Memory and Cognition*, 13, 464–73.

Shimamura, A., and Squire, L. R. (1989) Impaired priming of new associations in amnesia. *Journal of Experimental Psychology: Learning Memory and Cognition*, 15, 721–8.

Shimamura, A. P., Janowsky, J., and Squire, L. R. (1990) Memory for temporal order of events in patients with frontal lobe lesions and amnesic patients, *Neuropsychologia*, 28, 803–13.

Short, D. D., Workman, E. A., Morse, J. H., Turner, R. L. (1992) Mnemonics for eight DSM-III-R disorders. *Hospital and Community Psychiatry*, 43, 642–4.

Silber, M., Almkvist, O., Larsson, B., and Uvnas-Moberg, K. (1990) Temporary peripartal impairment in memory and attention and its possible relation to oxytocin concentration. *Life Sciences*, 47, 57–65.

Skilbeck, C., and Robertson, I. (1992) Computer assistance in the management of memory and cognitive impairment. In B. A. Wilson and N. Moffat (eds), *Clinical Management of Memory Problems*, 2nd edn, 154–88. London: Chapman & Hall.

Sloman, S. A., Hayman, C. A. G., Ohta, N., Law, J., and Tulving, E. (1988) Forgetting in primed fragment completion. *Journal of Experimental Psychology: Learning, Memory and Cognition*, 14, 223–39.

Smith, S. M. (1986) Environmental context-dependent memory: recognition memory using a short-term memory task for input. *Memory & Cognition*, 14, 347–54.

Smith, S. M., and Vela, E. (1992) Environmental context-dependent eyewitness recognition. *Applied Cognitive Psychology*, 6, 125–39.

Snoek, J. W., Minderhoud, J. M., and Wilmink, J. T. (1984) Delayed deterioration following mild head injury in children. *Brain*, 107, 15–36.

Spanos, N. P. (1986) Hypnotic behavior: a social-psychological interpretation of amnesia, analgesia, and 'trance logic'. *Behavioral and Brain Sciences*, 9, 449–502.

Spanos, N. P. (1992) Compliance and reinterpretation in hypnotic responding. *Contemporary Hypnosis*, 9, 7–15.

Sperling, G. (1960) *The Information Available in Brief Visual Displays*. Psychological Monographs, no. 498.

Spreen, O., and Strauss, E. (1991) *A Compendium of Neuropsychological Tests*. New York: Oxford University Press.

Squire, L. R. (1982) Comparisons between forms of amnesia: some deficits are unique to Korsakoff's Syndrome. *Journal of Experimental Psychology: Learning, Memory and Cognition*, 8, 560–71.

Squire, L. R. (1987) *Memory and Brain*. New York: Oxford University Press.

Squire, L. R., and Butters, N. (eds) (1992) *Neuropsychology of Memory*, 2nd edn. New York: Guildford.

Squire, L. R., and Frambach, M. (1990) Cognitive skill learning in amnesia. *Psychobiology*, 18, 109–17.

Squire, L. R., and Knowlton, B. J. (1994) Memory, hippocampus, and brain systems. In M. Gazzaniga (ed.), *The Cognitive Neurosciences*, 825–38. Cambridge, Mass.: MIT Press.

Squire, L. R., and Slater, P. C. (1975) Forgetting in very long-term memory as assessed by an improved questionnaire taxonomy. *Journal of Experimental Psychology: Human Learning and Memory*, 104, 50–4.

Squire, L. R., and Slater, P. C. (1983) Electroconvulsive therapy and complaints of memory dysfunction: a prospective three-year follow-up study. *British Journal of Psychiatry*, 142, 1–8.

Squire, L. R., Nadel, L., and Slater, P. C. (1981a) Anterograde amnesia and memory for temporal order. *Neuropsychologia*, 19, 141–5.

Squire, L. R., Slater, P. C., and Miller, P. L. (1981b) Retrograde amnesia and bilateral electroconvulsive therapy. *Archives of General Psychiatry*, 38, 89–95.

Squire, L. R., Amaral, D. G., Zola-Morgan, S., Kritchevsky, M., and Press, G. (1989) Description of brain injury in the amnesic patient N.A. based on magnetic resonance imaging. *Experimental Neurology*, 105, 23–35.

Squire, L. R., Knowlton, B. J., and Musen, G. (1993) The structure and organization of memory. *Annual Review of Psychology*, 44, 453–95.

Squires, E. J., Hunkin, N. M., and Parkin, A. J. (1996) Memory notebook training in a case of severe amnesia: generalizing from paired associate learning to real life. *Neuropsychological Rehabilitation*, 6, 55–65.

Squires, E. J., Hunkin, N. M., and Parkin, A. J. (submitted) Can errorless learning facilitate the learning of novel associations in amnesia?

Stacy, A. W. (1995) Memory association and ambiguous cues in models of alcohol and marijuana use. *Experimental and Clinical Psychopharmacology*, 3, 183–94.

Steinglass, H. P., Bobring, K. H., Burgart, F., Sartori, G., and Schugens, M. (1994) Training of cognitive functions in alcoholics. *Neuropsycholoigcal Rehabilitation*, 4, 49–62.

Stuss, D. T., Alexander, M. P., and Palumbo, C. L. (1994) Organizational strategies with unilateral or bilateral frontal lobe injury in word learning tasks. *Neuropsychology*, 8, 355–73.

Sunderland, A., Harris, J., and Baddeley, A. D. (1983) Do laboratory tests predict everyday memory? *Journal of Verbal Learning and Verbal Behavior*, 122, 341–57.

Talland, G. A. (1965) *Deranged Memory*. New York: Academic Press.

Tart, C. T. (1972) *Altered States of Consciousness.* New York: Doubleday.

Taylor, P. J., and Kopelman, M. D. (1984) Amnesia for criminal offences. *Psychological Medicine,* 14, 581–8.

Tessler, M., and Nelson, K. (1994) Making memories: the influence of joint encoding on later recall by young children. *Consciousness and Cognition,* 3, 307–26.

Thigpen, C. H., and Cleckley, H. M. (1957) *The Three Faces of Eve.* New York: McGraw-Hill.

Thoene, A. I. T., and Glisky, E. L. (1995) Learning of face–name associations in memory-impaired patients: a comparison of different training procedures. *Journal of the International Neuropsychological Society,* 1, 29–38.

Thorndike, E. L. (1913) *Educational Psychology.* New York: Teachers' College Press.

Trennery, M. R., Crosson, B., DeBoe, J., and Leber, W. R. (1989) *Stroop Neuropsychological Screening Test.* London: NFER-Nelson.

Tulving, E. (1962) Subjective organization in free recall of 'unrelated' words. *Psychological Review,* 69, 344–54.

Tulving, E. (1972) Episodic and semantic memory. In E. Tulving and W. Donaldson (eds), *The Organization of Memory,* 382–403. New York: Academic Press.

Tulving, E. (1985) How many memory systems are there? *American Psychologist,* 40, 385–98.

Tulving, E., and Thomson, D. M. (1973) Encoding specificity and retrieval processes in episodic memory. *Psychological Review,* 80, 352–73.

Tulving, E., Schacter, D. L., and Stark, H. (1982) Priming effects in word-fragment completion are independent of recognition memory. *Journal of Experimental Psychology: Human Learning and Memory,* 8, 336–42.

Tulving, E., Kapur, S., Craik, F. I. M., Moscovitch, M., and Houle, S. (1994) Hemispheric encoding/retrieval asymmetry in episodic memory: positron emission tomography findings. *Proceedings of the National Academy of Sciences USA,* 91, 2016–20.

Verfaellie, M., and Roth, H. L. (1996) Knowledge of English vocabulary in amnesia: an examination of premorbidly acquired semantic memory. *Journal of the International Neuropsychology Society.*

Victor, M., Adams, R. D., and Collins, G. H. (1971) *The Wernicke–Korsakoff Syndrome.* Philadelphia: Davis.

Wagstaff, G. F. (1981) *Hypnosis: Compliance and Belief.* Brighton: Harvester Press.

Wagstaff, G. F., and Mercer, K. (1993) Does hypnosis facilitate memory for deep processed stimuli? *Contemporary Hypnosis,* 10, 59–66.

Waldfogel, S. (1948) *The Frequency and Affective Character of Childhood Memories.* Psychological Monographs, 62, no. 291.

Walker, S. (1992) Assessment of language dysfunction. In J. R. Crawford, D. M. Parker and W. W. McKinlay (eds), *A Handbook of Neuropsychological Assessment,* 177–222. Hove: Erlbaum.

Walsh, K. W. (1985) *Understanding Brain Damage.* Edinburgh: Churchill Livingstone.

Warburton, D. M., and Rusted, J. M. (1991) Cholinergic systems and information processing capacity. In J. Weinman and J. Hunter (eds), *Memory: Neurochemical and Abnormal Perspectives,* London: Harwood Academic Publishers.

Warrington, E. K. (1984) *Recognition Memory Test*, London: NFER-Nelson.

Warrington, E. K., and James, M. (1991) A new test of object decision: 2D silhouettes featuring a minimal view. *Cortex*, 27, 377–83.

Warrington, E. K., and McCarthy, R. A. (1988) The fractionation of retrograde amnesia. *Brain and Cognition*, 7, 184–200.

Warrington, E. K., and Weiskrantz, L. (1970) Amnesic syndrome: consolidation or retrieval? *Nature*, 228, 628–30.

Warrington, E. K., and Weiskrantz, L. (1982) Amnesia: a disconnection syndrome? *Neuropsychologia*, 20, 233–48.

Watson, J. B. (1914) *Behavior: An Introduction to Comparative Psychology*. New York: Holt.

Wechsler, D. (1945) A standardised memory scale for clinical use. *Journal of Psychology*, 19, 87–95.

Wechsler, D. (1955) *WAIS Manual*. New York: The Psychological Corporation.

Wechsler, D. (1981) *Manual for the Wechsler Adult Intelligence Scale Revised*. New York: Psychological Corporation.

Wechsler, D. (1987) *Wechsler Memory Scale Revised*. New York: Psychological Corporation.

Weeks, D., Freeman, C. P. L., and Kendell, R. E. (1980) ECT: II. Enduring cognitive deficits? *British Journal of Psychiatry*, 137, 26–37.

Weiner, R. D. (1984) Does electroconvulsive therapy cause brain damage? *Behavioral and Brain Sciences*, 7, 1–53.

Weingartner, H., Kaye, W., Smallberg, S., Cohen, R., Ebert, M. H., Gillin, J. C., and Gold, P. (1982) Determinants of memory failure in dementia. In S. Corkin, K. L. Davis, J. H. Growdon, E. Usdin and R. J. Wurtman (eds), *Aging*, Vol. 19: *Alzheimer's Disease: A Report of Progress*, 171–6. New York: Raven Press.

Weiskrantz, L. (1985) Issues and theories in the study of the amnesic syndrome. In N. M. Weinberger et al. (eds), *Memory Systems of the Brain*, 380–415. New York: Guildford.

Wernicke, C. (1881) *Lehrbuch der Gehirnkrankheiten für Aertzte und Studirende*, vol. 2, pp. 229–42. Kassel: Theodor Fischer.

West, R. L. (1986) Everyday memory and aging. *Developmental Neuropsychology*, 2, 323–44.

West, R. L., and Cohen, S. L. (1985) The systematic use of semantic and acoustic processing by younger and older adults. *Experimental Aging Research*, 11, 81–6.

Wetzel, C. D., Janowsky, D. S., and Clopton, P. L. (1982) Remote memory during marijuana intoxication. *Psychopharmacology*, 76, 278–81.

White, N., and Cunningham, W. R. (1982) What is the evidence for retrieval problems in the elderly? *Experimental Aging Research*, 8, 169–71.

Whiting, S., Lincoln, N., Bhavnani, G., and Cockburn, J. (1985) *Rivermead Perceptual Assessment Battery (RPAB)*. Windsor: NFER-Nelson.

Williams, J. M. G., and Broadbent, D. E. (1986) Autobiographical memory in suicide attempters. *Journal Abnormal Psychology*, 95, 145–9.

Williams, J. M. G., Watts, F. N., MacLeod, C., and Mathews, A. (1988) *Cognitive Psychology and Emotional Disorders*. Chichester: Wiley.

Wilson, B. A. (1982) Success and failure in memory training following a cerebral vascular accident. *Cortex*, 18, 581–94.

Wilson, B. A. (1987) *Rehabilitation of Memory*. New York: Guildford.

Wilson, B. A. (1991) Long-term prognosis of patients with severe memory disorders. *Neuropsychological Rehabilitation*, 1, 117–34.

Wilson, B. A. (1995) Management and remediation of memory problems in brain-injured adults. In A. D. Baddeley, B. A. Wilson, and F. N. Watts (eds), *Handbook of Memory Disorders*, 451–79. Chichester: Wiley.

Wilson, B. A., and N. Moffat (1992) *Clinical Management of Memory Problems*, 2nd edn. London: Chapman and Hall.

Wilson, B. A., Cockburn, J., and Baddeley, A. D. (1985) *The Rivermead Behavioural Memory Test*. Bury St Edmunds: Thames Valley Test Company.

Wilson, B. A., Ivani-Chalian, R., and Aldrich, F. K. (1991) *The Rivermead Behavioural Memory Test for Children aged 5–10 years*. Bury St Edmunds: Thames Valley Test Company.

Wilson, B. A., Baddeley, A. D., Shiel, A., and Patton, G. (1992) How does post-traumatic amnesia differ from the amnesic syndrome and from chronic memory impairment? *Neuropsychological Rehabilitation*, 2, 231–43.

Wilson, B. A., Baddeley, A. D., Evans, J., and Shiel, A. (1994) Errorless learning in the rehabilitation of memory-impaired people. *Neuropsychological Rehabilitation*, 4, 307–26.

Wilson, B. A., Baddeley, A. D., and Kapur, N. (1995) Dense amnesia in a professional musician following herpes simplex virus encephalitis. *Journal of Clinical and Experimental Neuropsychology*, 17, 668–81.

Wilson, B. A., Alderman, N., Burgess, P. W., Emslie, H., and Evans, J. J. (1996) *Behavioural Assessment of the Dysexecutive Syndrome (BADS)*. Bury St Edmunds: Thames Valley Test Company.

Wilson, R. S., Kaszniak, A. W., and Fox, J. H. (1981) Remote memory in senile dementia. *Cortex*, 17, 41–8.

Wingfield, A., Stine, E. L., Lahar, C. J., and Aberdeen, J. S. (1988) Does the capacity of working memory change with age? *Experimental Aging Research*, 14, 103–7.

Winocur, G. (1982) *Learning and Memory Deficits in Institutionalized and Non-institutionalized Old People. An Analysis of Interference Effects*. New York: Plenum Press.

Winocur, G., and Kinsbourne, M. (1978) Contextual cueing as an aid to Korsakoff amnesics. *Neuropsychologia*, 16, 671–82.

Winograd, E. (1976) Recognition memory for faces following nine different judgments. *Bulletin of the Psychonomic Society*, 8, 419–21.

Winograd, E., Sebel, P. S., Goldman, W. P., and Clifton, C. L. (1990) Indirect assessment of memory for music under anaesthesia. In B. Bonke, W. Fitch, and K. Millar (eds), *Memory and Awareness in Anaesthesia*, 181–4. Lisse/Amsterdam: Swets & Zeitlinger.

Wolf, A. S. (1980) Homicide and blackout in Alaskan natives. *Journal of Studies on Alcohol*, 41, 456–62.

Wollen, K. A., Weber, A., and Lowry, D. H. (1972) Bizarreness versus interaction of mental images as determinants of learning. *Cognitive Psychology*, 3, 518–23.

Wrightson, P., McGinn, V., and Gronwall, D. (1995) Mild head injury in preschool children: evidence that it can be associated with a persisting cognitive defect. *Journal of Neurology, Neurosurgery and Psychiatry*, 59, 375–80.

Yapko, M. D. (1994) Suggestibility and repressed memories of abuse: a survey of psychotherapists' beliefs: response. *American Journal of Clinical Hypnosis*, 36, 185–7.

Yarnell, P. R., and Lynch, S. (1973) The ding: amnestic states in football trauma. *Neurology*, 23, 196–7.

Yates, F. A. (1966) *The Art of Memory*. London: Routledge and Kegan Paul.

Young, A. W., Aggleton, J. P., Hellawell, D. J., et al. (1995) Face processing impairments after amygdalectomy. *Brain*, 118, 15–24.

Zangwill, O. L. (1967) The Grunthal–Storring case of the amnesic syndrome. *British Journal of Psychiatry*, 113, 113–28.

Zola-Morgan, S., and Squire, L. R. (1985) Complementary approaches to the study of memory: human amnesia and animal models. In N. M. Weinberger, J. L. McGaugh and G. Lynch (eds), *Memory Systems of the Brain*, 46–78. New York: Guildford.

Zola-Morgan, S., Squire, L. R., and Amaral, D. G. (1986) Human amnesia and the medial temporal region: enduring memory impairment following a bilateral lesion limited to field CA1 of the hippocampus. *Journal of Neuroscience*, 6, 2950–67.

Name Index

Subject Index